Learning Culture through Sports

Exploring the Role of Sports in Society

Edited by

Sandra Spickard Prettyman
Brian Lampman

Rowman & Littlefield Education
Lanham, Maryland • Toronto • Oxford
2006

Published in the United States of America
by Rowman & Littlefield Education
A Division of Rowman & Littlefield Publishers, Inc.
A wholly owned subsidiary of The Rowman & Littlefield Publishing Group, Inc.
4501 Forbes Boulevard, Suite 200, Lanham, Maryland 20706
www.rowmaneducation.com

PO Box 317
Oxford
OX2 9RU, UK

British Library Cataloguing in Publication Information Available

Library of Congress Cataloging-in-Publication Data

Learning culture through sports : exploring the role of sports in society / edited
by Sandra Spickard Prettyman, Brian Lampman.
    p. cm.
  Includes bibliographical references.
  ISBN-13: 978-1-57886-379-2 (hardcover : alk. paper)
  ISBN-13: 978-157886-380-8 (pbk. : alk. paper)
  ISBN-10: 1-57886-379-1 (hardcover : alk. paper)
  ISBN-10: 1-57886-380-5 (pbk. : alk. paper)
  1. Sports—Social aspects—United States. I. Prettyman, Sandra Spickard,
1957-   II. Lampman, Brian, 1973-
  GV706.5.L43 2006
  306.4'83—dc22
                                      2005028200

Contents

Part I: Youth Participation and Sport

Part II: Gender and Sexuality in Sport

Part III: Race and Ethnicity in Sport

Part IV: Sport and the Media

Part V: Sport and Violence

Part VI: Sport and Schools

Contents

Acknowledgments

No book is written in isolation or without the inspiration and influence of countless others, and this book is no exception. The words and ideas of writers, researchers, commentators, and athletes such as Paul Robeson, Martina Navratilova, Jack Johnson, Arthur Ashe, Donna Lopiano, and Mitch Albom had an impact on our view of sport and society, moving us to take up this project. Many of these people are deeply committed to sport, and also deeply committed to issues of social justice, serving as powerful role models for us. We also need to thank our mentors, our teachers, and our colleagues for constantly pushing us to think through our ideas and question the world. Without their guidance, wisdom, and support this book may never have come to fruition. Brian is especially indebted to academic mentors Harry McLaughlin and Keith Harrison, and his athletic model for successful relationships, David Carlson of the Burns Park Soccer Club. Sandra must thank her former teacher and advisor, friend, and mentor Rebecca Martusewicz, whose intellectual rigor and commitment to social justice continue to infuse her thinking and writing. In addition, we both owe debts of gratitude to our families. Brian would like to thank his wife, Justina, for her unconditional love, support, and daily inspiration. Brian hopes his son, Kale, grows with a love and respect for others and a desire to work for social justice. Brian also has his parents to thank for their support of his athletic endeavors and encouragement in his academic accomplishments. He would like to thank his brother and sister for their love, encouragement, and assistance with his snap-hook drive and poor jump shot, respectively. Sandra has her children to thank for her interest in sport; it is because of their experiences, both positive and negative, that she came to recognize the importance of sport in our world. It is also due to their influence that she became an "athlete" herself, something for which she is deeply grateful. She also thanks her partner, Tim, for listening incessantly to ideas about and stories from the book; it is more than he ever wanted to know about sport. Their love, support, and commitment to social justice continue to inspire her. These people, and countless others, have influenced us and made this book what it is. We hope, for them, with them, and through them, that this book will contribute to changing the game in positive ways.

Introduction: Why Study Sport?

Sandra Spickard Prettyman
University of Akron

The slogan "Winning is everything" is often proclaimed in our country, from T-shirts to commercials to school banners. And on school playgrounds and sporting fields, the words "You throw like a girl" are often used to denigrate particular players. Caricatures of American Indians continue to fill billboards and sport stadiums, even in our nation's capital, despite the outcry of many American Indian organizations and supporters. These words, images, and the actions associated with them have meanings and say much about the role of sport in our world and in our lives. Yet sport is rarely examined critically, despite the fact that it is an integral part of our society and an important force in our lives. While we often complain about certain aspects of sport, rarely are solutions explored. In addition, over 30 million young people participate in youth sport activities and programs each year. While the numbers of those who go on to play sports as adults is much lower, you can find adults on soccer fields and basketball courts across the country. Millions more participate by watching, either in person or on television. Others, young and old, reject or resist organized sport programs, although a growing number of people are turning to alternative forms of sport for activity and entertainment.

Thus, it is fair to say that sport plays an important role in the lives of millions of Americans. Even if we do not play a sport, our lives are influenced by it, in part because we are inundated with images and ideas about sport. In addition, there is a great deal of value placed on the behaviors and attributes associated with sports and athletes. A commonly held assumption is that young people can (and should) learn about and enjoy physical activity through participation in organized sport programs. Another assumption is that participating in sport helps us learn important behaviors, values, and skills. However, to figure out whether these assumptions are true, it is important to examine them from different perspectives. Have they always been true (a historical perspective)? Are they true for some groups of people in some situations (a sociological perspective)? How do individuals respond to sport and these assumptions (a psychological perspective)? These perspectives provide a foundation for this book. We believe it is important for all of us to examine this important force in our lives, and this examination should encompass multiple perspectives.

A CRITICAL SOCIOLOGICAL PERSPECTIVE

There are many books that talk about what sport is and its benefits, or that talk about the demographics of sport participation and its rewards and benefits. However, there are very few books that examine what sport means in our lives today and how these meanings are constructed. This book examines sport in relationship to the meanings it holds for individuals, for groups of people, for organizations, and for society, and provides a broad context in which to engage in this examination. The perspective taken by the authors in this book is that there are complex relationships between sport and our society, and between sport and our lives. To best understand these relationships, we need to take a step back and try to imagine the connection between the individual and the social, between the patterns, practices, and events in the broader social world and in our own lives. This is often referred to as "the sociological imagination." Three different, but connected, approaches to understanding the world help to develop this perspective: the historical, the comparative, and the critical.

In many ways, everything we study is historical in nature. It is difficult to imagine how we could study sport, for example, without studying its history, especially if we want to create any changes in it. This attention to the historical is not so we can predict the future, but so we can better understand the present. A comparative approach allows us to examine sport from perspectives other than our own, especially from other cultural perspectives. This comparative analysis insures that our own beliefs about the world do not diminish those of others. Lastly, a critical approach to sport means that we critique the way sport currently exists in our world. It does not mean that these authors are antisport, only that they ask questions about and examine taken for granted assumptions about the way the world and sport work. This critical approach allows us to engage in examinations and discussions of contradictions and complexities in sport and in society, thus moving us toward thinking and acting critically to create change where necessary.

When these approaches are used, it becomes clear that sport is more than just something we do for fun, or even for a living; it is linked to the political, social, economic, and historical contexts in which we live. This view might challenge the way you typically think about sport. If so, we hope it causes you to be more reflective about sport in your world. This reflection can help you think carefully about your own views and beliefs about sport, evaluate them in light of new information and ideas, and decide whether or not you want to hold onto those views and beliefs or reevaluate your position on them. One benefit of engaging in a critical examination of sport is that it allows us to better understand our own positions and provides us with the tools to adequately defend those positions. Without such tools, it is difficult for us to separate fact from fiction, and to recognize how our own ideas are influenced by social, economic, political, and historical influences. The goal is to be able to examine a variety of different viewpoints, including our own, through a critical lens.

This is certainly no easy task, and we recognize that for many people it will be difficult to engage in such a critical analysis. We have become accustomed to taking things for granted, and to not questioning the way the world operates. As a result, some of the ideas in this book may make you uncomfortable, or angry, or upset. We will call those feelings *cognitive dissonance*, which refers to a situation where our thinking is challenged by new ideas that are not in harmony with what and how we currently think. However, it is this cognitive dissonance that can move us forward in our thinking and challenge us to either defend our own ideas or reconsider those ideas in light of new information.

THINKING CRITICALLY VERSUS BEING CRITICAL

The authors in this book examine the role of sport in American society, but this does not mean they provide justifications for the way sport currently operates, is understood, or is consumed. Rather, they take a critical approach that asks readers to think about and reflect on the relationship between sport and the larger society of which it is a part, as well as our own relationship to sport and the world. The goal is to create a social consciousness about sport that helps take readers beyond simplistic slogans and taken for granted assumptions. We hope this critical analysis helps readers make sense of their world and how it works, as well as their relationship to it. Such a critical analysis is often construed as being negative. However, these authors are not antisport but rather are practicing what is often considered the highest form of commitment and dedication. Leaders like Thomas Jefferson and J. William Fulbright believed that criticism is the highest form of patriotism, since it is only with criticism that we can recognize our flaws and work to eliminate them. Critique can actually serve as a more powerful form of support than blind acceptance of current practices, whether speaking of government or sport. Applied to sport, this idea encourages the development of critical analysis and criticism as a service to and a support of sport, and one means by which we can help move sport toward better practices.

The critical analyses undertaken by the authors in the following chapters demonstrate this service and commitment to the ideals of sport. This is not a criticism of sport itself, or of those who participate in it. Rather, it is a means by which to uncover and acknowledge the ways in which negative forces such as discrimination, injustice, and abuse currently operate through and in sport. Thus, the critical perspective taken by these authors is a way for them to acknowledge their commitment to sport while at the same time to work for change. However, more often than not, our society tends to shy away from critical analysis, whether about sport or anything else. Instead, we often want easy answers to difficult questions and issues. This assumes it is not worthwhile to identify and understand injustices and abuses unless we have a plan for reform ready to go. However, the goal of critical analysis is not to present a preplanned course for change, but to engage the community in furthering their understanding and reflection on the issues. This means it is the responsibility of all those associated with and concerned about the institution to work for change.

Given the above statements, it is clear that this book has a particular perspective on sport and its role in society, one that recognizes both the flaws and the benefits of sport in our world. This perspective certainly represents a value judgment that is not neutral in nature. However, we would argue that values and bias are present in all of the sciences, social and natural, and that true neutrality and objectivity are not possible. Instead, these authors write about sport as accurately, intelligently, and critically as they can, recognizing its strengths and its weaknesses. A major benefit of such a critical, sociological perspective is the diversity of ideas that can be pursued and the ways in which such a diversity of ideas can lead to debate as we try to make sense of ourselves and our world. Such debate can once again move us forward in our thinking and create change, both in ourselves and in our world.

OVERVIEW OF THE BOOK

We have chosen to break the book into parts that each deal with particular issues that reflect both possibilities and problems for sport. First, part I, "Youth Participation in Sport," has chapters that examine how sport influences young people, in both positive and negative ways, and about the purposes it supposedly serves. Jay Coakley writes about how and why sport programs became organized entities for young people, also exploring new and developing trends in sport and society. Chapters by Bob Bigelow and his colleagues and Fred Engh both address the issue of how we can make sport a better institution for kids, one that actually promotes the ideals and purposes it sets out to accomplish. Their chapters represent different perspectives on this problem and approaches to it, highlighting the need for continued conversation around these issues. Finally, Martha Ewing and Peggy McCann discuss the goals and outcomes of youth sport participation, recognizing the potential it has, as well as the problems it poses, in the lives of young people.

The next two parts deal with gender and sexuality and race and ethnicity in sport. Authors in both parts address issues that face all of us as we negotiate the world of sport, and specifically focus on much of the discrimination and bias that is present. Margaret Duncan examines the impact and influence of Title IX, as well as its future in our current world, using her own experience as a vehicle to explore this important piece of legislation. Natalie G. Adams and Pamela J. Bettis analyze cheerleading and whether or not it can or should be considered a sport, as well as how its participants conceive of it. The chapter by Sandra Spickard Prettyman explores the role of coaches, power, and language in students' experiences with sport. Eric Anderson's chapter discusses the link between sport and homophobia. Richard Lapchick's chapter addresses some of the new racial stereotypes in sport, and Brian Lampman explores the importance of pursuing issues of race with secondary students to help them better interrogate its influence and impact in their lives. Athlete, former coach, and ESPN commentator Bill Curry presents a retrospective on the importance of the huddle and sport in bringing players together, physically and culturally. Finally, Ellen J. Staurowsky presents a critical analysis of the use of American Indian mascots in sport.

Part IV presents several authors who examine the relationship between sport and the media, including Stephen D. Mosher's retrospective analysis of the importance of popular music, flags, and anthems in the relationship between sport and patriotism. Maureen Smith examines the new role of "girl power" and its relationship to female athletes and athletic females, and author Kyle W. Kusz looks at the link between images of white masculinity in the new millennium by examining two popular cultural texts, *Jackass* and *8 Mile*. C. Keith Harrison and Quaylan Allen explore the work of Stuart Scott of ESPN and hip-hop's impact on our culture. The next part examines sport and violence and includes chapters on hazing and its detrimental effects by Joe Gervais, and perceptions of athletes as role models and criminals by Earl Smith and Angela Hattery. In the final part of the book, C. Keith Harrison, Eddie Comeaux, and others provide evidence about the scholar-baller program and the importance of promoting academics and athletics; John R. Gerdy presents a new model for the relationship between sport and schools; and Rob Renes (re)examines the meaning of success, especially in relationship to sport and schooling.

These authors present cutting-edge research and writing about a variety of issues facing the world of sport today. Whether we consider ourselves sport fans or not, whether we are (or were) athletes or not, it is clear that sport influences all of our lives. It is everywhere around us, in film and television and advertising, on our clothing and apparel, in our language and communication patterns. Even our decision to actively ignore it sends a message about sport. Recognizing its importance in our world, and our lives, brings us closer to understanding the relationship between sport and society, and thus how to create change, possibly in both of them. Sport is not just a game, but is a serious piece of our culture that needs to be examined critically from multiple perspectives. Hopefully, this examination can help us change the game in positive ways.

I

YOUTH PARTICIPATION AND SPORT

Organized Sports for Young People:
A 20th-Century Invention

Jay Coakley
University of Colorado, Colorado Springs

ORGANIZED YOUTH SPORTS ARE UNIQUE

Most children around the world play physical games. But organized sports with coaches, referees, official playing fields, and uniforms for players are a luxury that many people cannot afford. Organized youth sports are special types of physical games. They require facilities and spaces designed for the games being played. They depend on adults who have the money, time, and skills to organize and administer programs and teams. And they exist only when there are children who have the time and interest to participate in activities that have rules, schedules, practices, and competitions controlled by adults. In regions of the world where children must work to help their families survive, there are few, if any, organized youth sports: Playing fields and facilities don't exist, adults don't have the resources to organize and manage them, and children are too busy working.

THE EMERGENCE OF ORGANIZED
YOUTH SPORTS IN THE UNITED STATES

Playing organized sports is such a common experience in the United States that many children and teenagers take them for granted. This is especially true among children from families and communities that have the resources that are needed to organize and sponsor sport programs and make sure that there is easy access to participation opportunities. Children in low-income families and poor communities are less likely to take organized youth sports for granted because they often lack the resources needed to pay for participation fees, equipment, and transportation to practices and games, and their communities do not have resources to build and maintain sport fields and facilities.

Organized youth sports first appeared during the early 20th century in the United States and other wealthy nations. They were originally developed when educators and developmental experts realized that the behavior and character of children were strongly influenced by their social surroundings and everyday experiences. This led many people to believe that if you could organize the experiences of children in particular ways, you could influence the kinds of adults that those children would become.

This belief that the social environment influenced a person's overall development was very encouraging to people interested in progress and reform in the United States at the beginning of the 20th century. It caused them to think about how they might control the experiences of children to produce responsible and productive adults. They believed strongly that democracy depended on responsibility and that a growing capitalist economy depended on the productivity of workers.

Progressive reformers in the United States were influenced by educators in England who thought that organized sports were ideal activities for molding the characters of young boys. In fact, the very first organized youth sports were developed in exclusive private boys' schools in England. The headmasters at these schools thought that playing organized sports would help the sons of wealthy and powerful people in British society become future leaders in business, government, and the military.

After they heard about organized sports in elite British schools, it wasn't long before reform-oriented adults in the United States developed organized sports, especially team sports, for boys in schools, on playgrounds, and in church groups. These adults hoped that playing organized team sports would teach boys from working-class families a set of values related to work, productivity, obedience to authority, and teamwork in the pursuit of competitive success. They also hoped that playing sports would help boys from middle- and upper-class families develop into strong, assertive, competitive men who would eventually become the captains of industry, government, and the military.

Many reformers worried that most middle- and upper-class American boys were learning too many feminine values because they were raised primarily by their mothers and taught by women. Their fathers worked long hours and were seldom at home, so there was a fear that boys were not learning what they needed to know to become strong, productive men. Organized sports, they believed, could be used to offset the feminine influence of mothers and teachers and teach boys the lessons that would enable them to become men who would maintain the power and influence of the United States.

At the same time that sports programs were organized for boys, girls were encouraged to participate in activities that would help them learn how to be good mothers and homemakers. Most people during the early 20th century, even progressive reformers, believed that it was more important for girls to learn domestic skills than sport skills. School curricula and playground activities reflected this belief. Historically, many people believed that girls were naturally suited to be wives and mothers, not athletes or leaders in society. In fact, many people, including doctors, believed that playing vigorous physical activities were dangerous to the overall health and well-being of girls and women. Strenuous physical activities were widely thought to cause women problems in childbearing, damage their breasts and reproductive organs, cause them to have menstrual problems, and lead them to develop masculine biological traits. However, it was also believed that girls needed to learn about sports so that when they became mothers they could provide the guidance and support that their sons would need as they learned to play sports and become strong, productive men.

History shows that youth sports in the United States were initially organized around the idea that boys must learn how to be men in a competitive, capitalist society where productivity was valued, and in a political context in which a strong military was believed to be a requirement for national security and economic expansion. In the 19th century the United States had fought the Mexican-American War, the Civil War, and the Spanish-American War, and had witnessed wars and political conflicts in Europe that led to World War I between 1914 and 1918. In light of this economic and political context, youth sports were seen as a valuable training ground for disciplining the bodies and minds of the boys who were expected to be the next generation of workers, industrial and military leaders, and soldiers.

Some organized youth sport programs during the first 75 years of the 20th century permitted or encouraged the participation of girls, and on rare occasions, boys and girls participated together in youth sports during those years. Gender-mixed participation, when it did occur, involved younger children. Gender segregation at all ages was the rule, and it was nearly universal for young people over the age of 12. This was due to the belief that if boys and girls played together and came to know each other as friends, they would not be interested in getting married and having children.

Youth sports for girls prior to the 1980s in most societies, including the United States, were organized around concerns about motherhood and sexuality. Therefore, they emphasized physical coordination and good health rather than physical contact, the physical domination of opponents, or the perfection of high-level physical skills. While many boys could play on sport teams sponsored by their schools, there were few if any school-sponsored sports for girls. Many schools did sponsor annual play days for girls, which meant that once a year they had official track and field events in which girls could compete. These continued to exist through the 1960s, but they were like glorified PE classes and seldom inspired girls to develop physical skills or define physical competition as a valuable activity in their lives.

Of course, there were exceptions to these patterns, and some girls did develop impressive physical skills and played in certain competitive sports. But organized youth sports through most of the 20th century were developed around prevailing cultural ideas about how boys and girls should grow up and what they were supposed to learn in the process of becoming productive adults in a capitalist society. They were also developed around the beliefs that boys from poor and working-class families, many of whom were the sons of recent immigrants to the United States, would learn values that would make them productive workers, while at the same time boys from more established middle- and upper-class families would learn to be political, economic, and military leaders. These ideas and beliefs about gender and social class served as guides for the adults who dedicated considerable time, energy, and money to developing organized sports in communities and schools.

ORGANIZED YOUTH SPORTS IN RECENT HISTORY

When the first wave of the Baby Boom generation (that is, children born between 1946 and 1964) moved through childhood during the 1950s and

1960s, organized youth sports grew dramatically. Programs in the United States were funded by a combination of public, private, and commercial sponsors. Local parks and recreation departments sponsored programs. The YMCA, the Boys and Girls Clubs, and many religious organizations and churches added programs of their own. Entrepreneurs developed commercial clubs for children whose parents could afford to pay for private lessons and exclusive sport participation opportunities.

Parents also entered the scene as active promoters of youth sports. They were eager to have the characters of their sons built through organized, competitive games. Fathers became coaches, managers, and league administrators. Mothers did laundry and became chauffeurs and short-order cooks so their sons were always ready and properly suited up for practices and games.

Most organized youth sports through the mid 1970s were for boys 8–14 years old. The programs usually emphasized a combination of fun and competition as preparation for future occupational success. Girls' interests in sports were largely ignored and seldom encouraged. Girls were expected to stay close to home or to sit in the bleachers and watch their brothers' games. Some had the chance to be high school cheerleaders, but not athletes. Before the 1970s few girls ever had the chance to play on organized youth teams or varsity sports in junior or senior high school because there were no teams.

It wasn't until the mid 1970s that the women's movement, the health and fitness movement, and government legislation prohibiting sex discrimination in public school programs all came together to stimulate the development of new sport programs for girls. The most significant government legislation was Title IX of the Education Amendments to the Civil Rights Act. Signed into law by President Richard Nixon in 1972, Title IX prohibits gender discrimination in schools that receive money from the federal government. This meant that because playing sports was defined as educational, girls and boys must have the same opportunities to participate on sport teams, just as they must have the same opportunities to take math and science classes.

Although it took at least 6 years for the government to enforce Title IX, youth sports for girls began to grow through the late 1970s and 1980s to the point that many girls now have nearly as many sport participation opportunities as boys have. However, participation rates among girls remain lower than rates among boys because playing sports continues to be connected more strongly with masculinity and becoming a man than with femininity and becoming a woman. Furthermore, some girls continue to be discouraged by notions that "girls are not as good as boys" in sports, and that "playing like a girl" means that one is not playing correctly—that is, as a boy or man would play. Furthermore, some girls who have learned to define gender in limited or homophobic terms continue to be discouraged when they hear messages that playing certain sports is unfeminine or a sign of being a lesbian.

Even though traditional ideas about masculinity and femininity still influence participation in youth sports, playing sports is now an accepted part of the process of growing up in most wealthy nations, including the United States. This is especially true among middle- and upper-class families, where plentiful resources enable parents, communities, and organizations to sponsor, organize, and administer many programs for young people. Some of these programs now provide participation opportunities for children as young as 4 years old.

Many parents encourage their sons and daughters to play organized sports today. A few parents may wonder if their children should play in sports programs where winning is emphasized more than overall child development, but many parents seek out the win-oriented programs, hoping their children will become the winners and receive college scholarships and multimillion-dollar professional sport contracts, or at least learn to be successful in a competitive, capitalist economy. Of course, some parents also encourage their children to engage in noncompetitive physical activities outside of organized programs, and many children seek these activities as alternatives to adult-supervised organized sports.

NEW SPORTS FOR YOUNG PEOPLE

As youth sports such as soccer, football, basketball, and baseball have become highly structured and tightly controlled by adults, many children no longer define them as fun. Some young people don't like adults controlling their every move at practices and games, and they don't want their parents to control every minute of their day by signing them up for organized sports 12 months a year. In addition, some kids desire the non–rule-bound, noncompetitive nature of some alternative sports. Consequently, activities such as skateboarding, snowboarding, BMX biking, rollerblading, Frisbee, and dozens of other alternative or action sports are seen as increasingly attractive among young people. These activities allow participants to be expressive and spontaneous as they enjoy using their bodies and developing physical skills largely on their own terms rather than participating in the hypercontrolled setting of organized sports.

Physical educators, sociologists, and recreation specialists now study these activities and the young people who participate in them. As a sociologist I have watched these action sports for hundreds of hours and talked with many young people committed to them. I am amazed at the physical skills they have developed as they practice on their own and learn with and from their friends. To the surprise of many adults, young people in these action sports have developed skills without coaches, physical educators, and parents telling them how to do things correctly. Furthermore, no one has lectured them about why they must work hard if they want to master skills—they have learned this on their own.

At the same time that alternative and action sports have become popular with millions of young people, there are corporations and media companies that want to turn them into organized, competitive sports complete with spectator events and media coverage. In addition, some parents and community agencies want to regulate and organize these sports to make them safer and more accessible for all children. The corporations and media companies are interested in profits, whereas parents and community agencies are interested in protecting children and keeping them out of trouble.

Some young people buy into the profit motives of corporations and media companies and accept their emphasis on consumption and organized competition. Some young people willingly conform to the wishes of parents and other adults who want to regulate their activities to make them more safe, inclusive, and trouble free. And some young people resist any efforts to organize their activities in ways that might subvert the freedom, expression, creativity, and spontaneity that make them so exciting.

People who study sports in society are increasingly interested in what happens in these new sports for young people. Will they become hyperorganized like other youth sports? Will they be areas where young people take a stand and resist what they see as the overorganization and commercialization of childhood and adolescence? Will the X Games be used as a model for what alternative sports should be, just like the NFL has become a model for organized youth football? The questions will be answered as more research is done.

PROBLEMS IN YOUTH SPORTS

Organized youth sports are not without problems. Some sport programs have become so expensive that many young people are excluded from them for financial reasons. At the same time, many communities have cut publicly funded programs due to the budget crises local governments face. Instead of sponsoring programs as they have done in the past, local parks and recreation programs now allow club-based youth sport organizations to rent public playing fields and facilities. These club programs often have entry fees that make them too expensive for some children to join.

Organized youth sport programs often come in two major forms: recreational, participation-oriented programs on the one hand, and competitive, skills-focused programs on the other hand. The latter programs often receive the majority of community resources, and many parents think that their sons and daughters ought to play in such programs because they are good preparation for making high school teams and developing skills that will lead to everything from social acceptance to occupational success. Competitive, skills-focused programs tend to be highly organized, they emphasize winning and success in postseason tournaments, and they have demanding practice and competition schedules. In some cases, the coaches of these teams demand year-round commitments from children as young as 8 years old. This has created a situation where many children now specialize in a single sport and even a single position or event in a sport for 12 months a year. This form of specialization prior to 14 or 15 years old often constrains overall physical and social development and destroys the motivation of young athletes.

As youth sports have become more serious and demanding, burnout has become a new problem. Burnout occurs when young people, especially during early adolescence, feel that they have lost personal control over the conditions of their sport participation. This causes stress, and when stress becomes excessive, burnout becomes common. When burnout occurs, playing sports becomes tedious rather than fun, and young people drop out and experience a sense of failure even though they may have been age-group champions. Burnout can be dangerous when it causes a young person to reject the guidelines that provided structure in their lives and to withdraw from the people who provide them with support.

The seriousness and demands of youth sports affect more than young people; they also affect parents. In fact, stories about "Little League parents" have become the stuff of urban legends in U.S. culture. Obnoxious and sometimes violent parents and coaches have been described in newspapers, magazines, and television programs. Some parent-child relationships have been strained because of pressures and disagreements around youth sport participation and performance.

Many parents today feel that it is their moral obligation to find the best programs for their children and then encourage their children and their children's coaches to meet lofty expectations for success. These parents often believe that if they do things the right way, their children will earn college scholarships or even professional contracts and prize money in their sports. In the process, their children's accomplishments become evidence that parents use to establish and reaffirm their moral worth as mothers and fathers. This, of course, puts significant pressure on children to perform well and to continue playing a particular sport even when they would like to expand their interests, become involved in other activities, and develop a wider range of skills and experiences.

CONCLUSION

Movement and physical activities are a part of the lives of nearly all children around the world, but organized youth sports are a luxury. They require resources and "free time" among children and adults. They exist only when adults can take the time to organize them, when children have the time to play them, and when there is a widespread belief in society that childhood experiences strongly influence a person's development and character.

Youth sports have a unique history in every society where they exist. However, they have always been organized in ways that emphasize experiences and values that are defined as important by adults in the society as a whole. When sports were seen primarily as activities that turned boys into men, organized youth sports were open to boys and generally closed to girls. In this way, youth sports served to reaffirm traditional ideas about masculinity and femininity and perpetuate certain forms of gender inequality.

Participation patterns in youth sports are also influenced by other social factors such as social class, race and ethnicity, and physical (dis)abilities. When family income is low, children may not have opportunities to play organized sports. Cultural traditions and ideas about skin color and ethnic heritage often influence children's choices of what sports they will play. Stereotypes related to skin color and ethnicity may influence how people evaluate the physical abilities of particular children and whether they encourage children to play certain sports. The widespread notion that sports exemplify ideals of bodily perfection has also interfered with providing youth sports for children with disabilities. Even today there are few sport participation opportunities for children with disabilities, and there are few examples of children with disabilities who participate with their able-bodied peers in organized youth sports.

We face interesting challenges for the future related to youth sports. One the one hand, our goal is to make sure than all children have opportunities to play sports as they grow up. On the other hand, our goal is to provide organized sports in which children can develop and display physical skills without being discouraged by those adults who have lost perspective about what makes sports fun for children. The stakes associated with youth sports have become very high as we try to help young people develop interests in physical activities that will keep them fit and healthy through their lives. Instead of emphasizing rules, competitive outcomes, postseason playoffs, and championships, the focus in organized youth sports should be providing contexts in which young people learn to love the experience of participating in physical activities. This occurs most often when sports enable young people to learn physical skills, face exciting challenges, display physical competence, and share their sense of physical empowerment with other participants.

THINKING ABOUT SPORTS

- Why are organized youth sports more common in the United States than in countries like Mexico or Afghanistan?

- Coaches in the past have been known to shame boys and men who did not play well by saying that they "played like a bunch of girls." How has this orientation influenced youth sport participation opportunities available to girls through most of the 20th century?
- What are the differences between organized youth basketball programs and skateboarding, and why would some young people prefer to skateboard than play in an organized basketball league?
- As you look at the organized youth sports that exist in your community, what are the most serious problems in the programs and leagues that you know about?
- If you could change two things about organized youth sports, what would you change, and what goals would you hope to achieve by making these changes?

SUGGESTED READING AND WEBSITES

Bigelow, B., Moroney, T., and Hall, L. (2001). *Just let the kids play*. Deerfield Beach, FL: Health Communications, Inc. (A book written to help parents prevent other adults from turning sports into activities that undermine fun.)

Center for Sports Parenting. Institute for International Sport. www.sportsparenting .org/csp/. (A web-based program that offers immediate and practical guidance to parents, coaches, educators, administrators, officials, and others involved in youth sports.)

Coakley, J. (2004). *Sports in society: Issues and controversies*. New York: McGraw-Hill. (Chapter 5, "Sports and Children: Are Organized Sports Worth the Effort?" provides a detailed discussion of social issues associated with youth sports today.)

Engh, F. (1999). *Why Johnny hates sports*. Garden City Park, NY: Avery Publishing Group. (The Director of the National Alliance for Youth Sports discusses why organized youth sports are failing our children and what we can do about it.)

Institute for the Study of Youth Sports. Michigan State University College of Education. http://ed-web3.educ.msu.edu/ysi/. (The institute sponsors research on the benefits and problems of youth sports, produces educational materials, and provides educational programs for coaches, officials, administrators, and parents.)

MomsTeam. MomsTeam Media, Inc. www.momsteam.com. (Information at this parents' site is designed to create a safer, saner, less stressful, and more

inclusive youth sports experience; it is directed at mothers of children in organized youth sport programs.)

Murphy, S. (1999). *The cheers and the tears: A healthy alternative to the dark
side of youth sports today*. San Francisco: Jossey-Bass. (A respected sport psychologist outlines some of the major benefits and problems in youth sports today; he provides excellent information about families and parents as well as
suggestions for change.)

National Alliance for Youth Sports. www.nays.org. (A nonprofit organization
with the goal of making sports safe and positive for America's youth.)

Nu-Way Sports. www.youth-sports.com. (The site offers information, advice, and
instructional products for parents, coaches, and children involved in youth
sports.)

Ryan, J. (1995). *Little girls in pretty boxes: The making and breaking of elite
gymnasts and figure skating*. New York: Doubleday. (A journalist for the *San
Francisco Chronicle* wrote this in-depth look at the lives of U.S. girls and
young women in elite gymnastics and figure skating.)

Urban Youth Sports. Center for the Study of Sport in Society, Northeastern University. www.sportinsociety.org/uys.html. (The site focuses on issues in
Boston, but it provides a useful model for what might be done in other cities to
overcome barriers that limit youth sport participation.)

2

An Open Letter to Communities: What Community Leaders Can Do to Improve Youth Sports

Bob Bigelow, Bruce Svare, Richard Irving, Steve Fisher, and Doug Abrams, The Partnership for Youth Development through Sports

Over the past decade, prominent advocates and researchers have explored the serious problems that plague youth sports today. Thoughtful people have written dozens of books and articles and have held countless symposiums that pinpoint parental overinvolvement and misbehavior, coaches who place winning ahead of children's needs, and overspecialized programs with seasons that are simply too long. Still the problems persist. For example, we have visited many communities whose travel basketball leagues for fifth and sixth graders have 40 or more regular season games before playoffs. This is about 10 games more than most major Division I college basketball programs play. Despite all the writings and symposiums, more and more youth sports leagues seem to be moving toward this destructive "more is better" mentality, which remains a major reason why so many young athletes face increasing risk of injuries and burnout.

Not-for-profit organizations, educational institutes, and national youth sports organizations have offered a number of solutions to these nationwide problems. Most of the "solutions" focus on offering administrators, coaches, and parents educational and training programs designed to change adult attitudes about youth sports. The hope is that changed attitudes will produce changes in the ways adults organize sports programs and how they behave at their children's games. Some communities have even launched their own initiatives in response to crises. In 2000, the Jupiter-Tequestra (FL) Athletic Association became the first community-wide organization to require parents to take a course on how to behave at their children's sporting events. According to a CNN.com News report (July 10, 2000), the requirement was prompted by the increasing number of incidents of inappropriate and often violent behavior among parents of young athletes. To enroll their children, parents now must take an online, video-based course in good behavior offered through the National Alliance of Youth Sports.

Parents and coaches have been told to behave for years, even decades, but things just don't seem to be getting much better. Many thoughtful people in the youth sports community have identified the problems over the years, but we still have not found the solutions that work.

We contend that despite many, many initiatives devoted to adult education and training, the overall youth sports environment has not fundamentally improved over the last 10 to 15 years. Doug Abrams knows this all too well. Doug is a professor specializing in child law at the University of Missouri, and he has tracked youth sports incidents reported in newspapers and magazines around the country for over a decade. He compiles media reports of these incidents and distributes them in his free daily e-newsletter entitled simply *Today's Articles*. Hundreds of people across America who are interested in youth sports receive Doug's daily e-mail.

From his years as an expert observer, Doug maintains that negative examples of adults misbehaving have not lessened in either quantity or severity. Problems range from the worst high-profile incidents (such as the deadly fight in 2000 between two parents at an informal Massachusetts youth hockey scrimmage) to the more frequent adult misbehavior many of us see on sports fields every weekend. When asked recently whether he believes things are getting better or worse, Doug offered this:

I have coached youth hockey since 1968, and I have watched adult civility in youth sports spiral downward since the early 1990s. At one time, adults who acted like lunatics were shunned as outcasts. But many sports programs today encourage lunacy by tolerating, and even rewarding, adult misconduct. Too often, the worst misconduct comes from members of the board of directors, who see board membership as a license to get away with it. Trouble at the top produces trouble in the ranks.

Most parents want sports to be a positive influence in their children's lives. But even if only 10% of parents raise trouble in a typical program, we should measure their damage in decibels rather than sheer numbers. Who can have fun in a 200-family program saddled with 20 sets of troublemaker parents? (D. Abrams, telephone interview, March 2005)

If things were really getting better, the number and severity of incidents Doug tracks each day would dramatically lessen. Ultimately, his e-newsletter should no longer be needed. Unfortunately, that's just not the case today.

THE SOLUTION LIES IN CHANGING THE STRUCTURE AND GOALS OF YOUTH SPORTS PROGRAMS

We believe that to remedy the ills of youth sports in America, adults need to change the very structure and goals of today's youth sports programs. We must reduce the emphasis on competition as the chief goal, and rather promote youth sports as a central aspect of education for every child who wishes to participate. Overemphasizing competition inevitably whittles down the number of kids who play, shutting out not only the ones who are made to feel they aren't good enough, but also the talented ones who get burned out from adult-imposed pressure. On the other hand, sports-as-education stresses skill development, healthy exercise and fitness, enjoyment, socialization, recreation, and just plain fun. The objective is to meet children's primary needs for fun and participation and to assure all children the benefits that come from meeting these needs.

Changes to the structure of today's youth sports programs, like any fundamental change, will face fierce resistance from people heavily invested in the status quo. The detractors will likely include many of the overinvolved parents, coaches, and administrators who are often the "big players" in the local youth sports scene. These folks are the ones who fervently believe that having their kids on a great winning team is far more important than meeting the most fundamental needs for participation and fun that the vast majority of children have (including their own).

Despite this resistance, we argue that there is a need to change the way youth sports programs are structured and operated because, contrary to what most people continue to believe, *mere adult training and education will not solve the problems.* Scientists often tell us that human beings respond to their environment as well as their beliefs. To produce meaningful behavior change, sometimes we have to focus on the environment itself as the number one priority.

An ongoing online survey conducted by Bob Bigelow on his website (2005) shows that most respondents remain very concerned about the problems besetting youth sports. Virtually everyone suggests the traditional solution of more training for parents and coaches. The survey solicits responses from adults who participate in all aspects of youth sports, including coaches, officials, administrators, and parents. All major sports are represented and include programs offered through national youth sports agencies as well as local "parks and rec" programs. Here's what the survey takers recommend (based on results as of April 12, 2005):

- 94%—More training for coaches, officials, and administrators
- 73%—A better focus on developing skills in children
- 58%—Fairer playing time
- 58%—Improved parent behavior

Numerous communities and programs have indeed offered more training during the past two decades, including programs offered by not-for-profits, youth agencies, educational "institutes," and even the national youth sports organizations themselves. Why, then, aren't things getting better, and why isn't all this training and education working?

UNDERSTANDING THE ROOT CAUSE

The answer lies in the fundamental emotions that parents, coaches, and other adults experience when they see their kids participate in sports. This insight is provided best by Dr. Shane Murphy, a prominent youth sports psychologist with over 3 decades of experience at all levels of youth sports, from recreational play to Olympic training and development programs. Here is what Dr. Murphy (1999) says in his watershed book *The Cheers and the Tears*:

> There are deeper motivations behind the involvement of families in youth sports. . . . [P]arents have a deep and powerful love for their children. The power of this love cannot be underestimated. In my experience, this love leads parents to adopt certain attitudes when it comes to their child's involvement in youth sports: they want the best for their child; they want to protect their child from harm; they hope that their child will excel; they fantasize about what might be.
>
> The result of these attitudes is that parents usually become *very emotionally involved* in the youth sports experience . . . because the parent *identifies* so strongly with the child.

But there is little a parent can do but watch once a child pulls on a uniform and goes out onto the field to compete with others of the same age. Naturally this *loss of control* can generate a great deal of anxiety for the concerned parent.

There are few life experiences that can generate the anxiety and tension of watching your own son or daughter participate in a sporting contest. *There is a strong, visceral and emotional connection because of the adult's identification with the child.*

This process of identification helps us understand what happens to youth sports parents as they become more involved in their child's endeavors.

The over-identified parent mistakes his own feelings and goals for those of the child. (pp. 49–52)

The key point Dr. Murphy is making is that the most overinvolved adults—the 20 among the 200 as Professor Abrams puts it—are responding to fundamental, visceral emotions that they find very difficult to overcome; yet these emotions are very normal for virtually all parents who care about their children. The implication is that more fundamental solutions are needed than just parent education and training in order to really change how adults behave at youth sports events.

The truth is that some parents are less able than others to control these visceral emotions. Some parents just respond too intensely when they see their child "on stage" at the Saturday ball game. Most of them are not bad people. In fact, if you saw these out-of-control sports parents in another context, such as mowing their lawns in the neighborhood the very morning of the game, you might never suspect that they will become some of those parents yelling the most at the soccer match for their 10-year-olds that very afternoon! Many other parents, in addition to the 20, also feel these strong emotions, but some are just a bit better at gritting their teeth and being less vocal. Yet the underlying angst is there for many, many other adults who participate in youth sports.

THE NEED FOR CHANGING THE VERY ENVIRONMENT OF MOST YOUTH SPORTS PROGRAMS

While admittedly important, training and education simply cannot overcome the strong emotions parents feel when their kids are involved in youth sports. Short educational sessions, parent pledges, and "good behavior" signs on the field do not neutralize these innate parental emotions that can drive "overin-volved" behavior. We must change the environment within youth sports pro-grams that encourages these strong emotions. By so doing, we can dramati-cally lessen those very emotions that can drive misbehavior, and no longer have to rely on simply providing parents instructions about how to behave.

Parents can all relate to those times when we have seen our kids on stage at a school play. We typically experience the gut-wrenching emo-tions of watching our children perform, and we dread that they will forget their lines! We rejoice when they succeed and sometimes even believe we have the next Marlon Brando or Katharine Hepburn. Youth sports put kids on a similar stage every week, and in an environment that is frankly much more stressful than any school play. The sports environment remains competitive in even most "recreational" programs that enroll the vast ma-jority of our child athletes.

Imagine for a moment an educational process in which parents could watch their kids in class every day. You can bet many would be intensely rooting for their kids to get most every question right and an A on that day's quiz. Of course, this intensity is one reason why most schools limit how of-ten parents can come and visit their child's class. Classroom teaching is grounded in models developed over time by professional educators who gauge the needs of all children, and not just the gifted few. Youth sports need similar grounding, and this is why we believe the solution lies in changing the very structure of today's typical youth sports programs. School physical educational programs stress fitness, skills, and recreation, but most youth sports programs stress competition by applying adult sports models to children. Competition means setting up teams and leagues with stand-ings, similar to high school, college, and pro sports. At the worst, very young children are often placed on teams by adults participating in pro-style "drafts." In the end, we tolerate far too many prepubescent "losers" who drop out for every "winner" that might make the high school varsity team.

Kids' needs are very different from those of adults. It has been well documented that kids place fun and participation well above winning and losing. This was shown clearly in a landmark 1992 study of over 26,000 children conducted by Michigan State University's Institute for the Study of Youth Sports (Seefelt, Ewing, & Walk, 1992). That is why schools and professional educators focus on learning and participation and don't form kids into fixed teams and leagues as they play and learn in the school gym.

Most youth sports programs do exactly the reverse, placing kids on fixed teams within leagues. This placement alone creates a natural environment that permits—indeed encourages—parents, coaches, and other adults to misbehave when the focus on competition runs head on into the emotions that Dr. Murphy so eloquently describes.

The very structure must change to an environment where sports-as-education is the number one priority. This would replace our current model, which puts competition at the forefront. A better structure can meet kids' needs for participation, learning, and fun without many of the elements of adult-oriented play models. This structure would emulate the "recess play" Bob Bigelow, with Tom Moroney and Linda Hall, describes in his book *Just Let the Kids Play* (2001). This model focuses on how kids used to play sports, before adults began overorganizing just about everything our kids do. The Recess Model gives kids a chance for a greater role in how they play rather than having adults running the whole show. Kids used to pick their own teams, resolve their own disputes (most of the time), and make sure scores were as close as possible by balancing their contests. Close games are more fun for children. "Teams" were also fluid from game to game, formed from groups of kids in the local neighborhood. Kids could play with different friends each game and gain the benefits of greater socialization. Ideally, local organized youth sports programs for children under the age of 12 should also have fluid teams, so that kids and coaches make new relationships throughout the year in an environment that deemphasizes individual wins and losses.

Kids certainly enjoy competing, and they do play to win during the game. But when the game is over, kids will tell you that in the grand scheme of things, participation is ultimately more important than who wins or loses. And we should remember that when kids balance out their games in the natural course of their free play, everyone pretty much gets a .500 record!

THE CRITICAL ROLE OF COMMUNITY
LEADERS IN FOSTERING CHANGE

The community's role is crucial in creating change. In 2001, the National Alliance for Youth Sports sponsored a symposium on how to improve youth sports. Key leaders and educators from all over the country attended and developed a series of groundbreaking recommendations for communities on how they could sponsor positive change and realign youth sports programs to fit an educational model. Central to this model is recasting the role of coaches to that of mentors similar to the teachers in our schools. Sports should become an extension of a child's education with the focus on learning rather than pure athletic competition. Positive sports participation grounded in educational principles can help children develop many important values as they learn and grow. This development is impossible for many kids today, as sports have become such a negative experience that over 70% of children quit playing by the age of 13, according to the National Alliance of Youth Sports. Pressure to compete and win can cause kids of all abilities to turn away from organized sports—not only the kids who don't feel they're "good enough," but also "the stars," who are regularly expected by their parents and coaches to live up to an unrealistic level of performance.

We believe that community leaders can help drive educational change and thereby provide an effective alternative to relying on youth sports programs to police themselves. Most youth sports organizations have entrenched cultures that rely on adult-oriented models to interact with kids. These models are driven by adults' competitive emotions that are wrapped up in the performance of their own children and "their teams." On top of that, coaches often feel a responsibility to "their kids" and parents to not let them down by losing too many games. If they do, the parents may judge them as not very good coaches. This frame of mind puts competition ahead of education and often emphasizes tactical play to win games, rather than development of skills in all the kids on a team. Individual parents who seek positive change may be cast as troublemakers for trying to rock the boat, and they are typically not in positions to influence how youth sports programs are run anyway. The inertia of "the way we do things around here" is powerful indeed, and it is difficult to swim against the tide!

Trying to change programs from within can be a long and arduous task. The Positive Coaching Alliance is an excellent organization dedicated to retraining coaches and parents in how they view youth sports and interact with kids. The PCA has undertaken its meritorious mission for several years. On its website (as of this writing) the organization indicates it has conducted over 1,700 workshops for 68,000 coaches, parents, and administrators, covering 680,000 kids who participate in youth sports. These numbers are impressive, but they are still under 2% of the over 4 million volunteer coaches and 40 million–plus children who participate in organized youth sports programs each year. In addition, according to Bob Bigelow, we must consider that turnover in volunteer coaches typically occurs every 3 to 4 years, so that some of these 68,000 coaches undoubtedly have "retired" since they were trained.

Youth sports reform efforts are not only time-consuming, but they also must wend their way through local political pressures that often haunt the administration of these programs. Jupiter, Florida, has installed community-driven mandates for how programs must operate and how parents and coaches must behave. By responding to what were perceived as out-of-control adults at a particular time, the community created a true legacy solution that will outlive the turnover in parents, coaches, and administrators who participate in their youth sports programs.

Richard Irving, founder of Character through Sports (2004), and Bruce Svare, founder of the National Institute for Sports Reform (2004), have worked community-driven change processes in basketball leagues in both Laconia, New Hampshire, and the Albany, New York, area. They have helped install processes that have key community leaders supporting a sports-as-education focus. Their efforts have influenced how their programs are run, have led to new requirements for training coaches, and have created more controls for parental behavior. While not an overnight process, involvement of key community leaders, especially from the school district and parks and recreation department, can help transcend the inertia of individual youth leagues and move more rapidly to positive goals.

COMMUNITIES HAVE THE POWER TO CHANGE YOUTH SPORTS FOR THE BETTER!

How can communities sponsor and promote change? Frankly, communities hold the power of the permit to the fields and other facilities operated by parks and recreation departments and the school district. These authorities can deny permits to programs that fail to measure up to community standards. Community leaders have a moral and ethical responsibility to ensure safe and positive experiences for all children. This responsibility is well established in the classroom, and it should extend to our youth sports programs in our community facilities as we move toward an educational mission and abandon adult-oriented models that perpetuate youth sports' most serious problems. Implementing the use of fluid teams in local programs for children 12 and under is a good place to start (Fisher, 2005). Bob Bigelow's online survey shows that 46% of people believe that there should be more involvement by community officials in improving youth sports programs (Bigelow, 2005). This means nearly half want their local community leaders to get involved.

In a word, adult models stress teams, competition, performance, and all the attributes we enjoy in high school, college, and professional sporting events. These models, however, simply do not fit the needs of younger children. They drive adults to behave in ways inconsistent with the central reasons why kids play sports, namely to have fun, learn new skills, and enjoy playing with friends. Communities and their leaders must step up and take a forceful role in how these programs are run. Examples of success stories are out there. We call on community leaders to get involved and create more positive youth programs that keep kids playing in a positive environment where fun is always first!

REFERENCES

Bigelow, B. (2005, April 12). *Bob Bigelow youth sports survey*. www.bob bigelow.com.

Bigelow, B., Moroney, T., & Hall, L. (2001). *Just let the kids play: How to stop other adults from ruining your child's fun and success in youth sports*. Deerfield Beach, FL: Health Communications, Inc.

Fisher, S. (2005). *New play models for youth sports*. Winchester, MA: The Partnership for Youth Development through Sports.

Irving, R. (2004). *Harnessing the potential of youth athletics: Better kids through better sports*. Winchester, MA: The Partnership for Youth Development through Sports.

Murphy, S. (1999). *The cheers and the tears: A healthy alternative to the dark side of youth sports today*. San Francisco: Jossey-Bass.

National Alliance for Youth Sports (2001). *Recommendations for communities developed through the national summit on raising community standards in children's sports*. West Palm Beach, FL: Author.

Seefelt, V., Ewing, M., & Walk, S. (1992). *An overview of youth sports programs in the United States*. East Lansing, MI: Institute for the Study of Youth Sports at Michigan State University. Commissioned by the Carnegie Council on Adolescent Development, Washington, DC.

Svare, B. (2004). *Reforming sports before the clock runs out*. Delmar, NY: Bordalice Publishing, Inc., Sports Reform Press.

Zarrella, J. (2000, July 10). Florida youth league requires parents to learn sportsmanship. www.cnn.com/2000/HEALTH/07/10/kids.sports.parents.

3

Time Out! For Better Sports for Kids

Fred Engh
National Alliance for Youth Sports

Few will dispute that the violence that unfolded at the rink in Reading, Massachusetts, in July of 2000, in which Thomas Junta beat Michael Costin to death in a dispute over rough play at a youth hockey practice, marked one of the darkest days in the history of organized sports. It also left much of the country wondering how a hockey practice for children disintegrated into a brawl that left a father of four dead, and the altercation became a frightening national symbol of parental rage at youth sporting events. The deadly incident, now more than 5 years old, continues to serve as a grim reminder of how youth sports can be sabotaged by senseless violence between adults. It still stings and still seems unfathomable. Yet as we peer across today's youth sports landscape, the question that now resonates is whether it is any safer for children to step onto a field, court, or rink today to participate in an organized athletic program than it was in 2000 when that fight between Mr. Costin and Mr. Junta became forever etched in our memories.

Surprisingly, in many parts of the country the answer to this question is a resounding no. What transpired in Reading has done little to slow the violent tide sweeping across many of this country's youth athletic facilities. While the majority of today's parents are a supportive and caring group who do a wonderful job with their children, the unfortunate fact of the matter is that there are an ever-increasing number who are disrupting youth sports events with their vicious words, fiery tempers, and out-of-control actions. These are the parents who are turning what should be a good experience for children into a negative one, and not just for their own children, but everyone else involved in the program, as well.

For example, the following are just some of the many incidents that have taken place since that horrific afternoon:

- Two dads pummeled a man whose son played for the opposing team during a hockey tournament game in New Jersey because they believed the squad was using an illegal player. The two were arrested and face up to 5 years in prison under a new state law.
- More than 30 adults brawled following an under-14 soccer tournament game in California that led to several arrests, including one on suspicion of assault with a deadly weapon.
- A father was arrested on a battery charge after he stormed the field and punched the referee in his 7-year-old son's flag football game in Florida.
- Two women assaulted a mother who was left unconscious following a youth baseball championship game in Utah.
- A baseball coach for children ages 12 and 13 was taken into custody on accusations that he grabbed and wrestled an umpire to the ground in Wisconsin.
- An assistant coach allegedly jumped over the boards and grabbed the referee in a dispute over a penalty during a game involving mostly 13-year-olds in Manitoba, Canada.
- Two men were arrested for allegedly kicking a man in the head repeatedly in a brawl that involved about 25 youngsters and adults that began after a youth football game in California.
- A father was sentenced to 60 days in jail and fined $1,000 for misdemeanor charges of assault and battery for hitting his son's coach after a summer baseball game in New Mexico.

Clearly, the simple and sad fact is that fisticuffs involving coaches and parents can emerge pretty much at any community's field, rink, or gym at any time. Anyone who argues otherwise is grossly misinformed regarding the youth sports climate that currently exists.

Athletic competition places children in a vulnerable position, and the natural impulse for parents is to try and control things to ensure that nothing bad happens. This is an extremely difficult position to be in, wanting to control something—the competition—that by its very nature is uncontrollable. Furthermore, there can often be a fine line between knowing when to cheer and when to chill out. While many wonderful parents successfully walk this behavioral tightrope, far too many others blatantly cross the line, and the results are typically disastrous.

Parents want—and deserve—the very best for their children. Whether it's a dance recital, spelling bee, or soccer game, they want their children to succeed. But once scoreboards and shiny championship trophies creep into the picture, the world of organized youth sports becomes a volatile mix. Parental motives suddenly become skewed, perspective is lost, and reasonable behavior vanishes. It is ironic that nobody yells at a child who forgets some lines during a play, who misspells a word during a spelling bee, or who hits the wrong key during a piano recital. But when it comes to sports, a youngster who drops a ball, misses a tackle, or allows the opposing team to score is often going to hear about it from the parents. Human behavior is a tricky subject when it comes to organized sports for children. Three factors that greatly influence parental attitudes when it comes to their children's sports participation are fear, ego, and greed.

Fear literally consumes some parents, who fear their children striking out, missing a ground ball, or dropping the potential game-winning touchdown pass. Many parents harbor fears that their children won't meet their lofty expectations and will be forced to ride the bench during the season. These fears can even carry over into other areas, such as the children not even liking sports and wanting to pursue other interests, and many parents are desperate to do anything to prevent such a fate.

Too often parents are guilty of thinking too far ahead. They worry about how their children aren't going to be chosen for the all-star team that summer if they don't start improving soon. Parents wonder if their children will be good enough for the travel team in a few years, how their daughter compares athletically to the girl down the street who is about the same age, if their son will be talented enough to start on the varsity team as a junior, and so on. There are countless individuals who go through life with low self-esteem, and becoming a parent typically doesn't do much to ease those feelings. Oftentimes the way they visualize themselves directly affects how they behave when their children do not meet expectations. They take it personally, believing that it is not the children who have failed, but they themselves. These are the parents who yell, scream, and complain because it is their egos that are shattered when their children don't measure up to expectations.

To a certain degree it is wonderful to see parents showing support for their children and offering encouragement. But when the underlying reasons for this encouragement and support evolve from an effort to satisfy their own egos, that is when their behavior shows signs of crossing the line. Too often what also transpires is that parents who haven't been able to make a mark on the world themselves are guilty of trying to make that mark through their children. This is the behavior of the parent who vicariously shares the child's experience, which, when it creeps into parental actions, can severely tarnish the parent-child relationship. Parents struggle to detach their self-image as adults from their children's prowess in the competition. Suddenly, when the children make mistakes or don't fulfill the warped expectations placed on them, the parents take it personally. So it is not the children but the adults who have failed. In these types of situations it becomes extremely difficult for parents to separate their children's performance in sports from their own identities.

It is also important to note that few things in life can compare to the joy, frustration, triumph, and disappointment parents will experience watching their children participate in sports. There is simply no denying the fact that parents feel a wonderful sense of pride watching their child sink a game-winning basket, score a big touchdown, or hit a home run in the bottom of the ninth inning to help lead their team to a victory. When a youngster plays like a champion, the parent feels like one. There is a powerful emotional reaction in seeing your own flesh and blood succeed. It often takes over in full force once the games begin, and it can take parents on a roller-coaster ride of emotions.

These days there is also a lot of money to be made in sports, and parents are well aware of the cash windfalls that an athletically gifted child can generate. But if parents allow visions of athletic stardom to become the focal point of their thinking, with their ultimate goal of attaining multimillion-dollar contracts, hefty signing bonuses, and shoe endorsements, the results are typically disastrous. Oftentimes parents become so delusional about the abilities of their children that they mistakenly believe that if the coach doesn't give them extra playing time or allow them to play certain positions that they are depriving the children of the chance to secure scholarships to prestigious universities. It is scary to think about the number of children who are being scarred for life by parents eyeing big payoffs, especially considering just how few children actually reach those elite levels. For example, approximately 0.09% of high school football players will eventually be drafted by an NFL team, according to the NCAA (National Collegiate Athletic Association, 2004). It also reports that 0.03% of high school basketball players will be drafted by an NBA team, and 0.02% of girls basketball players will be drafted by a WNBA team.

I created the National Alliance for Youth Sports back in 1981 because, as the father of seven sports-playing youngsters, I was concerned about volunteer coaches who, despite their best intentions, were oftentimes ill prepared to work properly with a group of children in a sports setting. I never imagined that youth sports would deteriorate so quickly in so many communities that the Alliance and our thousands of volunteers around the country would be forced to refocus our efforts on simply ensuring a safe environment for youngsters to participate. Too many youngsters are having their sports experiences tarnished and their emotional well-being scarred by horrific acts of violence among parents and coaches that spill over from the stands and sidelines onto the playing field. These certainly aren't the types of environments that are conducive to fun and learning, or the catalyst for a lifetime of wonderful sports memories.

A recent survey on adult violence in youth sports that was done by *SportingKid* (2003) magazine found that 95% of the more than 3,300 respondents said that it was time to do something on a national level to stop violent behavior before it escalates to serious injury or death. Furthermore, 85% said they were supportive of a national effort to put a stop to inappropriate behaviors in youth sports. More telling—and disturbing—than anything was the fact that 84.25% said they have witnessed violent parental behavior (shouting, berating, abusive language) toward children, team coaches, or officials at youth sporting events; and 79.8% responded that they have personally been victims of inappropriate behavior.

Clearly, these numbers signal a significant problem regarding adult behavior around the country and the need for youth program directors and league administrators to adopt policies that prevent these types of behaviors from infringing on a child's participation and enjoyment of a sport.

WHAT'S BEING DONE TO STOP THE VIOLENT AND NEGATIVE ADULT BEHAVIOR PLAGUING YOUTH SPORTS

The National Alliance for Youth Sports unveiled its public service campaign—Time Out! For Better Sports for Kids—in 2001 to address the physical and emotional abuse of children, the rampant cheating and total disrespect being shown toward opponents, and the hostile environments children are forced to play in that are ultracompetitive and reward a win-at-all-cost approach. Two vital components of this reform movement are the *Recommendations for Communities* (2001) and parent sportsmanship training offered through the Parents Association for Youth Sports (PAYS).

RECOMMENDATIONS FOR COMMUNITIES

There are approximately 90,000 facilities around the country that are funded by local tax dollars that are used for youth sports programs. Roughly 70% of these programs are overseen by parent interest groups that are handed these facilities to use without having to go through any type of training or instruction in the areas of spectator and coaching behavior, which is a major reason for the violence epidemic we're witnessing now (National Alliance for Youth Sports, 2001).

Well-meaning volunteers who fill coaching and administrative roles, but who typically have not received any type of training or instruction on what the position entails, run most of these sports programs. Furthermore, many parents overstep the boundary of good behavior simply because they've never been told their roles and responsibilities in youth sports. When all these factors are mixed together, it can create a volatile environment.

Because of the rampant violence and growing concern among recreational professionals who oversee sports programs across the country regarding the safety of today's participants, the Alliance convened many of the nation's top recreation leaders for the National Summit on Raising Community Standards in Children's Sports in Chicago in 2001. The three-day summit focused on exploring the escalating problem of violence in youth sports and—more importantly—allowed leaders the opportunity to trade insights on viable approaches and effective policies for restructuring and retooling youth sports programs in order to prevent violence from affecting their programs. The result of the summit was the document *Recommendations for Communities*, which has become the voice of what the nation's most knowledgeable and respected leaders in the field of recreation wholeheartedly believe needs to be implemented to alter the destructive course many communities are currently traveling.

Any interested group seeking to enact positive changes in its programs, or that is looking to put protective measures in place to safeguard its programs, can download the *Recommendations for Communities*—at no cost—from the National Alliance for Youth Sports' website at www.nays.org/IntMain.cfm?Page=33&Cat=1&textarea=Recommendations. "I love the Recommendations, they have been great. I hand out more copies of that than anything," said Andrew Holzinger, the athletic coordinator for Palm Beach County (Florida) Parks and Recreation. "Now we are not a sole voice trying to do something. It allowed us to be able to say that these are the standards, and this is what needs to be done" (National Alliance for Youth Sports, 2003.)

In brief, *Recommendations* encourages communities to do three things. First, it is necessary to appoint a trained and knowledgeable supervisor to oversee children's sports. Next, it is important to hold adults who are granted the use of facilities accountable for what happens in their programs. Last, communities must insure that parents and coaches go through a program that addresses good sportsmanship and the importance of living up to a set code of behavior prior to the start of the season. The Recommendations for Communities must be adopted to restore order and civility to youth sports, and help insure that every child who steps onto the local field, court, or rink has a safe and rewarding experience. It is up to concerned individuals within their respective communities to take a stand and exercise leadership for positive change at the local level. There is simply too much at stake to let all the problems that have been well documented continue to destroy organized sports. The adult behaviors we're seeing at youth athletic events around the country are truly disgraceful. It would be even more disgraceful if we simply sat back and failed to do anything about it. An increasing number of communities around the country have taken proactive steps by implementing the Recommendations for Communities.

The three steps for implementing the Recommendations for Communities are the following:

1. Adopting a community philosophy that makes youth sports safe and positive for children
2. Appointing a professional youth sports administrator to ensure adherence to the philosophy
3. Holding everyone associated with the program accountable for his or her behavior

I believe the Recommendations for Communities must be adopted to restore order and civility to youth sports and to help insure that every child who steps onto the local field, court, or rink has a safe and rewarding experience. It is up to concerned individuals within their respective communities to take a stand and exercise leadership for positive change at the local level. There is simply too much at stake to let all the problems that have been well documented continue to destroy organized sports.

CONCLUSION

Sports are one of the greatest tools to help children develop positive character traits and life values. Unfortunately, the grim reality is that the youth sports system that is currently in place in many communities across the country actually facilitates the emotional and physical abuse of children and encourages inappropriate behavior. It's time that we raised the standard for how sports programs are conducted in communities. If we are going to put an end to these incidents of physical, emotional, and psychological abuse that are occurring, we need to take a look at what's happening around the country very seriously and restrict who is allowed to use a community's public facilities.

Until we treat youth sports with the same importance that we do our educational system, we will continue to encounter problems. A positive youth sports program is not something that anyone should ever simply hope turns out well. It requires work at all levels. The blueprint for returning sports back to their rightful place exists in the *Recommendations for Communities*. Highly respected recreation leaders from around the country have spoken, and the steps they firmly believe need to be implemented have been outlined. The *Recommendations for Communities* is the voice of reason.

REFERENCES

National Alliance for Youth Sports. (2001). *Recommendations for communities developed through the national summit on raising community standards in children's sports*. West Palm Beach, FL: Author. Also available at www.nays.org/IntMain.cfm?Page=33&Cat=1&textarea=Recommendations.

National Alliance for Youth Sports. (2003, August). Palm Beach County Parks and Recreation adopts stricter requirements to ensure safety of everyone using its facilities. (Press release.)

National Collegiate Athletic Association. (2004). *Estimated probability of competing in athletics beyond the high school interscholastic level*. Retrieved November 27, 2005, from www.ncaa.org/research/prob_of_competing/.

Survey says: End the madness—NOW. (2003, March/April). *SportingKid*, 13–14.

4

Motivation and Outcomes of Youth Participation in Sport

Peggy McCann and Martha Ewing
Institute for the Study of Youth Sports,
Michigan State University

If we were to walk down any street, school hallway, or college campus in the United States, it is very likely that we would not walk far before seeing children, teenagers, and adults sporting their favorite team's ball cap, jersey, or team jacket. When we pick up the local newspaper, the lead story is generally focused on the big game performance of high school and college athletes. Parades, dances, and other celebrations are planned to honor the achievements of our local sport heroes. Clearly, adults, children, and adolescents value sport achievement (Chase & Dummer, 1992).

Given that sport achievement is highly valued in our society, many have come to believe that sport participation offers a number of positive outcomes for children. On occasion, we hear or read testimonials (especially in the media) from parents, coaches, and fans that sport builds character, keeps children involved in a structured activity and out of trouble, and teaches teamwork and discipline. Undoubtedly, there is a strong conviction in the United States that the benefits of participation in sport far outweigh the risks. But what exactly are the benefits of sport participation, particularly for children and adolescents?

Seefeldt (1987) explained that the benefits of sport participation could be categorized by their ability to provide young athletes with the opportunity to (1) develop physical skills and improve fitness, (2) learn social and emotional skills, (3) develop moral values, and (4) increase perceived competence, self-esteem, and self-confidence. Essentially, sport participation is viewed as a means to achieving *positive* physical, social, and personal outcomes. Physical benefits may include enhanced strength and cardiovascular fitness (endurance), as well as the development and improvement of sport skills. Social benefits may consist of making new friends or being with existing friends, learning teamwork, and improving upon or forming new relationships with adults. Personal benefits may consist of increasing one's level of self-esteem, confidence, beliefs about one's ability in sport, and overall general attitude.

As one can imagine, the benefits of participation in sport are far reaching and cannot be thoroughly covered in this writing. It is the intent and purpose of this chapter to focus on the personal benefits and outcomes of participation in sport. Specifically, we focus on the personal attribute of motivation, examining why children and adolescents participate in and drop out of sport. Factors that are impacted by or influence one's motivation are discussed as well. These factors include perceptions of competence, sportsmanship, and character development.

MOTIVATION

Many of us have watched or participated in a sporting event in which we have observed varying behavior among the athletes. Some athletes seem to never give up despite how badly they are being beaten, while others tend to give up under the easiest of circumstances. Why is it that some athletes seem to have such high levels of effort and are always strategizing, while others do not seem to care? Most would agree that an individual's level of motivation explains these types of behavior.

Numerous individuals talk about motivation, but do people know what it means? Simply put, motivation is the direction and intensity of one's effort (Sage, 1977). The direction of effort refers to whether an individual seeks out, approaches, or is attracted to a situation or a task. For instance, a student may sign up for a math class, a runner may enter a marathon, or a mother may attend a parenting seminar. The intensity of one's effort is related to the amount of effort an individual expends in a certain situation. For example, children may register to participate in a soccer league, but some will put forth greater effort in practice sessions than in games. Some will not want to practice, but play very hard in games.

As one might conclude, this definition of motivation is vague and often leads to misunderstandings and unrealistic expectations in sport. Many view motivation as an internal trait. You are either born with it or you are not! Often, coaches have a difficult time understanding why athletes do not seem to practice hard or achieve in critical situations. Additionally, coaches may develop motivational strategies, such as providing rewards in the form of stars for football helmets or patches for letter jackets, but fail to understand that while some athletes work harder to earn the reward, other athletes may actually be turned off or work less hard. In essence, some athletes may interpret rewards as a form of control rather than as information about their ability in sport. Consequently, these athletes have a lower level of motivation than what the coach expected.

Essentially, there are individual differences in how athletes respond to situations in sport. The impact of motivational strategies on athletes' subsequent behaviors varies as well. Given that individuals respond differently depending on the situation or personal psychological variables, it is important to examine how motivation impacts changes in both behavioral and psychological outcomes. These outcomes may include perceptions of competence, enjoyment, and reasons for participating in sport and physical activity.

PARTICIPATION MOTIVATION

Participation motivation refers to the reasons that individuals adopt for initiating, continuing, and sustaining involvement in sport and physical activity, as well as the reasons people give for discontinuing or dropping out of sport (Weiss & Ferrer-Caja, 2002). It is estimated that 45 million children under the age of 18 years participate in school and nonschool (i.e., club, YMCA, and recreational) sport programs (Ewing, Seefeldt, & Brown, 1996; Seefeldt, Ewing, & Walk, 1993). Although children who participate in sport vary in many ways, the reasons they give for participating in sport, as well as discontinuing their participation, are very similar. Several studies (i.e., Ewing & Seefeldt, 1989; Sapp & Haubenstricker, 1978; Wankel & Kreisel, 1985) have been conducted over the past 20 years examining the reasons why children (11–18 years old) participate in sport, and in every study children cite fun as the number 1 reason. Other reasons included in the top 10 are learning/improving skills, being with friends, getting into shape, and the exciting and challenging aspects of participating in sport (see Table 4.1). Understanding why children and adolescents participate in sport is important because the goal is to keep children involved in sport. If the motives of youth are known, then sport can be structured to meet the wants and needs of its participants.

Unfortunately, a trend is occurring in the United States indicating that most children start to drop out of sport by the age of 13. This pattern of consistent decline continues to about the age of 18. At this age, only a relatively small percentage of America's youth are participating in sport (Ewing & Seefeldt, 1989). For example, 25.3% of gymnasts participated in their sport as 10-year-olds, but only 3.3% continued to participate by the age of 18 (Seefeldt et al., 1993). Other studies have reported similar results (see Gould & Petlichkoff, 1988; Orlick, 1973, 1974; Sapp & Haubenstricker, 1978). Reasons cited by young children for dropping out of sport include lack of playing time, an overemphasis on winning, too much pressure, lack of fun, and conflict with the coach (e.g., Orlick, 1973, 1974). Adolescents frequently cited time as a major reason for discontinuing sport participation. For example, many expressed the need to get a job so they would have money for gas, clothes, and general "stuff."

The dropout rate of children's sport participation is cause for great concern. For example, in 2002, then secretary of the U.S. Department of Health and Human Services ([USDHHS], 2002) Tommy Thompson called for families, communities, and businesses to work together in creating innovative ways for children to become involved in physical activity. Thompson further stated that "We need to stop the guilt ridden lectures and show kids enjoyable things that they can do to improve their health.

Table 4.1. Top 10 Motives for Participation and Withdrawal in Youth Sports

Motives for Participation	*Motives for Withdrawal*
1. To have fun	1. Lost interest
2. To improve sport skills	2. Not having fun
3. To stay in shape	3. It took too much time
4. To do something they are good at	4. Coach was a poor teacher
5. For the excitement of competition	5. Too much pressure

Adapted from Ewing and Seefeldt, 1989.

That way, they'll want to spend more time on the playground and less time on their Play Stations" (p. 1).

Thompson's urging stemmed from a recent study indicating that the prevalence of obesity and overweight children and adolescents had more than tripled over the past 2 decades (National Center for Health Statistics [NCHS], 2000). This inactivity among children and adolescents will likely cause a major economic burden on the economy. Sedentary lifestyles, such as inactivity and unhealthy eating patterns, can contribute to obesity, cancer, cardiovascular disease, and diabetes (USDHHS, 2002). Because inactivity is unhealthy behavior for children and adolescents and will likely lead to sedentary lifestyles as an adult, it is critical that children be encouraged to participate in regular physical activity (Garcia et al., 1995).

Data from the Youth Risk Behavior Surveillance (Center for Disease Control and Prevention, 2003) indicate that all children are at risk for inactivity, but this is most prevalent for African Americans, Hispanic children, and girls of all ages. This significant lack of inactivity, particularly for African American and Hispanic children and adolescents, likely contributes to differences among obesity levels of African American, Hispanic, and European American children and adolescents. Prevalence of obesity among African American and Hispanic children is 18.3% and 17.3% respectively, while obesity among European American children (14.1%) is lower. Although diseases associated with physical inactivity tend to manifest later in life, behavioral patterns exhibited in childhood tend to persist into adulthood (Kelder, Perry, Klepp, & Lytle, 1994). It is, therefore, necessary to increase or maintain the activity patterns of children. Obviously, participation in sport is one way to accomplish this goal. But, what are the smaller steps that must be taken to ensure that this goal is met? One method is to focus on the positive psychological outcomes of participation in sport, including enhancing one's level of perceived competence.

PERCEIVED COMPETENCE

Perceived competence is defined as the judgments that individuals form about their capabilities (Harter, 1978, 1981). In other words, how good do children and adolescents think they are at a particular sport? Research has consistently indicated that individuals, particularly children and adolescents, who participate in sport and have high perceptions of competence demonstrate higher levels of enjoyment, perceptions of internal control (believe they are responsible for their successes and failures), motivation to continue to participate, effort, and performance (Brustad, 1988; Ebbeck & Weiss, 1998; Scanlan & Lewthwaite, 1984; Weiss, Bredemeier, & Shewchuk, 1986; Weiss & Horn, 1990).

In addition, sport participants have been found to demonstrate varying levels of perceived competence, which are dependent upon the role they play on a team. For example, starters have been found to have higher levels of perceived competence as compared to those first to substitute and those considered benchwarmers (Petlichkoff, 1993a, 1993b). Results such as those reported in this study clearly indicate that perceived competence could be nurtured and developed by giving all players the opportunity to practice, develop, and demonstrate their skills.

Perceptions of competence have also been found to differ between very young children (4–7), middle school–aged children (8–13), and adolescents (14–18). Very young children do not differentiate between effort and ability (Nicholls, 1978). Children at this age believe that they are very good because they put forth great effort. For example, a child might say, "If I try my best to shoot a basketball, I am good, regardless of whether I make the basket." As children age, however, they are able to differentiate between effort and ability. Therefore, they believe that if they have to work hard on a task, they must have low ability. Trying hard to make a basket indicates that I am not very good at shooting. Conversely, easily making 10 jump shots in a row means high ability.

How children form their perceptions of ability is important to understand as well. Essentially, what are the criteria that children use for forming their judgments about their competence? Research in sport and physical activity has demonstrated that perceptions of physical competence in younger children (i.e., 8–9 years old) increase with positive feedback from coaches and parents, while conversely, perceptions of physical competence in older children (i.e., 10–13 years old) increase when they perceive that they have outperformed peers in a sport or physical skill (Horn & Hasbrook, 1987; Horn & Weiss, 1991; Weiss, Ebbeck, & Horn, 1997). Adolescents ages 14–15 tend to rely on peer comparison as well, whereas older adolescents (16–18 years old) rely more on internal information, such as skill improvement and effort exerted, as well as goal achievement and attraction to their sport (Horn, Glenn, & Wentzel, 1993). Hence, the saliency of information sources differs among age groups of children.

This difference in the saliency of sources is important to understand especially for those adults involved in organized youth sports. Children prior to the age of 6 or 7 do not understand how to use ability to establish their perception of competence. This is the good news, as preschool age children are often willing to practice a skill longer than those older children who compare how they perform a skill relative to others. If early elementary age youth see that they cannot run as fast or throw or kick a ball as far as others, or other children make fun of how they perform a skill, these children may decide they lack the ability to succeed in sports. Children between the ages of 8 and 15 must be encouraged to focus on more internal information as well as peer comparison because reliance on only peer comparison may lead to detrimental outcomes. These include lower perceptions of competence, perceptions of external control (a belief that others are responsible for their success and failure), and a tendency to display unsportsmanlike behavior (Duda, Olson, & Templin, 1991; Horn & Hasbrook, 1987; Weiss et al., 1997). Parents and youth coaches are also key players during these skill-building years. Youth must be praised for practicing skills, and parents should spend time playing catch or shooting baskets to encourage their work ethic.

SPORTSMANSHIP AND CHARACTER DEVELOPMENT

How often have you heard the saying that sport builds character? Historically, there is a belief that sport is a vehicle for building character or developing moral values, such as sportsmanship. Character encompasses many characteristics including compassion, fairness, sportsmanship, and integrity (Shields & Bredemeier, 1995). Sportsmanship (also referred to as sportspersonship) reflects behaviors that indicate a full commitment toward participation, respect and concern for the rules and officials, respect for social conventions (e.g., shaking hands after the contest), respect and concern for the opponent, and avoiding poor attitudes (Vallerand, Briere, Blanchard, & Provencher, 1997).

The development of character and sportsmanship does not happen automatically. The key to this development is the promotion of quality youth sport programs with competent leadership (Ewing, Gano-Overway, Branta, & Seefeldt, 2002; Shields & Bredemeier, 1995; Smoll & Smith, 1989). In fact, teaching and modeling of appropriate behaviors have been found to be effective strategies in developing moral behaviors in young athletes (Bredemeier, Weiss, Shields, & Shewchuk, 1986; Debusk & Hellison, 1989). All too often, however, we hear news accounts of coaches, parents, and spectators behaving badly. For example, two coaches were involved in incidents with their teams in which the coach's behavior was questionable. One incident involved a coach who paid two children (age 8) $1 to beat up another child on the team. The coach was apparently dissatisfied with this player and wanted him off the team. In the second incident, a coach of 13-year-old hockey players pulled his goalie from the ice to allow the other team to score. The reason: If his team won they would then be forced to play a tougher opponent in the tournament. If his team lost or tied, however, they would face a weaker opponent. The coach's team was winning by one goal with time winding down in the game.

Parents play a role in their children's character development through sport as well. Children's perceptions of the importance of sport participation are impacted by their parents' behaviors (Greendorfer, Lewko, & Rosengren, 2002). Hence, how a parent behaves at a sporting event or a child's competition may impact the child's behavior. In essence, the child will internalize the parent's beliefs and in all likelihood will behave similarly. In our own research we have seen how the behavior of parents at their children's sporting events might be cause of great concern. For example, while observing a youth sport soccer game, our research team observed the parents (approximately 20 parents) being *very* involved in the action on the field. They were standing very close to the field of play and yelling instructions constantly to the children. In fact, it was very difficult for our research team to determine who the coach was for the team. In addition, because this was a group of young athletes, the field was modified to half the size of a regular soccer field. The sheer size of the field, therefore, made it appear as if the parents were practically on top of the action. The constant barrage of messages to the players was very distracting to our research team, and one can only imagine how distracting and confusing these messages were to the participants. In a similar observation of another soccer game we observed the parents laughing at an opposing player when the ball hit her in the face (Haubenstricker, Ewing, & McCann, 2002).

ROLE OF PARENTS IN ATHLETE MOTIVATION AND OUTCOMES

Regardless of whether the parent is a coach or spectator on the sideline, children interpret parents' level of involvement in a variety of ways. In the literature, this interpretation is examined through looking at the constructs of parental support and pressure. Brustad (1988) found that for both boys and girls (ages 9 to 13) who participated in an agency-sponsored youth basketball game, higher levels of enjoyment were predicted by perceptions of low parental pressure and an intrinsic motivational orientation. Similarly, tennis players between the ages of 6 and 18 who perceived high parental support reported higher levels of enjoyment and self-esteem (Leff & Hoyle, 1995). Gender differences, however, did exist in the players' perceptions of support from their mothers and fathers. Females perceived greater support from both parents than did males. In addition, males perceived higher levels of pressure from their fathers than from their mothers, whereas females perceived similar levels of pressure from both parents. These results point to the importance of examining the subjective interpretation of athletes from the perspective of their socialization histories. Males and females are often socialized differently into sport, and this socialization is often a reflection of the parents, particularly the father (Greendorfer & Lewko, 1978).

Hellstedt (1990) examined the perceptions of parental support and pressure with 13-year-old alpine ski racers. He was interested in the athletes' perceptions of degree of parental pressure to compete, their continued participation in the sport, and the athlete's subjective affective response. The results indicated that the majority of the athletes perceived a moderate to excessive level of pressure from their parents. What was surprising, however, was that many of the athletes did not perceive this pressure as negative, but rather positive. Parents are skating on thin ice with adolescent children. While adolescents are trying to learn to be independent during these years, parents must provide guidance and support. Adolescents still want to be loved and made to feel special while maintaining a distance to show their independence.

ROLE OF COACHES IN ATHLETE
MOTIVATION AND OUTCOMES

The coach becomes an important source of competence information during the middle childhood years (Horn et al., 1993; Horn & Hasbrook, 1987; Horn & Weiss, 1991; Weiss et al., 1997). During this time period, coaches can have a tremendous impact on a young athlete's psychological and motivational processes. Specifically, the type and frequency of coaches' feedback have been found to greatly influence athletes' perceptions. For example, Smith, Smoll, and colleagues (Barnett, Smoll, & Smith, 1992; Smith & Smoll, 1990; Smith, Smoll, & Curtis, 1979; Smith, Smoll, & Hunt, 1977; Smoll, Smith, Barnett, & Everett, 1993) found that Little League coaches who received a training program that encouraged the use of positive, instructional, and supportive feedback had a much lower player attrition rate than untrained coaches. In addition, young baseball players who were low in self-esteem responded better to coaches who provided supportive and instructional feedback and also had significantly greater increases in their self-esteem at the end of the season. These studies clearly indicate the importance of other significant people, such as coaches, and the need for supportive and instructional feedback to build competence and self-esteem.

Horn (1984, 1985) was interested in the relationship between coaches' behaviors and athletes' perceptions also. Her focus, however, shifted from coaches' interactions with the team as a whole to coaches' interactions and behaviors with individual athletes. She examined the relationship between coaching behaviors and self-perceptions (e.g., perceived competence, perceived performance control, and expectations of success) among 12-to-15-year-old softball players. Results from these studies indicated that coaches' practice behaviors were significantly associated with players' self-perceptions, but coaches' game behaviors were not. These results suggest that players perceived coaches' practice behaviors to be more salient indicators of their ability than coaches' game behaviors. Overall, results suggested that greater frequency of no reinforcement (saying nothing at all) was associated with lower perceptions of competence. In addition, greater instances of positive reinforcement for mastery attempts and performance were also associated with lower perceived softball competence. Finally, criticism for performance errors was linked to increases in perceived competence. These seemingly contradictory findings were explained by the contingency and appropriateness of the coach's feedback. Those athletes who were low in expectancies for success, as compared to athletes expecting higher levels of success, likely received more frequent positive reinforcement for easy tasks, therefore perceiving this information as an indication that they possessed low competence in softball. On the other hand, those athletes expecting success who frequently received criticism from coaches may have perceived this information as coaches having higher expectations, thereby resulting in more positive beliefs in competence. These results, again, highlight the complex nature of feedback and how interpretations of feedback often are not what are intuitively expected. It is also critical to understand that the positive perception of criticism from a coach works best for athletes who are in high school or older.

CONCLUSION

Youth development in sport is the result of a complicated interaction of personal and contextual factors. The purpose of this chapter is to cover only a small percentage of these variables. Our focus is to enlighten the reader about some of the positive developmental outcomes that result from participation in sport. In addition, we examine how motivation plays a large role in forming these positive outcomes. As you think about how sport fits into your life, we hope that you take the information you have learned and apply it to your thinking about your own reasons for participating and not participating in sport. We also encourage you to think about the ways in which sport has impacted your thoughts, and how other significant people influence your perceptions about your sport experience. Finally, we encourage you to expand your horizons and delve deeper into the topic of sport and its impact on psychological and social processes. Keep in mind that we have only provided you a small glimpse into this area and that other topics, such as aggression, stress, burnout, and athletic injury in sport, are important to consider as well.

REFERENCES

Barnett, N. P., Smoll, F. L., & Smith, R. E. (1992). Effects of coach-athlete relationships on youth sport attrition. *The Sport Psychologist, 6,* 111–127.

Bredemeier, B. J., Weiss, M. R., Shields, D. L., & Shewchuk, R. M. (1986). Promoting moral growth in a summer sport camp: The implementation of theoretically grounded instructional strategies. *Journal of Moral Education, 15*, 212–220.

Brustad, R. J. (1988). Affective outcomes in competitive youth sport: The influence of interpersonal and socialization factors. *Journal of Sport and Exercise Psychology, 10*, 307–321.

Center for Disease Control and Prevention. (2003). Youth risk behavior surveillance: United States 2003. *Morbidity and Mortality Weekly Report, 53*, 1–100.

Chase, M. A., & Dummer, G. M. (1992). The role of sports as a social status determinant for children. *Research Quarterly for Exercise and Sport, 63*, 418–424.

DeBusk, M., & Hellison, D. (1989). Implementing a physical education self-responsibility model for delinquency-prone youth. *Journal of Teaching in Physical Education, 8*, 104–112.

Duda, J. L., Olson, L. K., & Templin, T. J. (1991). The relationship of task and ego orientation to sportsmanship attitudes and the perceived legitimacy of injurious acts. *Research Quarterly for Exercise and Sport, 62*, 79–87.

Ebbeck, V., & Weiss, M. R. (1998). Determinants of children's self-esteem: An examination of perceived competence and affect in sport. *Pediatric Exercise Science, 10*, 285–298.

Ewing, M. E., Gano-Overway, L. A., Branta, C. E., & Seefeldt, V. D. (2002). The role of sports in youth development. In M. Gatz, M. A. Messner, & S. J. Ball-Rokeach (Eds.), *Paradoxes of youth and sport* (pp. 31–48). Albany: State University of New York Press.

Ewing, M. E., & Seefeldt, V. (1989). *Participation and attrition patterns in American agency-sponsored and interscholastic sports: An executive summary.* Final Report. North Palm Beach, FL: Sporting Goods Manufacturers' Association.

Ewing, M. E., Seefeldt, V. D., & Brown, T. P. (1996). *Role of organized sport in the education and the health of American children and youth.* Background Report on the Role of Sports in Youth Development. New York: Carnegie Corporation of New York.

Garcia, A. W., Norton-Broda, M. A., Frenn, M., Coviak, C., Pender, N. J., & Ronis, D. L. (1995). Gender and developmental differences in exercise beliefs among youth and prediction of their exercise behavior. *Journal of School Health, 65*(6), 213–219.

Gould, D., & Petlichkoff, L. (1988). Participation motivation and attrition in young athletes. In F. L. Smoll, R. A. Magill, & M. J. Ash (Eds.), *Children in sport* (3rd ed., pp. 161–178). Champaign, IL: Human Kinetics.

Greendorfer, S. L., & Lewko, J. H. (1978). Role of family in members in sport socialization of children. *Research Quarterly, 49*, 146–152.

Greendorfer, S. L., Lewko, J. H., & Rosengren, K. S. (2002). Family influence in sport socialization: Sociocultural perspectives. In F. Smoll & R. Smith (Eds.), *Children and youth in sport* (pp. 89–111). Dubuque, IA: Brown and Benchmark.

Harter, S. (1978). Effectance motivation reconsidered: Toward a developmental model. *Human Development, 21*, 34–64.

Harter, S. (1981). A model of intrinsic mastery motivation in children: Individual differences and developmental change. In W. A. Collins (Ed.), *Minnesota symposium on child psychology* (Vol. 14, pp. 215–255). Hillsdale, NJ: Erlbaum.

Haubenstricker, J., Ewing, M., & McCann, P. (2002). *Evaluation of the Volunteers, Administrators, and Coaches Initiative (VAC)*. East Lansing: Michigan State University, Institute for the Study of Youth Sports.

Hellstedt, J. C. (1990). Early adolescent perceptions of parental pressure in the sport environment. *Journal of Sport Behavior, 13*, 135–144.

Horn, T. S. (1984). Expectancy effects in the interscholastic athletic setting: Methodological considerations. *Journal of Sport Psychology, 6*, 60–76.

Horn, T. S. (1985). Coaches' feedback and changes in children's perceptions of their physical competence. *Journal of Educational Psychology, 77*, 174–186.

Horn, T. S., Glenn, S. D., & Wentzell, A. B. (1993). Sources of information underlying personal ability judgments in high school athletes. *Pediatric Exercise Science, 5*, 263–274.

Horn, T. S., & Hasbrook, C. A. (1987). Psychological characteristics and the criteria children use for self-evaluation. *Journal of Sport Psychology, 9*, 208–221.

Horn, T. S., & Weiss, M. R. (1991). A developmental analysis of children's self-ability judgments in the physical domain. *Pediatric Exercise Science, 3*, 310–326.

Kelder, S. H., Perry, C. L., Klepp, K. I., & Lytle, C. C. (1994). Longitudinal tracking of adolescent smoking, physical activity and food choice behaviors. *American Journal of Public Health, 84*, 1121–1126.

Leff, S. S., & Hoyle, R. H. (1995). Young athletes' perceptions of parental support and pressure. *Journal of Youth and Adolescence, 24*(2), 187–203.

National Center for Health Statistics. (2000). *Health, United States*. With adolescent health chartbook. Table 69, updated on 7/27/2000. Retrieved December 15, 2005, from www.cdc.gov/nchs/hus/hus00.pdf.

Nicholls, J. (1978). The development of the concepts of effort and ability, perception of academic attainment, and the understanding that difficult tasks require more ability. *Child Development, 49*, 800–814.

Orlick, T. D. (1973, January/February). Children's sport: A revolution is coming. *Canadian Association for Health, Physical Education, and Recreation Journal*, pp. 12–14.

Orlick, T. D. (1974, November/December). The athlete dropout: A high price for inefficiency. *Canadian Association for Health, Physical Education, and Recreation Journal*, pp. 21–27.

Petlichkoff, L. M. (1993a). Group differences on achievement goal orientations, perceived ability, and level of satisfaction during an athletic season. *Pediatric Exercise Science, 5*, 12–24.

Petlichkoff, L. M. (1993b). Relationship of player status and time of seasons to achievement goals and perceived ability in interscholastic athletes. *Pediatric Exercise Science, 5*, 242–252.

Sage, G. (1977). *Introduction to motor behavior: A neuropsychological approach* (2nd ed.). Reading, MA: Addison-Wesley.

Sapp, M., & Haubenstricker, J. (1978). *Motivation for joining and reasons for not continuing in youth sport programs in Michigan.* Paper presented at the AAHPER National Convention. Kansas City, MO.

Scanlan, T. K., & Lewthwaite, R. (1984). Social psychological aspects of competition for male youth sport participants: I. Predictors of competitive stress. *Journal of Sport Psychology, 6*, 208–226.

Seefeldt, V. D. (1987). *Handbook for youth sport coaches.* Reston, VA: National Association for Sport and Physical Education.

Seefeldt, V., Ewing, M., & Walk, S. (1993). *Overview of youth sports programs in the United States.* Unpublished manuscript commissioned by the Carnegie Council on Adolescent Development.

Shields, D. L. L., & Bredemeier, B. J. L. (1995). *Character development and physical activity.* Champaign, IL: Human Kinetics.

Smith, R. E., & Smoll, F. L. (1990). Self-esteem and children's reactions to youth sport coaching behaviors: A field study of self-enhancement processes. *Developmental Psychology, 26*(6), 987–993.

Smith, R. E., Smoll, F. L., & Curtis, B. (1979). Coach effectiveness training: A cognitive-behavioral approach to enhancing relationship skills in youth sport coaches. *Journal of Sport Psychology, 1*, 59–75.

Smith, R. E., Smoll, F. L., & Hunt, E. (1977). A system for the behavioral assessment of athletic coaches. *Research Quarterly, 48*, 401–407.

Smoll, F. L., & Smith, R. E. (1989). Leadership behaviors in sport: A theoretical model and research paradigm. *Journal of Applied Social Psychology, 19*, 1522–1551.

Smoll, F. L., Smith, R. E., Barnett, N. P., & Everett, J. J. (1993). Enhancement of children's self-esteem through social support training for youth sport coaches. *Journal of Applied Psychology, 78,* 602–610.

U.S. Department of Health and Human Services. (2002). *HHS urges community partnerships to improve physical activity.* Washington, DC: U.S. Department of Health and Human Services, Government Printing Office.

Vallerand, R. J., Briere, N. M., Blanchard, C., & Provencher, P. (1997). Development and validation of the multidimensional sportspersonship orientation scale. *Journal of Sport and Exercise Psychology, 19,* 197–206.

Wankel, L. M., & Kreisel, P. S. J. (1985). Factors underlying enjoyment of youth sports: Sport and age group comparisons. *Journal of Sport Psychology, 7,* 51–64.

Weiss, M. R., Bredemeier, B. J., & Shewchuk, R. M. (1986). The dynamics of perceived competence, perceived control, and motivational orientation in youth sports. In M. R. Weiss & D. Gould (Eds.), *Sport for children and youths: Proceedings of the 1984 Olympic Scientific Congress* (pp. 89–102). Champaign, IL: Human Kinetics.

Weiss, M. R., Ebbeck, V., & Horn, T. S. (1997). Children's self-perceptions and sources of physical competence information: A cluster analysis. *Journal of Sport and Exercise Psychology, 19,* 52–70.

Weiss, M. R., & Ferrer-Caja, E. (2002). Motivational orientations and sport behavior. In T. S. Horn (Ed.), *Advances in Sport Psychology* (2nd ed., pp. 101–171). Champaign, IL: Human Kinetics.

Weiss, M. R., & Horn, T. S. (1990). The relation between children's accuracy estimates of their physical competence and achievement-related characteristics. *Research Quarterly for Exercise and Sport, 61*(3), 250–258.

II

GENDER AND SEXUALITY IN SPORT

5

Title IX: Past, Present, and Future

Margaret Duncan
University of Wisconsin, Milwaukee

A TALE OF TWO WOMEN

It's the summer of 1965, and I'm shooting hoops with my best friend Carolyn Groff. Every evening we play h-o-r-s-e on the blacktop behind her garage. The backboard was mounted for Carolyn's two older brothers— who are now grown up and have moved away—so we get to practice our shots without any annoying older-brother commentary. We spend hours perfecting our layups, but mainly we play just for fun. Once the weather gets cold, our evening basketball games are a thing of the past.

But in November in junior high phys ed class, we start our unit on indoor basketball. I discover that I'm one of the best players in my class. It's thrilling: I can shoot from almost anywhere on the court and make a basket. My gym teacher, Mrs. Shoemaker, is extravagant with her praise. "Fantastic, Margaret," she says. I am euphoric. Every day I look forward to 11:30 gym class.

All too soon, though, we move on to a unit on social dancing. Once we do, I think wistfully of my basketball prowess. There are no more chances to play real basketball on a team of girls. The boys have a regular basketball team and compete with other junior high school teams, but we are supposed to be content to watch them from the bleachers. Carolyn and I attend some of the games, but it's disheartening; I yearn to be out there on the court. My homeroom teacher, Mr. Boehm, is the boys' basketball coach. He knows I'm in love with basketball and teases me gently. "Margaret," he says, "we could have won that game if you'd been on the team." That's as close as I get to basketball glory.

A generation later, my daughter Elizabeth is now 14, the same age as I when I ended my basketball "career." She has a cornucopia of sport choices. She considers soccer, volleyball, basketball, swimming, and track, and finally settles on the low hurdles. Alongside the boys, she trains hard in the weight room twice a week. We come to her track meets and applaud her victories. We commiserate with her when she loses. At the end of the track season we attend the athletic banquet, where she receives praise for her hard work. Elizabeth assumes that girls have always had these opportunities and have always been encouraged to play sports. She has no sense as I do that being on an athletic team is a privilege, an opportunity that wasn't accorded to girls of my generation. This is the difference that Title IX has wrought.

The effects of Title IX are the centerpiece of this chapter. However, to grasp how this legislation shaped the sporting opportunities of girls and women, it is necessary to understand its historical and political context. As readers will see, for women and girls, sport has been the field on which bitter and sometimes protracted power struggles take place — with stakes higher than anyone might imagine. Although the history of women's sport is, at least in part, a history of male control, there have always been women and girls who contested the notion of sport as a masculine domain. These women embodied strength, skill, and discipline, proving themselves worthy of the title "athlete."

The passage of Title IX was, in some ways, a turning point for female athletes, even when — as has often been the case — its promise was not fulfilled by sport institutions. This chapter describes women's striving for parity in sport.

A BRIEF HISTORICAL OVERVIEW OF SPORT AND WOMEN'S PHYSICALITY

Any survey of girls' and women's sport must begin with society's view of the female body, since the two are intimately connected. Much of what has been written about the female body focuses on White middle- or upper-class girls and women. Historians have written less about the physicality of girls and women of color. Yet it is important to acknowledge that generalizations about privileged girls and women do not necessarily apply to historically marginalized groups such as African and African American women, Latinas, and Asian Americans. Where possible, this overview will draw distinctions among different groups of women.

The Exclusion of Women and Girls from Sport

It is fitting that a historical survey begins with the ancient Greek Olympic Games, the earliest and most prestigious competition. These games were to set the tone for later athletic competitions insofar as the competitors were exclusively elite males (nonslaves). Women were prohibited from participating in the Games, and married women were forbidden even to view the Games, upon pain of death (*FAQs*, 2001).

This early exclusion of women from sports and physical activity was echoed during later historical periods, although there were always some women and girls who ignored the strictures of convention. The Victorians viewed the middle- and upper-class White woman's body as a frail and delicate vessel (except when she was engaged in rigorous domestic labor!). Not only was she thought to be physically incapable of vigorous movement, she was morally obligated to conserve her precious "vital force" for childbearing (Lenskyj, 1986; Smith-Rosenberg & Rosenberg, 1987). Male doctors warned against exercise on the grounds that it might displace the uterus, interfering with a woman's reproductive function (Gerber, 1974; Lenskyj, 1986). In addition, male authorities warned that vigorous physical activity might lead a woman to cultivate traits that were antithetical to true womanhood (meaning the roles of wife and mother), such as a certain independence of spirit, a determined will, and a developed intellect (Cahn, 1994).

Challenges to the Established Victorian Gender Order

The invention of the baby carriage posed a challenge to Victorian mores. It allowed upper- and middle-class Victorian mothers, previously housebound, to become mobile. Later, the invention of the bicycle offered even greater mobility (Cahn, 1994; Lenskyj, 1986; Nelson,

1998). The bicycle permitted women of all classes to become physically active, as even working-class women could afford to rent this vehicle (Nelson). Bloomers, an early precursor to women's trousers, allowed women more freedom of movement than the heavy and restricting folds of fabric that made up women's skirts (Gerber, 1974; Nelson). These innovations cleared the way for women's later participation in physical activity.

The Status of Women of Color

The myth of women's frailty applied only to White women, and then mainly when it suited men's purposes. Black women were regarded quite differently. During the 19th century, the image of the Black woman was strongly influenced by the "Hottentot Venus," Sarah Baartman. Baartman was a Khoi Khoi woman of South Africa, brought to England and Europe by two European men, who exhibited her as a physical curiosity (Brady, 2001). Her large, protruding buttocks were a distinguishing feature that signified hypersexuality to the repressed Victorians, and they were attracted and repelled in equal measure by her exoticism (Brady; McKeown, 2003). The notion of Black hypersexuality was reinforced by African slave women who were brought to the auction block nude and closely scrutinized by prospective buyers (Collins, 2000). When Black female slaves were raped by White slave owners and bore their children, the association of Black women with sexual promiscuity was intensified (Collins, 2000). Thus, unlike White women, Black women were strongly identified with the body and its sexual appetites.

Yet when it suited their purposes, Whites simultaneously regarded Black women as gender*less*. On the plantation, Black slave women in the fields toiled as hard as men. Sojourner Truth's famous "Ain't I a Woman" speech (1851), delivered in 1851 at the Women's Convention in Akron, Ohio, was a poignant testament to the ease with which White men exploited Black women for the purposes of expediency:

> That man over there says that women need to be helped into carriages, and
> lifted over ditches, and to have the best place everywhere. Nobody ever
> helps me into carriages, or over mud-puddles, or gives me any best place!
> And ain't I a woman? Look at me! Look at my arm! I have ploughed and

planted, and gathered into barns, and no man could head me! And ain't I a woman? I would work as much and eat as much as a man—when I could get it—and bear the lash as well! And ain't I a woman!

Black women were thus viewed as a species apart from White women, and as such, their physicality was acceptable, especially when they were needed in the fields. The advent of two World Wars, however, changed the way women, both Black and White, thought about themselves and their physical capabilities.

The Temporary Reign of Rosie the Riveter

Nowhere was the retreat to expediency (for women of color *and* White women) more obvious than during the two World Wars. When men went off to fight, women were needed in the factories to produce the goods that fueled the war effort. In a stunning ideological about-face, suddenly women were deemed competent to undertake work that was distinctly *nondomestic*, for example, to labor in munitions plants (Gerber, 1974). Rosie the Riveter reigned! Yet once the wars were over, women were told in no uncertain terms that their jobs belonged to the returning soldiers. Because physical activity could be deeply satisfying, many women wanted to keep working, and some continued to do so, despite societal resistance (Gerber, 1974).

College Athletics for Women

Although the largely male medical profession continued to impose restrictions on women's involvement in physical activity, especially during their "monthly incapacity" (Lenskyj, 1986; Smith-Rosenberg & Rosenberg, 1987), exercise and physical training became popular offerings at women's colleges in the early 1900s (Cahn, 1994). Authorities debated the merits of competition and the appropriateness of certain sports for women. Female physical educators recommended athletics, but only in moderation; they created separate women's programs that emphasized playfulness, health, and cooperation (Cahn, 1994). Highly competitive games were deemed masculine and inappropriately aggressive for young women (Cahn, 1994; Smith-Rosenberg & Rosenberg, 1987).

"Feminine" Sports and the Health/Beauty Equation

Authorities debated the merits of certain sports for women. Throughout the 20th century, experts promoted aesthetically pleasing, noncontact individual sports for White women and girls (Metheny, 1965). Figure skating, gymnastics, synchronized swimming, dance, and of course, the ever popular cheerleading were all activities that lent themselves to traditional heterosexual images of femininity. Early on, popular magazines equated health with beauty, a theme that endures to this day (Cahn, 1994; Duncan, 1994; Spitzack, 1990). Exercises were one route to glamour, and discipline led to a well-proportioned figure, something, magazines implied, that every woman should strive for (Cahn, 1994; Duncan, 1994; Spitzack, 1990).

Some other types of sports, such as basketball, were acceptable for women, but only when the rules were modified in ways that made it clear to all that the women's game was but a pallid imitation of the real game, that is to say, the men's game (Lenskyj, 1986). Black women again proved the exception, as athletes like Alice Coachman, Wilma Rudolph, and Willye White excelled in track and field (Cahn, 1994). Yet coed sports, contact sports, team sports, and so-called "masculine" sports such as football, rugby, ice hockey, baseball, and wrestling were all anathema to conservative critics (Cahn, 1994). Girls and women who participated in these kinds of sports were characterized as "mannish" and often accused of lesbianism—usually in direct measure to their athletic successes (Griffin, 1998; Lenskyj, 1986). Derogatory labels were one method of social control, yet there were always women athletes who defied social convention (Cahn, 1994; Nelson, 1998).

Pioneering Women

Many sport experts believe that Mildred "Babe" Didrikson was the finest all-around athlete of the 20th century. She began her sport career playing high school basketball, dropped out to continue her basketball career for a company team, competed in softball, and then switched to track and field. During one track meet in 1932, she earned six gold medals and broke four world records. During the 1932 Olympics, she won two gold medals and one silver medal. Didrikson (who, like many successful athletes, was often charged with being boastful and "mannish") excelled at virtually every sport she tried, and eventually became a peerless golfer before succumbing to cancer (Schwartz, n.d.). Other sporting pioneers include Gertrude Ederle, the first woman to swim the English Channel; Althea Gibson, a world-class tennis player who won women's singles and doubles at Wimbledon in 1957; Sonja Henie, who won 10 consecutive world championships and 3 Olympic gold medals in figure skating; Shirley Muldowney, the first woman to win the National Hot Rod Association points title and the first person to win three NHRA championships; Nancy Lopez, winner of 48 LPGA tournaments; Joan Benoit Samuelson, who won the first women's Olympic marathon in 1984; and Jean Driscoll, who was victorious in seven consecutive Boston wheelchair marathons, tying Clarence DeMar's overall Boston marathon record.

Power Plays

Often men responded swiftly with punitive action when women dared breach the limits of traditional femininity. In 1967 Kathrine Switzer registered for the male-only Boston Marathon under the name K. Switzer. When Jock Semple, the organizer of the marathon, realized that K. Switzer was a woman, his reaction was telling: He physically attacked her, yelling, "Get out of *my* race" (*An Interview with Kathrine Switzer*, 2003, para 18). There could be no clearer statement of the relationship between men and sport. Men felt they owned sport, and female incursions into that realm were assaults on their masculinity.

Therefore, when Billie Jean King played Bobby Riggs in the much-hyped "Challenge of the Sexes" tennis match, the symbolic stakes were high. For some of the 50 million television viewers, King's victory over Riggs seemed to suggest a new era in sport, an era where women and men could compete as equals. Other spectators saw it as an anomaly, the exception that proved the rule of men's superiority.

As women entered the work force in greater numbers and showed themselves to be as capable as men in law, medicine, politics, academics, and business, sport became the last bastion of masculinity. For many men, sport was the lone arena—Bobby Riggs's defeat not withstanding—where it seemed that male superiority was indisputable. On the playing fields and in gymnasiums, men could still wield power over women, despite the threat of women's parity in other realms.

For this reason, sport carries tremendous symbolic weight in our society. And Title IX, because it legislates sport in educational institutions, is equally freighted with symbolic value. The degree of controversy generated by Title IX makes sense only if we understand that power is what is at issue.

THE MANDATES OF TITLE IX

On the face of it, Title IX is a straightforward directive. Enacted in 1972 it states,

> No person in the United States shall, on the basis of sex, be excluded from participation in, be denied the benefits of, or be subjected to discrimination under any education program or activity receiving Federal financial assistance. (Brake, 2000/2001, p. 46)

In practice, this law says that no educational institution receiving federal funding (and most college-level educational institutions do) can discriminate against girls and women in the context of athletic opportunities. In training and practice facilities, supplies, equipment, the scheduling of games and practice times, travel allowances, publicity, locker rooms, opportunities to receive coaching and academic tutoring, medical services, athletic scholarships, and recruitment of student athletes, girls must receive benefits equal to those given to boys. This law applies to athletics in secondary school (i.e., middle school, junior high school, and high school) as well as to athletics in college or university. It includes not only intercollegiate sport, but also interscholastic, club, and intramural athletics (Carpenter & Acosta, 2005).

However, the primary point of contention—and what has generated the most controversy—is the number of opportunities for women and girls to participate in competitive sports relative to those opportunities for men and boys (Brake, 2000/2001).

Since Title IX was enacted, the number of girls and young women who have participated in sport has increased exponentially. In 1970 only 1 high school girl in 27 played varsity sports. By 2004, that figure was 1 in 2.5

(Lopiano, 2005, #13). At the college level, the number of women competing in sports has more than tripled, from 31,000 to 128,208 (Women's Sports Foundation). Even the participation rates of younger girls (ages 6 to 11) have risen markedly (Brake, 2000/2001).

Women athletes' accomplishments have more than kept pace with these growing participation rates. The last decade has seen the advent of professional women's basketball, the proliferation of websites and magazines dedicated to women's sports and fitness, the stunning victories of American sportswomen at the 1994 Winter Olympics, the so-called "Olympics of the Women" (the 1996 Atlanta Summer Games), the 1999 Women's World Cup Soccer Championship, and numerous other sporting achievements.

Although these events suggest nothing less than a revolution in girls' and women's sport participation, they don't tell the whole story.

Arguments For and Against Title IX

It has been estimated that at least 80% of all colleges and universities have not complied with Title IX mandates. Although financial figures for high schools are not available, girls make up half the student population but benefit from only 39% of the sport program opportunities (Lopiano, 2005, #13). Schools continue to offer many more sporting opportunities to men and boys than they do to women and girls, and this holds true at both high school and college levels (Brake, 2000/2001; Messner, 2002). And the quality of those opportunities is better for boys than it is for girls (Brake, 2000/2001; Messner, 2002). As a 2000 survey by *The Chronicle of Higher Education* concludes, American college women athletes "still lack opportunities to participate at many institutions, and they often do not receive fair shares of scholarship funds, coaching salary budgets, recruiting budgets, and operating budgets" (as cited in Messner, 2002).

Despite these inequities, opponents of Title IX contend that it discriminates against men when, for example, men's sports programs are cut so that women's programs may be added. A lawsuit brought by the National Wrestling Coaches Association in 2002 made this very argument (Porto, 2003). Advocates of Title IX disagreed. They acknowledged that although cutting men's programs was one strategy that athletic directors have employed, making women's programs the "easy scapegoat to blame for [this] loss" (Lopiano, 2005, #11), there were many other ways to comply with Title IX without the wholesale elimination of men's teams. In fact, according to the provisions of the statute, an educational institution could be in compliance by meeting any one of the following three conditions:

1. [Provide] intercollegiate level participation opportunities for male and female students . . . in numbers substantially proportionate [within 5 percentage points] to their respective enrollments; or
2. show a history and continuing practice of program expansion which is demonstrably responsive to the developing interest and abilities of the members of [the underrepresented] sex; or
3. demonstrate that the interests and abilities of the member of [the underrepresented] sex have been fully and effectively accommodated by the present program. (Brake, 2000/2001, p. 48)

Clearly, Title IX does not mandate decreases in opportunities for men athletes. Rather its purpose is to provide opportunities and quality of treatment for women equivalent to those for men.

Advocates of Title IX also point out that sports such as football place a drain on athletic budgets, since—contrary to conventional wisdom—few are profitable (Porto, 2003). Rather than cutting nonrevenue sports such as men's wrestling, gymnastics, or swimming, capping football rosters would go a long way toward eliminating athletic budget constraints (Porto, 2003). In many Division IA schools, the percentage of money spent on the football team is greater than the budgets of all their women's sports combined (Porto, 2003).

Another argument that opponents of Title IX sometimes advance is that women and girls are simply not as interested in sports as men and boys; therefore, it doesn't make sense to provide equivalent opportunities and equivalent quality of treatment—that is, benefits—to girls and women. A similar sort of argument was the basis for a series of four well-known legal decisions about Title IX in *Cohen v. Brown University* (1991–1997). The key contention made by the university was that men as a class were more interested in sports than women as a class were. Instead of complying with one of the Title IX conditions mentioned above, Brown proposed that a survey about athletics be given to women and men, and based on those results, the university would provide sport opportunities corresponding to the students' interests (Brake 2000/2001).

The court rejected Brown's proposal because of its assumption that sex differences between women and men (that is, interest in sport) were natural and innate. Rather, the court pointed out that these differences were fostered by Brown's very own institutional practices. The court explained, "Interest and ability rarely develop in a vacuum; they evolve as a function of opportunity and experience" (Brake 2000/2001, p. 54). Thus, if women have limited opportunities to be involved in sport, they are less likely to develop interest and skill in sport than those with more opportunities (men). In brief, interests follow opportunity and experience.

The Future of Title IX

The most recent challenge to Title IX was the formation of the George W. Bush administration's Commission on Opportunity in Athletics in response to arguments such as those brought by the National Wrestling Coaches Association. The Commission created six proposals that would have substantially weakened the provisions of Title IX. However, in July of 2003, the Office of Civil Rights reaffirmed Title IX's three-part mechanism for measuring compliance and validated Title IX as a significant civil rights statute (*2003: A Victorious Year*, 2003). Given the public outcry against the weakening of this statute and the public support for it (*Athletics Data Connection*, 2002), it seems likely that Title IX will remain in force, at least for the near future. But because Title IX symbolically contests the assertion of male superiority and sports as sacrosanct masculine terrain, it will remain controversial, and during conservative political administrations, more vulnerable to attacks.

Amidst the controversy that Title IX has generated, it is easy to lose sight of the central issue: Title IX is a pledge to provide equitable educational opportunities for men and women. As a teacher, sport can communicate lessons about teamwork and cooperation, about competition and commitment, about goal setting and achievement, about balance and beauty. Why should women and girls be denied these potential benefits, benefits that men and boys have profited from for so long? Given what is at stake, the preservation of Title IX is a moral imperative.

REFERENCES

2003: A victorious year. (2003). Retrieved January 20, 2005, from www .womenssportsfoundation.org/cgi-bin/iowa/issues/history/article.html? record=974.

An interview with Kathrine Switzer. (2003, April 28). Retrieved November 8, 2005, from www.runnersweb.com/running/news/rw_news_20030428_KathrineSwitzer .html.

Athletics data connection. (2002, Winter). Retrieved January 27, 2005, from www.aacu.org/ocww/volume32_/data2.cfm.

Brady, J. E. (2001). Pumping iron with resistance: Carla Dunlap's victorious body. In M. Bennett & V. D. Dickerson, *Recovering the black female body: Self representations by African American women* (pp. 253–278). New Brunswick, NJ: Rutgers University Press.

Brake, D. (Fall 2000/Winter 2001). The struggle for sex equity in sport and the theory behind Title IX. *University of Michigan Journal of Law Reform, 13,* 13–149.

Cahn, S. K. (1994). *Coming on strong: Gender and sexuality in twentieth-century women's sports*. New York: The Free Press.

Carpenter, L. J., & Acosta, R. V. (2005). *Title IX*. Champaign, IL: Human Kinetics.

Collins, P. H. (2000). *Black feminist thought: Knowledge, consciousness, and the politics of empowerment* (2nd ed.). New York: Routledge.

Duncan, M. C. (1994). The politics of women's body images and practices: Foucault, the Panopticon, and *Shape* Magazine. *Journal of Sport and Social Issues, 18,* 48–65.

FAQs: Frequently asked questions about the ancient Olympic Games. (2001). *The Sport Journal, 14*(1). Retrieved November 8, 2005, from http://www. thesportjournal.org/2001Journal/Vol4-No1/olympicsfaq.asp.

Gerber, E. W. (1974). In E. W. Gerber, J. Felsin, P. Berlin, & W. Wyrick, *The American woman in sport*. Reading, MA: Addison-Wesley.

Griffin, P. (1998). *Strong women, deep closets: Lesbians and homophobia in sport*. Champaign, IL: Human Kinetics.

Lenskyj, H. (1986). *Out of bounds: Women, sport and sexuality*. Toronto: The Women's Press.

Lopiano, D. (2005, May 26). Issues and Action: *Title IX Q & A*. Women's Sports Foundation. Retrieved November 8, 2005, from www.womenssportsfounda tion.org/cgibin/iowa/issues/rights/article.html?record=888.

McKeown, J. (2003, Summer). Reproducing the Hottentot Venus: (Re)Sexualizing black women in popular hip-hop music videos. *Youth Action Forum*. Retrieved January 20, 2005, from www.youthactionnetwork.org/forum/ backissues/spring03.pdf, pp. 19–20.

Messner, M. A. (2002). *Taking the field: Women, men and sports*. Minneapolis: University of Minnesota Press.

Metheny, E. (1965). *Connotations of movement in sport and dance: A collection of speeches about sport and dance as significant forms of human behavior* (Brown Physical Education Series). Dubuque, IA: W. C. Brown.

Nelson, M. B. (1998). In L. Smith, *Nike is a goddess: The history of women in sports* (pp. ix–xix). New York: Atlantic Monthly Press.

Porto, B. L. (2003). *A new season: Using Title IX to reform college sports*. Westport, CN: Praeger.

Schwartz, L. (n.d.). Didrikson was a woman ahead of her time. Retrieved November 8, 2005, from http://womenshistory.about.com/gi/dynamic/offsite .htm?zi=1/XJ&sdn=womenshistory&zu=http://espn.go.com/sportscentury/ features/00014147.html.

Smith-Rosenberg, C., & Rosenberg, C. (1987). The female animal: Medical and biological views of women and their role in nineteenth-century America. In J. A. Mangan & R. J. Park (Eds.), *From "fair sex" to feminism: Sport and the socialization of women in the industrial and post-industrial eras* (pp. 13–37). London: Frank Cass.

Spitzack, C. (1990). *Confessing excess: Women and the politics of body reduction*. Albany: State University of New York Press.

Truth, S. (1851). "Ain't I a woman?" *Modern history sourcebook*. Retrieved January 10, 2005, from www.fordham.edu/halsall/mod/sojtruth-woman.html.

6

Liberties and Lipstick:
The Paradox of Cheerleading as Sport

*Natalie G. Adams, University of Alabama, and
Pamela J. Bettis, Washington State University*

It's Thursday night, and the girls' varsity basketball team is prepared to play a fierce game with a perennial rival. The girls enter the gym in their sweats or baggy shorts with their hair pulled back in ponytails and begin their warm-up routines. As is the case in many high schools across the country in recent years, the varsity cheerleaders begin their routines to support the girls' efforts. The cheerleaders wear the traditional shorts skirts, sleeveless vests, ribbons in their hair, and lots of bright lipstick. While the basketball players run layups, the cheerleaders entertain and encourage the small crowd. They perform a traditional cheer and then launch into their most demanding stunt. With one foot cradled in the palms of two girls, two flyers stretch their other legs high into the air and perform a liberty. Then they pop into a basket toss and are caught by the bases. The crowd claps enthusiastically for the cheerleaders' athletic abilities and then refocuses on the start of the basketball game. If asked who the athletes are in the gym, most spectators would answer that it is obviously the basketball players.

Most contemporary cheerleaders and their supporters would argue differently and would claim the status of athlete. In the past, cheerleaders were the pretty and popular girls who were best known for their social networking and their "eye candy" appeal to adolescent boys and men. Today's cheerleaders might not dispute the latter two characterizations, but they certainly wouldn't be satisfied with these two attributes only. Most of them see themselves as athletes, and they would acknowledge the grueling practices, dangerous stunts (such as a standing back handspring), and athletic skills necessary to make a squad. ESPN broadcasts to audiences around the world national cheerleading competitions that involve routines that are more akin to group gymnastics performances than to traditional cheerleading. Although enveloped in traditional markers of femininity such as lipstick and ribbons, cheerleaders and those associated with cheerleading would emphatically declare that cheerleaders are, indeed, athletes.

Are cheerleaders athletes? Should cheerleading be considered a sport? How did the paradox of cheerleading, a combination of lipstick and liberty stunts, come about? Why does any of this matter? The history of cheerleading and how this activity is understood in our society provides a means for us to explore critically the important role that gender has played and continues to play in sports (Adams & Bettis, 2003). It also offers us the opportunity to rethink specifically what cheerleading could become and more generally what the possibilities of sport in this society could be.

TITLE IX, THE DALLAS COWBOYS CHEERLEADERS, AND THE RECASTING OF CHEERLEADING

In 1972, Title IX of the Education Amendments Act was passed and opened the world of sports to women in unprecedented ways. Interestingly enough, during this same year, the world of professional football was introduced to the Dallas Cowboys Cheerleaders, who were adorned in patented halter tops and hot pants. Both events would significantly impact cheerleading and speak to its paradoxical position in the world of sports.

Prior to the 1940s, cheerleading, which had begun as an exclusively male activity in the late 1800s at elite male colleges, had been dominated by males. With many college-age men fighting in WWII, collegiate cheerleading squads needed new faces to entertain the football crowds left at home. Those new faces were women, and once men returned and tried to regain their positions on the squads, women refused to leave. By the 1950s, cheerleading had reconstituted itself as an almost exclusively female activity, and the image of the cheerleader was that of the all-American wholesome girl next door. Although cheerleaders were considered leaders of their school, their position at athletic events was clear. They were to support and adore the male athletes who were the center of attention. At this time, there were few school-sponsored sports available for girls; thus, being a cheerleader was one of the only opportunities girls had to participate in any form of physical activity. Title IX would dramatically change this.

With the passage of Title IX in 1972, when feminist sensibilities were high and new roles and expectations for women were circulating in society at large, cheerleading came under attack. "Why," many would ask, "would a girl want to be a cheerleader on the sidelines when she could be an athlete center-stage?" Feminists often grouped Playboy bunnies, Miss America contestants, and cheerleaders as symbols of how women were oppressed, denigrated, and demeaned in a patriarchal society. The Dallas Cowboys Cheerleaders, which were masterminded by Dallas Cowboys general manager Tex Schramm, were further evidence for feminists of how cheerleading perpetuated an image of women as sex objects whose primary goal in life was to satisfy men. Capitalizing on a sexual form of entertainment at male-dominated football events, the Dallas Cowboys Cheerleaders more resembled Las Vegas showgirls than they did their 1950s and 1960s cheerleading predecessors; however, calling them "cheerleaders" positioned them as the ultimate male fantasy—simultaneously wholesome and sexy girls.

Title IX and the controversial popularity of the Dallas Cowboys Cheerleaders might have combined to bring about the demise of cheerleading had not the cheerleading industry, particularly the newly formed Universal Cheerleaders Association, recognized that cheerleading and the image of the cheerleader had to be changed if this American cultural institution was to be preserved. And it did change. Tight athletic motions, difficult jumps, pyramid building (often three and four people high), trampolines, tumbling, and fast-paced, crowd-pleasing dances to popular music were introduced to cheerleaders in cheerleading camps across the United States in the mid to late 1970s. The selection process also changed. Prior to the 1970s, most cheerleaders were selected by their peers or teachers, but with the new image of the cheerleader as athlete, external judges now selected girls who could execute physically demanding cheer routines, tumbling passes, stunts, jumps, and dance moves. National and regional cheerleading competitions were also introduced at this time, and by the early 1980s, national TV networks, including the sports network ESPN, began broadcasting these competitions. Suddenly cheerleaders moved from the sidelines, where they were motivational spectators, to center court to become the competitors themselves. By the early 1990s, with the energized popularity of cheerleading, private gyms offered cheer classes and started cheerleading squads. Often called all-star cheerleading, these squads do not cheer for any team. Rather, they exist solely to compete in local, regional, and national competitions.

Forty years after the passage of Title IX, the number of girls participating in high school sports has increased 800%, and these female athletes now number 2.8 million. However, contrary to feminist expectations, the passage of Title IX did not bring about the demise of cheerleading. In fact, cheerleading continues to grow in popularity. Currently, there are 3.8 million cheerleaders in the United States. The vast majority (97%) are female; however, a record number of males are reentering the world of cheerleading, particularly at the all-star level. In many high schools and colleges, the softball team and the cheerleading squad are now competing for the same participants. Although many acknowledge that cheerleaders are often the top athletes at their school, cheerleading has yet to attain the official status of "sport." Why is the debate about cheerleading as a sport important? What does it reveal about the pervasive beliefs about gender and the "proper" role of men and women in society?

SPORT OR NOT A SPORT?
THE NEBULOUS POSITION OF CHEERLEADING

Within the sports world, there are diverse opinions about whether or not cheerleading is or should be considered a sport. Neither the National Collegiate Athletic Association (NCAA) nor the Department of Education's Office of Civil Rights, which oversees Title IX, considers cheerleading to be a sport, although there are approximately 20 state high school athletic associations that have recognized it as such. The formal position of the Women's Sports Foundation (2000) is that cheerleading is not and should not be considered a sport, even if cheerleaders have opportunities to compete against other cheerleading squads. The Foundation notes that cheerleading exists "to coerce audience enthusiasm and participation for an athletic team that is engaged in competition." Further, the Women's Sports Foundation warns that in spite of the gains made with the passage of Title IX, girls still have fewer opportunities than boys to participate in sports, and few schools are in compliance with Title IX; thus, it is unethical for colleges or high schools to "take existing and already funded extracurricular programs for girls [i.e., cheerleading] and find a way to put a different label on them in order to make them athletic teams or sports" (Women's Sports Foundation).

Many argue that this is exactly what the University of Maryland did. In 2003, this university became the first in the United States to recognize cheerleading as a sport under Title IX and instituted two cheerleading squads: the traditional "spirit" squad that cheers at athletic events and a competitive squad that is allowed to participate in competitive events but cannot cheer at athletic events. Only cheerleaders on the competitive squad are eligible for athletic scholarships. Critics of the University of Maryland's move question the motive (was it really done as a backdoor way to add more male sports or increase funding for male sports?) and the reason why cheerleading was chosen rather than other sports that exist at the club level, such as women's hockey. Since neither the National Collegiate Athletic Association nor the Department of Education's Office of Civil Rights recognizes cheerleading as a sport, the Maryland decision will certainly be a test case for whether or not cheerleading can count as a sport under Title IX provisions.

Interestingly, within the world of cheerleading itself, there is disagreement about whether or not such a move is in the best interests of cheerleaders and the activity itself. Participants and supporters of all-star competitive squads maintain that competitive cheerleading matches the definition of a sport in that its primary goal is competition. Many college and high school cheerleading coaches also support the categorization of cheerleading as sport since they yearn for the status, facilities, and funding that football, basketball, and baseball receive. Many state high school athletic associations also support the declaration of cheerleading as sport, but for mostly economic reasons. Since more and more all-star squads as well as high school squads compete in regional and national competitions, which are often held out of state, state high school athletic associations are eager to host state championships and keep the entrance fees for their own funds as well support local businesses.

However, the position of most cheerleading associations, many state high school athletic associations, and countless coaches and athletic directors at the high school and collegiate level is that cheerleading should not be categorized as a sport. If cheerleading were considered a sport, then all the regulations regarding practice times, miles traveled, and other restrictions would be problematic for cheerleaders' ability to compete in national competitions. Typically, those who oppose the move to declare cheerleading a sport prefer to call it an athletic activity. They contend that recognizing cheerleading as an athletic activity allows cheerleaders to enjoy many of the privileges associated with sport as well as the privileges associated with other school activities, such as the band, debate team, or school chorus.

Although there are mixed responses to the activity versus sport debate within the cheerleading world, the world outside of cheerleading has little doubt about the status of cheerleading. Three days after *USA Today* ran a feature story on the athletic nature of contemporary cheerleading, the ESPN-produced *Dan Patrick* television show asked its listeners to call in and express their opinions on the question, "Is cheerleading a sport?" This response was typical: "Cheerleading can't be a sport because the scoring takes place after the game is over." This allusion to cheerleaders and sex is certainly part of a continuing public image of cheerleading. One only has to note the numerous ways in which cheerleaders as erotic icons are used to sell products and promote professional athletic events. Further, the adult movie industry has certainly tapped into the erotic image of cheerleading with a plethora of best-selling adult videos featuring cheerleaders.

Thus, cheerleading operates in a very nebulous space in the world of sports. Its athletic nature is acknowledged, while simultaneously its status is denigrated. All the while, this demanding physical activity continues to grow in popularity. And the reason for this provides us with insight into how many adolescent girls tread the path to womanhood, that is, in a very delicate manner. Cheerleading offers adolescent girls and young women the opportunity to explore the physically, emotionally, and psychologically demanding world of the athlete while still being considered feminine and presumed heterosexual. This is perhaps the biggest appeal of cheerleading to so many girls and women. Through cheerleading, they can demonstrate athletic prowess, risk taking, confidence, assertiveness, and joy in the physicality of pushing their bodies without being called "dyke," "butch," or "tomboy."

SOLIDIFYING SEXUALITY AND GENDER IN SPORTS AND CHEERLEADING

In this country, with the exception of the military, sport is the most masculine and male-identified institution. Although Title IX has provided

girls and women with significant opportunities for their participation in
the world of sports, generally, female athletes are perceived as residing
outside the realm of normative femininity. Further, female athletes who
participate in what are traditionally considered masculine domains, such
as basketball, volleyball, softball, and track, are constantly asked to
prove their heterosexuality. Hence, female athletes' behavior and appearance is highly regulated to insure that off the court they exude a traditionally feminine persona. Often called the "Babe Factor," the traditional feminine and heterosexual markers female athletes are
encouraged to assume include being seen with a boyfriend, not granting
postgame interviews until showered and made-up, wearing dresses to
out-of-town games, and having long hair (Adams, Schmitke, & Franklin,
2005). They are to be "heterosexy athletes." Certainly, many female athletes resist these attempts to "girlie" their athletic image, but they often
do so at a personal and professional price, as evident when Martina
Navratilova publicly announced she was a lesbian and subsequently lost
numerous commercial endorsements.

Just like traditional athletes, cheerleaders also engage in physically demanding body movements. They often work out on weights and participate in strenuous conditioning exercises along with both their male and
female athlete counterparts; they sweat and suffer from injuries similar to
those other athletes suffer (e.g., pulled hamstrings, broken wrists, noses,
ankles). However, their lipstick, ribbons, short skirts, cheery attitudes, and
perennial smiles mark them as different from traditional athletes. Female
cheerleaders, for all their athleticism, are still perceived as feminine and
heterosexual, thus not gender deviant. Cheerleading and girls who cheer
do not challenge socially accepted roles of men and women. They do not
unsettle the acceptable gendered status quo. Candace Berry, coach of the
Greenup County Cheerleaders, who have won several national high
school competitions, illuminates this position of cheerleading quite well
when she notes, "Cheerleading offers budding young women something
that girls' basketball, track, soccer, softball can't offer: lessons in how to
be a lady, how to be tough without imitating men" (McElroy, 1999, p.
119). Coach Berry obviously assumes that her cheerleaders will be girls.
But what happens when males want to be cheerleaders? Like their female
athlete counterparts, they are often considered gender deviant, and their
sexuality and masculinity are constantly questioned.

With the introduction of competitive-only cheerleading, more and more boys and men have been attracted to its physically demanding skills and pace. Football players and basketball players join squads when they are out of season to keep in shape and to vie for a national championship. Their reentrance into this female-dominated activity has, in some ways, given it more legitimacy and status. However, the reentry of men into cheerleading should not suggest a reconfiguration of acceptable gendered roles, for on most coed squads, males play a very different role from that of female cheerleaders. This role is, indeed, a very distinctively masculine role. In fact, most coed squads operate with a clear division of labor. Most boys and men join cheerleading squads to demonstrate their gymnastics abilities and to use their muscular strength and power during stunt performances. They become the bases for the petite female flyers, who dazzle the crowds with their high flips and jumps. Male cheerleaders typically don't dance, and they execute only a limited number of movements, typically called "strong arm" movements.

This rigid adherence by men to a clear masculine role is not surprising since the sexual orientation of male cheerleaders is questioned as quickly as that of female athletes. By engaging in traditional male-associated activities such as providing the muscles for the stunts, male cheerleaders attempt to shore up their heterosexuality and masculinity and counter the name of cheerqueer or cheerfag that is often yelled at them. But what if male cheerleaders refused to do so? What if male cheerleaders and female cheerleaders tried on different ways of being masculine and feminine?

THE POSSIBILITIES OF CHEERLEADING

Because cheerleading straddles the divide between sport and activity and masculine and feminine norms, it offers a space to rethink the gendered identity of sports. Cheerleading's uncertain status provides the opportunity to envision what a more healthy and vibrant place sports could be for men, women, girls, boys, heterosexual, homosexual, lesbian, and bisexual participants. There is some evidence that this is, indeed, taking place.

Although uncommon, girls basing boys is becoming more and more prevalent, particularly at the competitive level. Since most squads are not coed, the phenotype of the typical female cheerleader has begun to change. In order to execute physically demanding pyramids and stunts, strong, muscular girls are needed to be bases, so squads are now seeking team members who can hold a 100-pound girl in the air and who possess the coordination to catch her when she soars downward.

Further, independent and non-school-affiliated gay and lesbian squads have formed throughout the country. Some, like CHEER San Francisco and its extended network of squads, perfect challenging routines and raise money for local charities. Other more nontraditional squads made up of young radicals disrupt every facet of cheerleading from their black combat boots to their pom-pons fashioned from garbage bags. Their cheers reflect their disdain for the traditional gendered roles of cheerleaders and the assumption of heterosexuality; in fact, many revel in being called jeerleader or queerleader. These cheerleading squads offer possibilities to rethink the purpose of cheerleading and how it might look.

However, the challenge remains for most cheerleaders found across high school and collegiate campuses. Are they willing to drop their lipstick, long hair, makeup, and often sexually provocative movements in order to achieve the status of sport? Should they be expected to? In order to gain legitimacy, why should girls be required to assume masculine markers so that the activity is labeled sport? Why can't you be a girlie girl and an athlete? Why can't you be a butch and an athlete? Why can't boys and men join cheerleading squads and not be labeled cheerqueers? What would the world of sport gain by opening up to these possibilities?

REFERENCES

Adams, N. G., & Bettis, P. J. (2003). *Cheerleader! An American icon*. New York: Palgrave.

Adams, N., Schmitke, A., & Franklin, A. (2005). Tomboys, dykes and girly girls: Interrogating the subjectivities of adolescent female athletes. *Women's Studies Quarterly, 33*(1 & 2), 17–34.

McElroy, J. T. (1999). *We've got spirit: The life and times of America's greatest cheerleading team*. New York: Simon & Schuster.

Women's Sports Foundation. (2000, July 20). *Cheerleading, drill team, danceline and band as varsity sports: The Foundation position*. Retrieved June 19, 2002, from www.womenssportsfoundation.org/cgi-bin/iowa/issues/rights/article .html?record=95.

7

If You Beat Him, You Own Him, He's Your Bitch: Coaches, Language, and Power

Sandra Spickard Prettyman
University of Akron

HOW CAN HE SAY THAT?

One of my sons came home from middle school to say that he wanted to run cross-country, and we encouraged him since we knew and liked several of the high school boys who ran on the team. One day, he came home and announced that he needed to win at the meet that Saturday because he didn't want "to be anybody's bitch." I was more than a little shocked by his use of language and asked him what he meant, not sure that he even fully understood the terms he was using, much less their implications. He went on to tell me that the coach had told them, "If you beat someone, you own him, he's your bitch. And since you don't want to be no one else's bitch, you better make sure you win." As we talked about the language, and why the coach would have used those words to convey his message, it was clear that this was not the first time that sexist, racist, and homophobic language had been used. I was saddened and angered by this coach's usage of language with his athletes, and by the messages that were being sent to these young people through it. When I approached the coach about it, I was told that such language was "just a way to get them to run faster" and really did not mean anything. The coach was unconvinced by my arguments that language does indeed mean something, and that we send messages about how we view the world, and other people, through it. He continued to utilize demeaning language and say that it was just "motivation" and I probably did not understand it since I was not an athlete. But I did understand it. I understood the sexism in it, the racism in it, and the homophobia in it. The more I interacted with the athletic world through my children, the more aware I became of the need to get involved, to help improve what were often negative practices, often done in the name of "winning" or "motivation." In part, that is where this study originated, in my need to better understand what "motivated" this coach's behavior, and to search for alternatives to it.

SPORTS, MASCULINITY, AND LANGUAGE

Hegemonic masculinity is a conceptual tool used today by researchers and theorists alike as they grapple with understanding the construction and effects of masculinity in contemporary culture. This form of masculinity is characterized by aggression, competition, physical prowess, and heterosexuality (Connell, 1987, 1989, 1993; Kimmel, 1996). It is the "norm" against which young boys and men are measured, by themselves and by the world around them. Connell argues that subordinate forms of masculinity, and various forms of femininity, develop in relationship to hegemonic masculinity, representing not only a hierarchy, but a power relationship as well (Connell, 1987, 1989, 1993). While much of the empirical work on hegemonic masculinity focuses on schools, there is a growing body of research on the role of sport in the construction of masculinities and its contribution to the development of hegemonic forms of masculinity. This research also links sexism, homophobia, and heterosexism to the world of sport and argues that sport, as a gendering process and institution, is one means by which boys learn what it means to be masculine, what it means to be "real" boys who will grow up to be "real" men.

Much of what young boys learn about masculinity and sport comes from their interactions with each other and with their coaches. Recent scholarship demonstrates the important role coaches play in the lives of their athletes, but there is a lack of empirical research on the role they play in identity construction, especially with young student-athletes. In addition, previous research on the power of language contends that it is a powerful tool in the construction of our understanding of the world. Language influences our values, attitudes, and beliefs about ourselves and about others and is therefore an important component in identity construction. While language is often a mirror of dominant ideological positions, it can also serve as a tool of resistance. An examination of coaches and their language therefore seems imperative if we are to better understand how and what student athletes learn about themselves and others from their experiences and interactions in sport.

This study is a qualitative examination of the influence that coaches' language has on middle school student-athletes. Using participant observation and interviews, I investigated two middle school track programs. These programs are in districts that are demographically similar yet have very different approaches to coaching and athletics. The study asked questions about the role of language in constructing and maintaining hegemonic forms of masculinity and sought to better understand the relationship between language, interaction, and the development of misogyny, homophobia, and heterosexism in student-athletes. The results of the study demonstrate that the interactions between coaches and student-athletes have a tremendous influence on what young people come to understand about themselves as gendered beings, as well as their understanding and treatment of others. Findings show that how coaches talk to and interact with their student-athletes can either legitimate or disrupt the current gender order, specifically the development of hegemonic masculinity. The dominant definition of masculinity learned through sport focuses on competition, technical competence, aggression, heterosexuality, and male superiority. According to many sociologists who study sport, this definition is harmful to both men and women and should be challenged with a view toward redesigning sport into a more humane and antioppressive institution. This study demonstrates that there are ways in which this can be accomplished, although more often than not, sport becomes gender as usual, and boys work hard to beat others so they can "own" them, so they can have a "bitch" instead of becoming one themselves.

THE RESEARCH IN PRISTINE AND POTTAWATAMIE

Pristine and Pottawatamie are demographically very similar. The majority of the population in both towns is White, they both have a population between 10,000 and 12,000, with average incomes between $67,000 and $80,000 (United States, Census Bureau, 2000). Data for this study comes from participant observations and interviews done at Pristine and Pottawatamie, which provided me with tremendous insight into the lives of these young athletes. I was able to observe during informational meetings, practices, meets, and other track events in each district. During these times, I very much played the role of observer, taking field notes, which were later transcribed and coded for analysis. Interviews occurred with students at various times, sometimes during the school day, and other times after practices or meets when they were available. All interviews took place in public spaces. Quotes transcribed from field notes represent near-verbatim speech from participant observations. Quotes from interviews represent verbatim transcription unless otherwise noted. Pseudonyms are used for the schools and all participants in the study.

I must note here that as a parent of young athletes, I am deeply concerned about these issues. I tried to monitor them by consistently journaling about the research and my role in it, detailing my feelings and trying to separate these out from the research itself. This process provided me with a mechanism by which to control for my subjectivity, but also allowed for a better understanding of my own reaction to and involvement in the research. I am deeply committed to making sure that students learn positive lessons through and in sports, a commitment that grows out of this subjectivity. Whether it is intended or not, students often learn sexist, racist, and homophobic lessons from their participation in sports, something that I hope this research addresses and can hopefully begin to shift.

STARTING THE SEASON: COME RUN WITH US

I had spent the last several months researching at Pristine Middle School and knew most of the kids by name, as well as most of the teachers. The kids knew I was interested in gender and school, as well as sports, and so one morning in class several of them mentioned there was a track meeting that night, and that I might want to go. I had seen the signs around the school and had briefly spoken to the teachers who were the track coaches for the boys' and girls' teams. I had not planned on going, although I would plan on going to as many meets as possible. But several students urged me to go. "Come on," they said, "it will be fun. We'll all be there." Right, I thought. How many of you will really show up? In Pottawatamie, very few students go out for the track team. Track and cross-country are seen as low-status sports, and students who participate in them are not seen as "real" athletes, except for those football players who do track to keep in shape. But they convinced me to attend, and I showed up that night to hear what the coaches had to say. On that night, this study was born.

I was shocked when I walked into the meeting that night. This was an informational meeting, and there were over 400 students and their parents in attendance. Pristine would end up with over 300 students participating in track, all of them excited and looking forward to a great season. Pottawatamie coaches, on the other hand, had a few announcements made in the middle school, but they never met with interested students and parents. High school track and cross-country runners did visit the middle school and talked to specific students their coaches had previously identified as potential assets to the team. They eventually had about 42 athletes participating in the program.

This early interaction with students set the stage for what was to come during the course of the season. Pristine coaches worked closely with their participants to develop them as student-athletes who were part of a team that cared about and supported each other. Respect was a key component of this program, and the coaches' language reflected this. At Pottawatamie, coaches were often not present at practices, or were working closely with only a few athletes. Participants were encouraged to look out for themselves, and the team aspect of the sport was largely ignored. Respect was almost never mentioned by Pottawatamie coaches, and the attitudes their athletes developed were vastly different from those of Pristine participants.

HOW TO OWN/EARN RESPECT

I was sitting in the stands at the Pottawatamie track, watching several young people do sprint work around the track. I heard the coach, who often worked with distance runners, behind me, and I turned to see the runners stretching out on the lawn.

> Now I want you boys to get out there and run like you mean it. None of this pussyfooting around anymore. We've got a big meet this week, and I want those kids to know we mean it, so run like you do, not like the bunch of wimps you are. Look, if you beat that son of a bitch, you own him . . . and that's why you run, you run to win. If you get beat, well, it's pretty clear what that means. So, I want you all out there working to own those wuss runners from Pristine. They might have a bigger team, but they're not better.

Gaining respect as a runner in Pottawatamie meant owning someone else, beating him, proving yourself as a winner, as a man. Otherwise, you were just a "wimp" and a "wuss," no better than the girls on the team, no better than those "wuss" runners from Pristine.

I turned my attention to the sprint coach on the field; he was working with two different runners, talking to them about the upcoming meet. The other sprinters were on the other side of the track, working on stretching out. I heard the coach say that each of them had a chance to win their event, if they could "show what they were really made of."

> Forget the rest of 'em, you boys need to focus on you and you alone. You've got a shot here, you've got some real talent, and that's what we want to develop. So, run hard, run fast, and run for yourself. It's your medal, your win. You want my respect as a coach, then you go for the win, for you, not for anybody else.

For this coach, winning is an individual—not a team—endeavor, and each athlete needs to look out for himself or herself. Competition is what life is about, and what running is about, and structures the interactions between runners. Heward (1991) argues that male identities are forged in relationship with other males in a climate of competition—competition for friendship, for influence, and for power—the type of climate clearly present in this interaction. This competition structures their relationship on the sporting field, not only with the other team, but also with each other. The question then becomes how much does this influence spill over into other facets of their lives?

Many young athletes turn to sport as a means to connect with others; however, what they find is that connection is not encouraged, only competition (Messner, 1992). Boys learn that

> it is not "just being out there with the guys—being friends," that ensures the kind of attention and connection they crave; it is being better than the other guys—beating them—that is the key to acceptance. (p. 33)

For Pottawatamie coaches, respect means winning, beating others, so you can own them and make them your "bitch." It has little to do with developing a team spirit, with respecting others and their abilities, or with improving yourself as a runner.

Pristine coaches took a very different approach. This team had a female coach who worked with the young women, and a male coach who worked with the young men. They often worked out together, whereas the Pottawatamie girls were most often just ignored. Both Pristine coaches spoke often with their teams about consistent self-improvement, about the "development of a team mentality," and about "looking out for others, both on your team and on other teams." Connection seemed to be an overriding theme for these coaches, consistent with the school they represented. I often heard these coaches talk to distance runners about strategies for helping slower runners improve, strategies for winning meets rather than races.

> Remember, this race is not about you, it's about a team, about a group of runners who run together to help each other improve and be better runners, better people. So, when you go out and run this weekend, remember that, run your race, but run it as part of a team. Know where your teammates are and what they need, and give it to them. Winning the race doesn't mean winning the meet; to do that we need to work together.

Pristine coaches seemed to focus on connection, on cooperation, and not only on competition. This does not mean they do not want their athletes to win, but winning individually, at all costs, is not the goal. Athletes earned respect on this team from working with others, from helping others to realize their potential, as much as from improving individually or winning an individual event.

These differences were reflected in students' responses to interview questions about why students run and what they hope to gain from it.

Like I run to be better than other guys, to prove, like, you know, that I can do it. I like the long races, it's like, takes like more to do it, and it seems like more, like harder, so I push. I don't want to be beat, so I do whatever I can, work hard, sweat, you know, work hard to win. (Mitch: Pottawatamie)

I don't know, I run because I'm good at it. The coaches and some other runners came and talked to me and asked me to run, like I was special, like good. So I work hard to be good, to win, so I can stay on the team, so the coaches will work with me. Some of the guys on this team are, well, like, you know, not very good, but if you're good, you get a lot of attention, and that's what I want, to be the best, to be there. (Jake: Pottawatamie)

Well, I wanted to run on the team because a lot of my friends were. I play football, but I knew that track was fun, and would help me in football too. We just wanna be out there together though. There are lots of us and we run to be out there, part of the team. Everybody works together, and we usually win, like because we just have so many people. But it's more about being the best you can be, about helping other people too, to be their best, their running best. (Brad: Pristine)

Well, like I run because it makes me happy. I'm not very good, but nobody seems to care and I'm still part of the team and I get to hang out and everything. I just work to try to get better, and you know, there's always lots of people, like coaches and other runners, who wanna help you get better, so I do what they tell me and I have gotten better, but I think they like me whether I'm a good runner or not, it's just we like all support each other, like friends, we're a team, but we're friends. No one yells at each other, that's what I like. A lot of other sports coaches yell at kids, I don't like that. Our coaches don't yell. Just to support us. (Josh: Pristine)

Pottawatamie coaches reinforce many of the components of hegemonic masculinity as it plays out in the society at large: competition, aggression, and being "better than" others, among others. Pristine coaches on the other hand seem effective at dislodging some of these tenets of hegemonic masculinity, developing caring and cooperation among their athletes. While it is too soon to tell if this disruption will have lasting effects, it is certainly a step in the right direction.

MISOGYNY, HOMOPHOBIA, AND ALL THAT STUFF

I was sitting in the bleachers in the rain at an invitational meet. I could see all the teams and their tents, athletes huddled underneath them, hoping the rain would end. The difference between the Pottawatamie team and all the others was that there were only boys under the tent; the girls were all sitting out in the rain. When I asked several parents in the stands what was going on, they replied that the boys' coaches said that the tent belonged to them, and therefore only the boys could use it. Despite the school's attempt to create a coherent track program, where boys and girls participated together and learned from and supported each other, these coaches clearly made the team into separate spheres. When such sex segregation occurs, in a structured environment sanctioned by adults such as coaches, a context is developed in which gendered identities and gender differences become normalized and appear as a natural part of the world (Messner, 1992; Thorne, 1997). When sport is perceived as an exclusively male enterprise, the link between masculinity and characteristics such as competition, physical aggression, and technical skill also becomes naturalized, thereby reinforcing hegemonic norms and devaluing girls and women and their abilities as athletes, as well as devaluing other forms and expressions of masculinity.

That afternoon in the rain, several of the boys decided they felt sorry for the girls and decided to let them under the tent. After a few minutes, the coaches asked them to leave, and then took their bags, blankets, and other gear and put them out in the rain. Such actions send a strong message to the boys about the importance of girls in the world of sport, and their place and value as members of the team. In addition, the coaches often told the boys that they were not allowed to cheer for the girls, because "they're a bunch of losers, and we don't want to be associated with them." The language and actions of the coaches represent misogynistic positions often present in the society at large and reinforce the status of boys as "real" athletes and winners.

This misogyny is represented in the following interview excerpts, demonstrating the power of these coaches' words in influencing the beliefs of their athletes.

Well, like the girls aren't very good anyway, so why cheer for them? Even if sometimes, like we want to cheer for them, but coach, he won't put up with it, so I don't. I think it's OK, like they have other people that cheer for them, and when they start winning, like being good, then maybe we'll cheer for them. It's like motivation for them to get better. (Mitch: Pottawatamie)

Girls are just girls, they will never like be as good as the guys, as fast as us. So, we need to focus on us, not on them. It would just be a waste of energy and cheering, so we just ignore them. They'll never get better if they don't push, like no pain, no gain. You know what I mean? So this is like, I don't know, paying your dues, like you have to prove yourself, and they haven't yet. (Brent: Pottawatamie)

Both Mitch and Brent indicate that their lack of support and cheering for the girls is motivation for them to do better, to improve. This attitude was also consistent with the language they heard from their coaches. In the previous section, I detailed how their coaches often used misogynistic, homophobic, and racist language when speaking with their athletes. Over and over, I heard how this was "motivational" language and not meant to hurt anyone or be derogatory. When asked whether they thought this language reinforced stereotypes, the coaches said their athletes knew better than to take it that way. The implication was that I didn't know anything about coaching, and therefore couldn't understand how athletes needed to be pushed in order to motivate them to endure the physical pain necessary for winning. But Mitch and Brent, and their other team members, clearly did understand the "motivation" their coaches were talking about, and in interview after interview I heard them demean the girls and their team, demean gays and lesbians, and equate both with not having the strength and determination to be winners, to be "real" athletes.

The misogynistic and homophobic language was rampant in Pottawatamie, and the coaches consistently equated poor performance with "wusses," "pussies," and "fags." In addition to owning someone that you beat, boys were consistently told that they needed to act like real men, which meant being able to endure pain, win at all costs, and be competitive. The following excerpts come from my field notes taken at practices and meets; they reflect the attitudes conveyed to Pottawatamie athletes from their coaches.

What are you a bunch of fags out there, get out there and show me what you're really made of. None of this pansy running, I want a real workout. (Coach 1:5)

If I wanted a bunch of sissies, I would have gone out and recruited them. But I got you, and I don't work with sissies, so don't act like one. We need this meet, so I don't care about your damn blisters or anything else, get out there and win. (Coach 1:8)

You don't wanna be out there like losers, like those girls, so get out there and kick some butt. (Coach 2:8)

I can't believe you let that fucking girl beat you, what are you, a fag, can't even run faster than a girl. We're gonna train the shit out in the next few weeks and you better take her the next time. We all look bad, like what are they gonna say. (Coach 2:9)

As I spoke with Pottawatamie athletes in interviews, their own language reflected the misogynistic and homophobic attitudes of their coaches. They repeatedly referred to boys who did not perform as well as "wusses" and "fags" and had little or no respect for them. They did not cheer for these boys, just as they did not cheer for the girls, for any loser. Such language and behavior represent the kind of "antagonistic cooperation" (Messner, 1992) prevalent in team sports. While publicly they are a team, working together for the good of the team, this is often a mask for the competitive struggle within the team, the struggle for survival, for status, for individual glory. These boys were making clear distinctions between who was masculine and who was not, who was a "real" man and who was not, who was in power and who was not. And those who were not were clearly linked to the feminine and to homosexuality. These boys were beginning to forge a masculine identity that was based on status through successful (winning and aggressive) athletic participation, and homophobic and misogynistic attitudes and behaviors.

Pristine coaches on the other hand began their season by having a talk with their student athletes to discuss what they expected from their athletes.

This is a team, and even though we have a boys' coach and a girls' coach, we are one team. We work out together, we support each other, we treat each other with respect. That's what we expect out of all our athletes, from you, from each of you, as we go through this season. We also expect that you will act as student ambassadors when we are here or at other schools. You know what language is acceptable and what is not. You know what behavior is acceptable and what isn't. And if we see or hear unacceptable behavior, you will not be participating on this team. You've all signed the code of conduct, that includes language and behavior that demand, so know it, respect it, or lose your privilege to be on this team. I know other teams and other athletes might not act or talk, or might talk and act different, but that's not what we do here. If you have questions or concerns, come to us, that's what we're here for. But treating others with respect, and encouraging others is our main goal on this team, not winning. Doing our best, for us and for others. That's what's important. (Coach 1:3)

This was a very different message from what the students in Pottawatamie heard on a daily basis. And the coaches in Pristine followed through with what they said. I did hear a student call another athlete a faggot, and he suffered immediate consequences. Coaches did not tolerate athletes who were disrespectful of other teammates or other teams and athletes.

As I interviewed students from Pristine, I found that their attitudes about others were fairly consistent with those of their coaches. The girls were respected and supported by the boys, and their value as members of the team was not questioned. I also rarely heard the use of homophobic language, other than the one time at a practice when a student used the word "faggot" and was then disciplined by the coaches.

I think running track is great. Like I play football in the fall, but I do this too, it's fun, it's, there's a lot of kids and we have fun, support each other, it's like fun. And the girls and boys can like be together, not like football, like all guys. I think it's good for us, we like can learn from each other. The girls, like lots of them are like really good, like better than the boys. They can challenge us to do better, but also like it helps us see how good we all are. (Ken: Pristine)

Well, well, I do field events and not as many girls do that, but some do, and some are like really good, we really do have a lot of girls. Like when we go to other schools they never have very many girls and so our girls are, and 'cause like they're really good, and so we win a lot, which is good, but I really want to just improve. Yeah, it's all about getting better, like me, but also like the team. We work hard to like work for each other. I think that's what I like about track is working with each other. Some of us are good, some aren't so good, but are good at other stuff, like maybe school or music or stuff, but we all support each other, and then like we can support each other other places too, like school. I don't know, it's just fun. (Kent: Pristine)

These students were clearly articulating different positions from those of students from Pottawatamie, about the role of women, about the value of the team, and about the place of competition. While winning was still important, more important seemed to be having fun, supporting each other, and working together. Homophobic and misogynistic language and behavior were not heard or seen, at least in my experience, on this team. The coaches set the tone for expectations about language and behavior, and the students' own language and behavior reflected that. We cannot know what will happen when these students move up to the high school, come into contact with other coaches, and have more pressure to "act like men." However, what is clear is that in Pristine there is a space where hegemonic forms of masculinity can be constructed in opposition to traditional norms based on competition, aggression, and technical competence.

CONCLUSION: DISRUPTING MASCULINITIES

The language that coaches use with student-athletes can and does influence the behaviors and attitudes of their athletes. When coaches use misogynistic and homophobic language, their athletes tend to adopt attitudes about girls and homosexuals reflective of those ideological positions. However, when coaches actively and publicly acknowledge the value of all students and demand respect for them from their athletes, they respond accordingly. Coaches in Pottawatamie developed athletes who upheld traditional hegemonic norms, athletes whose masculinity was not supportive of women and gays. Coaches in Pristine worked to develop athletes who were respectful and cooperative, athletes who would disrupt those hegemonic norms seen in Pottawatamie. Pristine track coaches and athletes were carving out a space where hegemonic norms could be questioned and overturned, where multiple forms of masculinity and femininity could be valued, and where everyone could be a "real" athlete. Such spaces and disruptions can serve as models for schools and coaches who want to create programs to serve the needs and interests of all students, not just those boys who want to win so they can "own" others.

REFERENCES

Connell, R. (1987). *Gender and power*. Stanford, CA: Stanford University Press.

Connell, R. (1989). Cool guys, swots and wimps: The interplay of masculinity and education. *Oxford Review of Education, 15*, 291–303.

Connell, R. (1993). Disruptions: Improper masculinities and schooling. In L. Weis & M. Fine (Eds.), *Beyond silenced voices*. Albany: State University of New York Press.

Heward, C. (1991). Public school masculinities: An essay in gender and power. In G. Walford (Ed.), *Private schooling: Tradition, change, and diversity*. London: Paul Chapman Publishing.

Kimmel, M. (1996). *Manhood in America*. New York: The Free Press.

Messner, M. (1992). *Power at play: Sports and the problem of masculinity*. Boston: Beacon Press.

Thorne, B. (1997). *Gender play: Girls and boys in school*. New Brunswick, NJ: Rutgers University Press.

United States Census Bureau. (2000). *Community facts sheet*. Retrieved November 18, 2002, from http://factfinder.census.gov/home/saff/main.html?_lang=en.

8

Pitching for Equality: Gay Athletes and Homophobia

Eric Anderson
University of Bath

Although athletic competitions date back to before the original Olympic Games in 769 BCE, organized team sports in American culture are relatively new. Sport in the United States was viewed largely as a waste of God's time, and people were thought better off spending their free time studying scriptures rather than playing games. This attitude began to change during the Civil War, as troops waited long periods of time between fighting and found sports, particularly an early form of baseball known as townball, an enjoyable activity. When the war ended, these soldiers brought their love for the game home. It was the industrial revolution, however, that was the catalyst for the valuing of sport in American culture.

Prior to the industrial revolution, children would return from school to find both mom and dad working the family farm. But because the industrial revolution brought people out of the farms and into the cities, children returned from school to find that dad was still working in the factory rather than working the family farm. This absence alarmed Americans, who feared that male youth, who were now spending large amounts of time with their mothers and female teachers, would grow to be "soft" or "weak," characteristics that were typically attributed to women and homosexual men. Capitalizing on the theories of Sigmund Freud, many believed that this would result in the "creation" of gay males. Therefore, sporting programs and other masculine-geared organizations (such as the YMCA and the Boy Scouts of America) were conceived as a solution.

In sport, young boys could be influenced by "proper" male role models, and a multitude of sporting programs were developed and flourished between the 1890s and 1920. Sport was utilized as a tool to turn young boys into sufficiently masculine heterosexual men who would be socially desirable. In other words, the sporting terrain was born from an antigay and antiwoman perspective. Women were not allowed to play sport, and homophobia in the sporting arena was so rampant that gay athletes would never have considered coming out of the closet.

While things have changed significantly for women in the sporting terrain, little has changed for gay men. The openly gay population is vastly underrepresented in sport. This is to say that there are fewer openly gay men in sport than there are in the general population. This, however, does not mean that there are fewer gay men in sport than in the general population; it merely indicates that gay males, for various reasons, have decided not to come out of the closet. For example, there has *never* been an openly gay professional baseball, basketball, football, or hockey player to come out while actively playing in the United States; and only a handful have come out after retiring. This is remarkable when one considers that tens of thousands of professional athletes have gone through the ranks of professional sports in the past 100 years. We are therefore left with the most pressing question, why are there so few *openly* gay athletes in team sports?

PERCENTAGES AND PROBLEMS:
IDENTIFYING AS GAY IN SOCIETY AND IN SPORT

Before engaging in a discussion of the percentage of gay men in sport, I must state that it is impossible to know what percentage of the general population is gay. There are two main reasons. First, it is impossible to force someone to admit to being gay or bisexual, and as long as there is homophobia, sexual minorities will be influenced to hide their sexuality from a disapproving populace. Second, it is hard to know what percentage of the population is "gay" because it is difficult to define exactly what it means to be gay or straight. The picture grows even more confusing when you consider that in addition to there being those who consider themselves gay, straight, and bisexual, there are also those who consider themselves asexual, intersexual, and transsexual.

After understanding that there are multiple sexual orientations, we then further complicate matters by categorizing sexuality along three other dimensions: sexual behavior (what you do), sexual orientation (what you want to do), and sexual identity (how you view yourself). For example, when I was in high school I knew I wanted romantic and sexual relationships with boys (sexual orientation), but because I was afraid to come out of the closet with my desires, I had relationships with girls instead (sexual behavior), even though I privately identified as gay and never felt emotionally connected to the women (Anderson, 2000). In this aspect, my sexual orientation and private identity were gay, while my sexual behavior and public identity were straight.

These complications aside, studies of the percentage of American males who identify as gay have various findings. They show that anywhere from 2.8% to 10% of American men identify as gay. For example, while 10% of the freshmen at UCLA identify as a sexual minority, 5% of the California voters identify as gay or lesbian. Thus, the only thing consistent about estimates of the gay population is that they vary. We will never know what percentage of the population is a sexual minority until our culture ceases to produce antigay attitudes (cultural discrimination), and our institutions such as schools, churches, and the government begin to give gays and lesbians equality in their policies—such as allowing gays to marry, to serve in the military, to be Boy Scouts, and to be treated equally in our school settings (not providing this equality is something we call institutional discrimination). As long as homophobia exists, sexual minorities will be influenced to hide their sexuality in much the same manner that the self-reporting of how many students have cheated on a test is likely to be unreliable. This obviously means that we can never know the percentage of gay or bisexual male athletes either. Indeed, it is *possible* that on any given sports team all the players can be closeted gay men, or vice versa; there simply is no way of knowing. When it comes to knowing what percentage of gay athletes are in sports, the only thing that can be said with certainty is that gay men and gay athletes do exist. Indeed, I've interviewed hundreds of them for my research.

My research shows that gay athletes exist at all levels, and in all sports (Anderson, 2005). There have been openly gay national champion swimmers, divers, tennis players, runners, and ice-skaters. There have been world record–holding track and field athletes, bodybuilders, and other individual sport athletes. There have been professional football players, baseball players, and soccer players who have come out of the closet after retiring, and I've anonymously interviewed active football players and a Stanley Cup–winning National Hockey League player for my research. For a more comprehensive list of famous gay athletes, you can examine www.outsports.com/outathletes.

What my research cannot say, however, is whether gay athletes are over- or underrepresented in sport. In other words, are there as many gay men in sport as there are in your typical English class? Since most boys are socialized into sport before they know what their sexual orientation is, we can conclude that the percentages *start off* about the same. So the question becomes, after gay boys are introduced to team sports, are they then attracted to or deterred from continuing to play them?

There are two schools of thought on this issue. The first maintains that the culture of team sports is so homophobic that when boys figure out they are gay (many know before they hit puberty, but most figure it out around puberty) they leave team sports for a safer environment like individual sports, theater arts, or intellectual pursuits. The second way of analyzing this is to understand that if gay boys (and men) are afraid of being known as gay, they might specifically seek team sports out because team sport athletes operate under the assumption of heterosexuality. In other words, stereotypes hold that baseball and football players are "straight," whereas athletes in ice-skating or kids in the band are more likely to be thought of as gay. Thus, team sports become highly desirable places for deeply closeted gay males. Team sport athletes are essentially cloaked in the assumption of heterosexuality, yet they are immersed in an incredibly homoeroticized activity. They get to be around highly sexualized and toned athletic boys and men, while being publicly perceived as heterosexual.

HOMOPHOBIA IN SPORT

Whether there are more gay athletes in sport than in the general population or not, one thing is certain: Being a gay athlete in an arena that was founded upon a homophobic premise is *difficult*. Team sports remain one of America's most homophobic institutions. There are several reasons for this. First, as mentioned at the beginning of the chapter, sport was founded on homophobic assumptions. At the time it was believed that people became gay or straight depending on their upbringing, and homophobia in and through sport was thought to deter boys from "becoming" gay. Although science clearly has demonstrated that neither heterosexuality nor homosexuality is the product of "choice" or one's childhood (most scientists agree that sexuality is largely biological in nature and out of individual control), sport has remained a homophobic arena because homophobia is essentially passed down through the generations. In other words, coaches and older players teach new players to be homophobic. Thus, homosexuality is not learned, but homophobia is.

Sport is also a homophobic arena because, at some level, the players recognize that it is a homoerotic environment. Some men, gay or straight, may be sexually aroused by engaging in sports with other boys. Homophobia therefore becomes the tool by which heterosexuals attempt to say, "No, I am not gay." However, because it is truly impossible for heterosexuals to "prove" they are "not gay," they repeatedly try to prove they are straight. In a homophobic culture, if a man says, "I'm gay," no one questions him; however, if he says, "I'm straight," it is not taken as fact, because people know that he could be closeted. So in a homophobic culture, such as a high school, heterosexual men (and closeted gay men) constantly attempt to dispel any notion of being thought gay, even if they are. They do this by frequently sexualizing women (often referred to as locker-room talk), when they talk about their heterosexual desires and activities, which are often made up. Most significant, they also denounce homosexuality through using words like "fag" and phrases like "that's so gay" as a way of subjugating homosexuality and distancing themselves from it.

Finally, sport remains a homophobic culture because younger boys want to be accepted by their teammates. If they join a team as high school freshmen, and all the older boys are using the term "fag" consistently, they are more likely to copy them as a way to fit in. They fear that if they don't denounce others as "fags," they may be more likely to be considered gay themselves. In this aspect, well over half the kids who use the word "fag" do not truly feel homophobic; they are simply trying to fit in (Smith, 1998). In fact, the most common thing I hear from people after they use the word "fag" is, "Oh. I didn't mean it that way." I usually respond with, Then don't use the word, because that's the way I take it."

My research also indicates that if older boys cease to allow the use of the word "fag" on a team, younger boys will quickly comply. One team I studied showed that the entire team frequently used the word until one of their teammates came out of the closet. As soon as he did, the team had a meeting and unanimously agreed to stop using the word "fag." When new athletes joined the team, they quickly complied with the tolerant atmosphere, and all agreed that the team atmosphere was much more enjoyable.

All of this places gay athletes in a strange social situation. They are immersed in a homophobic culture that provides them with a group of sexually attractive men to befriend, but they do not necessarily know who is homophobic and who is not. They hear people using the word "fag" and the phrase "that's gay," but they do not know in what context they mean it. Because of this, it is very difficult for gay athletes to accurately gauge the level of homophobia on their teams, and it scares them from coming out. To illustrate the paradoxical existence that closeted gay team sport athletes live, let us examine the story of "Blake," a high school basketball player in a small Indiana town.

BLAKE'S STORY

The wooden floor of the high school gym squeaks as Blake shuffles his 6-foot 4-inch 190-pound body up and down the court. Only a sophomore, Blake is already one of the best players in Indiana, drawing coverage from local media and praise from his community. Despite the fact that the rest of the team has gone home, Blake remains late into the evening, shooting basket after basket in order to better himself as an athlete. Blake had no dreams of superstardom when he began playing ball, but today he hopes that putting a ball through a hoop will not only provide him with the image of being heterosexual, but that it will also provide him with a college scholarship. "Basketball is my ticket out of here," he tells me. Blake hopes to escape the immense homophobia from his Midwestern home and community by relocating to a metropolitan area for college.

Blake grudgingly picked up basketball in the fourth grade because he perceived that popularity among boys was based primarily on athleticism, and he desired to raise his social standing among his peers. "I was actually more interested in reading," Blake tells me, "but that's not really cool.

I mean I really hated basketball; I'd much rather read a book; but other boys didn't do that. Everybody played basketball, and I wanted to fit in, so I did too." Blake learned long ago that male athletes are commonly perceived as incapable of being gay—a façade that he strategically takes advantage of as a basketball player.

It was during the sixth grade that Blake began to worry about a sexuality he increasingly recognized as "gay," and by the eighth grade Blake knew with certainty that he was what he feared. "It's not easy to be the thing that all the boys use as a put-down. It's what you call someone when you're trying to dis them, and I certainly did not want to be that!" So Blake learned to play both the game of basketball and the game of heterosexual passing. On the court he was "straight," but off the court he was able to shed the heterosexual façade via the Internet. "I met one gay friend online, and then another, and then I discovered XY.com where there are like thousands of gay teens online." Near the end of his eighth-grade year, he even ventured out to meet other gay boys and eventually found a boyfriend during his freshman year.

His boyfriend helped him realize that he was not alone, and that loving another boy was nothing to feel guilty about. "We dated for a few months, which at 14 seemed like forever, and then one day he just stopped calling. I couldn't figure out why he wasn't returning my calls or my e-mails." Blake began dealing with the taxing emotion of being rejected. Being closeted, however, Blake had no adult to turn to, nobody to express his anguish to. So he returned to venting online. "I was talking to a friend, asking him if he had heard from Chris." His friend responded, "Didn't you hear? Chris was killed in a car accident."

"I started to cry," he said. "So I ran to the bathroom and turned the radio up as loud as it went so nobody could hear me." Alone, Blake had nobody to turn to, nobody to hug him and hold him. He would have to mourn this devastating loss in secret. But while the blaring music cloaked his tears, it couldn't change his loneliness.

> I tried to tell myself that it didn't matter to me. But it did. I loved Chris. He was my first love, and I was young, and it hit me twice as hard. I only wished I could have told others; but I didn't have anyone I could talk to about it. I made a reference to him in a paper my freshmen year but I couldn't tell my teacher or my parents why he died, or who he was, or why I was upset. Hell, I couldn't even tell them that someone had died at all.

Blake's story highlights some of the hardships of concealing one's sexual identity. Blake repeated to me, "I just wish I could have talked to someone." His voice began to crack, and through muffled tears he angrily said, "If it had been a straight friend it would have been easy, but no, it was my boyfriend, and nobody wants to know about that. I was all alone."

Today, Blake walks the hallways of his rural high school publicly popular, but emotionally alienated. He describes his high school as "a typical jock high school." Ironically, where others think that Blake has it all, from where he stands, towering above the others figuratively and physically, he feels alienated. There are no openly gay students at his school, and Blake isn't even sure if there are any in his community. "If there are, I certainly don't know of them," he says with sadness.

Blake is also daunted by the insistent fear of being discovered as gay:

> I fear all the time that others will find out. That people's opinions of me will change if they find out that I'm gay. Like my teachers, they won't think the same of me; they make gay comments and say them in a derogatory manner. Even my own bro will say stuff about gay people. It makes it hard, I'm always thinking in the back of my mind, would you feel this way about me if you knew I was gay.

He adds, "My friends, it's the same thing with them. I have a lot of good friends, but a lot of them are religious, which strikes quite a bit of fear with me." Compounding matters, Blake fears that his parents may have an inclination that he is gay. "They don't want to think about it. Mom says, 'Blake you need to get a girlfriend.' 'Mom I don't want to,' I tell her. 'I don't have time. I'm too busy. I have to get my workout in.'" Basketball becomes the all-purpose excuse for Blake. It not only provides him with a veneer of heterosexuality, but it gives him something to do other than dating women.

Coming out is certainly something Blake ponders—daily—but he just has not been able to bring himself to come out yet. I asked him how he thought he would be treated if he were to come out to everyone in his town today.

> In all honesty, there will be some people who are not okay with it. But, at the same time, I think it might open a lot of people's eyes. Like the people at my school, they don't have any gay friends. They don't know any gay

people at all. They might just look at me and say Blake has been my best friend since I was little, and he's gay, and he's cool. I just hope they see me as the same goofy Blake.

His response is pleasantly absent of fears of being victimized by homophobic violence, partially because he embodies the ability to commit violence himself—he is tall and muscular. "Nobody would mess with me," he says. "I'm bigger and stronger than all the other guys at my school."

Blake's decision to postpone his coming out is complicated. Gay or straight, out of state tuition is expensive, and a scholarship for playing ball would help; Blake fears that coming out would hurt his chances, something hard to refute. "I definitely plan on coming out when I'm in college; there is no question about that. The question is, will I come out during my junior or senior year of high school?" Bravery is not so easily bought. Coming out in a small, homophobic town, in opposition to homophobic parents, teachers, and teammates, is more pressure than any million-dollar athlete would have to handle. It is, without doubt, as tough a decision as any 16-year-old should have to make.

COMING OUT IN SPORT—OPENLY GAY ATHLETES

Blake's isolation as a closeted gay athlete is the common story for closeted gay athletes. However, gay athletes do come out; and when they do, their stories are somewhat surprising. I interviewed a total of 50 openly gay high school athletes, most of whom were top-rated athletes. They came from all sports, from football to bowling. These athletes' stories show primarily that homosexuality is not antithetical to athleticism. Of the 50 gay athletes I studied, all but 6 were considered highly valuable to their teams. The sample included a number of athletes who were state champions as well.

The fact that so many of those in my study were excellent athletes tells us one of two things: either (1) gay athletes are better than straight athletes, or (2) at this point in time, only good gay athletes are coming out of the closet. Indeed, I maintain that the answer is the second. At present, only really good athletes seem to be coming out of the closet in the sporting realm because what is most important to athletes is winning. In other words, teammates are willing to tolerate gay athletes as long as they are good athletes. Gay athletes are able to sense this. However, at present, gay athletes must be more than good, and most come out only if they are good and they sense some general support from their teammates and coach. When all three conditions align, they are more likely to come out, although it is still more likely that they will not.

Once gay athletes do come out, they generally report a much more accepting environment than they had anticipated. Not one athlete in my study was physically or even verbally attacked by his teammates. Heterosexual teammates seemed to take one of two stances: (1) they tolerated the gay athlete but preferred that he not talk about it, or (2) they accepted the gay athlete, had many questions for him, and frequently enjoyed talking about it. It is, of course, the latter of the two that makes gay athletes feel more welcomed and more a part of their team.

THE CHANGING NATURE OF
HOMOPHOBIA IN SOCIETY AND IN SPORT

All of this is changing. Homophobia is on the decline in American culture, and this is particularly true of youth culture. Shows like *Real World* and *Queer Eye for the Straight Guy* have helped to lower the rates of homophobia among youth, and this has permitted more gays and lesbians to come out of the closet. And once people get to know a gay or lesbian, homophobia decreases. The Internet has also played an important role in decreasing homophobia. By providing a forum for gay men (and lesbians) to anonymously come to terms with their sexuality through a series of small steps, the Internet has accelerated the emergence of gay men from the closet. Gay youth generally create an anonymous screen name to enter gay chat rooms and instant message with other gay kids. After feeling comfortable enough, they often begin a slow process of revealing their true identity. Eventually, their online community leads to public meetings, and gay youth are therefore provided with much more opportunity to find other youth than they were prior to the Internet. They are better networked and emotionally equipped to come out because they have an online community of support. This has led to a greater coming out in general, which has therefore affected the number of gay athletes who come out.

Despite the emergence of gay athletes from the closet in the past few years, and despite the fact that evidence suggests that gay athletes are represented in solid numbers across most sports and at most levels, the institutions that govern sport have been virtually nonrespondent in addressing homophobia in athletics. Gay high school students are protected by law only in California, Connecticut, Massachusetts, Minnesota, Vermont, Washington, Wisconsin, and the District of Columbia. Therefore, in addition to sport remaining one of the last bastions of cultural homophobia, sport in American culture also remains one of the last bastions of *institutional* homophobia. Still, times are changing. A mix of legal actions and legislation is combining with popular culture to quickly erode homophobia in American culture. As these improvements are made in the culture in general, they will also affect the arena of athletics. Therefore, it is likely that gay male athletes will continue to come out at an ever-increasing pace, and they are more likely to be accepted by their teammates with each passing day. As they are increasingly tolerated, heterosexuals will find that the reduction of homophobia also benefits them.

This is because, in a homophobic culture, we can never truly know who is gay or lesbian, for someone we assume to be heterosexual could be closeted. Thus, heterosexuals continuously find their sexuality suspect. This is evident in the manner in which teens call each other "fag" in attempt to displace suspicion of homosexuality. In order to "prove" they are heterosexual, they generally try to align themselves with extreme masculinity. Essentially, they are frequently trying to prove they are heterosexuals, and limit their gender expression to do so. Reducing homophobia, however, allows heterosexuals to express a greater gender range, without fear of being called gay or lesbian. This is made popular in the notion of "metrosexuality" (Flocker, 2004) in which heterosexual men proudly cast off homophobia and feel free to associate with gay friends and to do things that are often considered "feminine," all while maintaining a heterosexual identity.

REFERENCES

Anderson, E. (2000). *Trailblazing: America's first openly gay high school coach.* Fountain Valley, CA: Identity Press.

Anderson, E. (2005). *In the game: Gay athletes and the cult of masculinity.* New York: SUNY Press.

Flocker, M. (2004). *The metrosexual guide to style: A handbook for the modern man.* New York: DaCapo Press.

III

RACE AND ETHNICITY IN SPORT

9

The New Racial Stereotypes

Richard Lapchick
University of Central Florida

ATHLETES AND CRIME

The beginning of the 21st century brought the hope that many social injustices would be rectified. However, surveys taken throughout the 1990s indicated that many inaccurate perceptions persisted, such as the majority of Whites surveyed continuing to believe that most African Americans are less intelligent, more prone to drug use, more violent, and more inclined toward violence against women than Whites are.

Sport culture, as it is currently interpreted, now provides Whites with the chance to talk about athletes in a way that reinforces these stereotypes of African Americans. Because African Americans dominate the most popular sports, Whites tend to "think Black" when they think about the major sports.

Each time any athlete gets into trouble, I receive many calls from writers and television producers seeking comments. After a fight involving a basketball or football player, the interrogation invariably includes, "What makes football or basketball players more inclined to get into fights?" I have never been asked this question of a hockey or baseball player, despite the fact that there are as many game fights in those sports.

After a reported incident of domestic violence involving a basketball or football player, the inevitable question is, "What makes football or basketball players more inclined to abuse women?" Equal numbers of hockey and baseball players are accused of domestic violence, yet I have never been asked this question about them.

Each year during the professional drafts in each sport I am asked, "What do you think about college or even high school football and basketball players jumping to the pros and missing their chance for an education?" I have never been asked that question about baseball or hockey, tennis or golf players who put higher education on hold to pursue athletic careers.

Shawn Fanning left Northeastern University early to turn pro and earn millions; he was called a genius for founding Napster. The dean of Northeastern University's School of Engineering told me that one of his biggest problems comes from companies attempting to lure away his top students each year. They leave for the money.

I believe that at least part of the systematic coupling of athletes and crime revolves around racial stereotyping. The media have persistently and consistently suggested that basketball and football players, who happen to be overwhelmingly African American, are more violent than athletes in other sports. As a result, many people, including women, fans, the media, sports administrators, and athletes themselves believe that certain athletes, especially basketball or football players, are more inclined to be violent in general and violent against women in particular.

Rosalyn Dunlap, an African American who was a five-time all-American sprinter who now works on social issues involving athletes, including gender violence prevention, said,

> Perpetrators are not limited to any category or occupation. The difference is that athletes who rape or batter will end up on television or in the newspapers. Such images of athletes in trouble create a false and dangerous mindset with heavy racial overtones. Most other perpetrators will be known only to the victims, their families, the police, and the courts. (R. Dunlap, personal communication, March 20, 1998)

Once while speaking to a group of distinguished international fellows at an elite academic institution, I asked members of the audience to write down five words they would use to describe American athletes. In addition to listing positive adjectives, not one missed including one of the following words: dumb, violent, rapist, or drug user. I regularly meet with NBA and NFL players, as well as with college student-athletes on dozens of campuses. There are a lot of angry athletes who are convinced the public is stereotyping them because of the criminal acts of a few.

Many American men have grown to dislike athletes. A typical man might crave the money and the fame that a pro athlete enjoys, but he recognizes that such athletic success is unattainable for him. After reading all of the negative press about athletes, he doesn't want to read that Mike Tyson felt he was treated unfairly by the justice system, knowing full well that Tyson made a reported $100 million in his postrelease rehabilitation program. He has little sympathy for the large number of pro athletes signing contracts worth more than $10 million a year. He is a microthought away from making egregious stereotypes about the "other groups" category. Whether it is an African American athlete or coach, or a White coach of African American athletes, when something goes wrong with a player, a national reaction is likely to be immediate. Tom "Satch" Sanders, who helped the Boston Celtics win eight world championships, is now vice president for player programs for the NBA. His office encourages and guides players to finish their educations, prepare for careers after basketball, and adjust to all the attention that NBA stars attract. Sanders presents a view complementary to Dunlap's. He proposes that the public has made a link between stereotypes for athletes and African Americans:

> Everyone feels that athletes have to take the good with the bad, the glory with the negative publicity. However, no one appreciates the broad-brush application that is applied in so many instances. Of the few thousand that play sports on the highest level, if four or five individuals in each sport— particularly if they were black—have problems with the law, people won't have long to wait before some media people are talking about all those athletes. (T. Sanders, interview, February 9, 1998)

APBnews.com released two revealing studies in 2000. The first was a study of NFL players on 2 teams that made it to the 2000 Super Bowl. The second was a study of the 16 NBA teams in the 2000 playoffs. In the NFL study, 11% of the players had a criminal history. That stood in dramatic contrast to the 35% to 46% lifetime arrest rate (taken from extensive studies in California and New York) for adult males under 30, the same age group as most NFL players. Most NFL players are between 18 and 30 years old, although most of those are between the ages of 21 and 30 (*Crime in the NFL*, 2000). In the study of NBA players, the arrest rate of those on the 16 playoff teams was 18%, again a fraction of the national figures for their comparable age group of males (*Crime in the NBA*, 2000).

Jeff Benedict's book *Pros and Cons* created a sensation in 1998 by saying that 21% of NFL players had arrest records. In an article he coauthored in 1999 for the statistics journal *Chance*, he said that the lifetime arrest rates for NFL players he documented in *Pros and cons* was less than half the arrest rate in the general population (Blumstein & Benedict, 1999).

Fans build stereotypes of athletes from media coverage of the athletes and the games. Fans, who are mostly White, observe sport through a media filter that is created by an overwhelming number of White men. There are 1,600 daily newspapers in America employing only 19 African American sport columnists. There are only two African American sport editors who work on newspapers in a city that has professional sport franchises (National Association of Black Journalists, 1998). The fact that the number of sport columnists, as reported at the 2000 conference of the National Association of Black Journalists, has almost doubled from 11 in 1998 is a positive sign. However, there are no African American sports writers on 90% of the 1,600 daily newspapers (National Association of Black Journalists, 2000).

I am not suggesting, nor would I ever suggest, that most or even many of the White news writers are racist. However, they were raised in a culture in which many White people have strong beliefs about what it means to be African American. The obvious result is that their reporting provides reinforcement of White stereotypes of African American athletes. According to the National Opinion Research Center Survey (1994), sponsored by the National Science Foundation for the University of Chicago, Whites surveyed share the following attitudes:

- Fifty-six percent of Whites think African Americans are more violent.
- Sixty-two percent of Whites think African Americans do not work as hard as Whites.
- Seventy-seven percent of Whites think most African Americans live off welfare.
- Fifty-three percent think African Americans are less intelligent.

Some White writers may have picked up these stereotypes in their own upbringing. When they write about an individual African American athlete or several African American athletes who have a problem, it becomes easy to unconsciously leap to the conclusion that fits the stereotype. Sanders said,

Blacks in general have been stereotyped for having drugs in the community as well as for being more prone to violence. However, now more than ever before, young black athletes are more individualistic and they resist the "broad brush." They insist on being judged as individuals for everything. (T. Sanders, interview, February 9, 1998)

But even that resistance can be misinterpreted by the public and by writers as off-the-court trash talking.

The athletes of the 21st century come from a generation of despairing youth cut adrift from the American dream. When the Center for the Study of Sport in Society started in 1984, one of its primary missions was to help young people balance academics and athletics. Since 1990, its mission has been extended to help young people lead healthy and safe lives.

Today our colleges are recruiting athletes

- who have witnessed violent death. If an American child under the age of 16 is killed every 2 hours with a handgun, then there is a good chance that young athletes will have a fallen family member or friend.
- who are mothers and fathers when they arrive at our schools. There are boys who helped 900,000 teenage girls get pregnant each year. Some student-athletes will leave after 4 years of college with one or more children who are 4 or 5 years old.
- who have seen friends or family members devastated by drugs.
- who have seen battering in their homes. An estimated 3% of American men are batterers, and an estimated 3 million women are battered each year.
- who were victims of racism in school. Seventy-five percent of all students surveyed by Lou Harris reported seeing or hearing about racially or religiously motivated confrontations with overtones of violence very or somewhat often.
- who grew up as latchkey kids. Either a single parent or two working parents head 57% of American families, Black and White alike (*MVP Fact Sheet*, 1997).

Not enough campuses or athletic departments have the right people to help guide these young men and women into their adult lives. College campuses desperately need professionals can deal with these nightmarish factors.

ACADEMIC ISSUES IN COLLEGE SPORT

The amount of media coverage devoted to student-athlete literacy problems makes such problems seem unique to athletes. The media rarely report that 30% of *all* entering freshman must take remedial English or mathematics. The same holds true for the media's portrayal of student-athlete graduation rates. Although college athletic departments should strive to increase the number of student-athletes who graduate, graduation rates for the student body as a whole have changed. Only 14% of entering freshmen graduated in 4 years. If an athlete does not graduate in 4 years, some call him dumb; others say the school failed him. Few note that he may be typical of college students.

Don McPherson nearly led Syracuse University to a national championship when he was quarterback in the 1980s. After 7 years in the NFL and CFL, McPherson worked until 1999 directing the Mentors in Violence Prevention (MVP) Program, the nation's largest program using athletes as leaders to address the issue of men's violence against women.

McPherson reflected on the image that associates athletes with a lack of intelligence:

> When whites meet an uneducated black athlete who blew opportunities in college or high school, they think he is dumb. They don't question what kind of school he may have to attend if he was poor, or how time pressures from sport may have affected him. If they don't make it as a pro athlete, they're through without a miracle. I met lots of "Trust Fund Babies" at Syracuse. They blew opportunities. No one called them dumb, just rich. We knew they would not need a miracle to get a second chance. I played at Syracuse at a time when being black and a quarterback had become more acceptable. But the stereotypes still remained. As a player, people still remember me as a great runner and scrambler. I had not dented their image of the physical vs. intelligent black athlete. (D. McPherson, interview, March 10, 1998)

McPherson led the nation in passing efficiency over Troy Aikman and won many awards, including the Maxwell Award, but he was most proud of being the quarterback with the highest passing efficiency rating in the nation.

I should have shattered the image of the athletic and mobile black quarterback and replaced it with the intelligent black quarterback. Unfortunately, stereotypes of football players, mostly black, still prevail. They make me as angry as all the stereotypes of black people in general when I was growing up. (D. McPherson, interview, March 10, 1998)

McPherson wore a suit to class and carried the *New York Times* under his arm. But McPherson said that those Whites who recognized his style were

surprised and said I was a "good black man," as if I were different from other black men. Most students assumed that I was poor and that football was going to make me rich. Like many other blacks on campus, I was middle class. My father was a detective and my mother was a nurse. (D. McPherson, interview, March 10, 1998)

Irrespective of color or gender, student-athletes graduate at a higher rate than non–student-athletes, yet it is difficult to get accurate reporting of this in the press. According to the NCAA's 1999 report:

- Fifty-eight percent of White male Division I student-athletes graduated vs. 57% of White male nonathletes. Forty-two percent of African American male Division I student-athletes graduated vs. 33% of African American male nonathletes.
- Seventy-one percent of White female Division I student-athletes graduated compared to 61% of White female nonathletes. Fifty-seven percent of African American female Division I student-athletes graduated vs. only 43% of African American female nonathletes.

Some disparities do appear when we compare White student-athletes to African American student-athletes:

- Fifty-three percent of White male Division I basketball student-athletes graduated versus 37% of African American male Division I basketball student-athletes.
- Seventy percent of White female Division I basketball student-athletes graduated compared to only 56% of African American female Division I basketball student-athletes (*NCAA Report of Graduation Rates*, 1999).

College sport does not own problems of illiteracy and low graduation rates. They belong to higher education in general and its inheritance of the near bankruptcy of secondary education in some communities.

The publication of graduation rates, long feared by athletic administrators, reveals scandalous rates, but it also shows poor graduation rates specifically for African Americans and Latinos. The predominantly White campuses of most colleges and universities are not welcoming environments for people of color. African American student-athletes arrive on most campuses and see that only 10% of the student body, 3% of the faculty, and less than 5% of top athletics administrators and coaches look like them. Unless there is a Martin Luther King Center or Boulevard, all the buildings and streets are named after White people (American Council on Education).

In many ways, the publication of graduation rates for student-athletes helped push the issue of diversity to the forefront of campus-wide discussions of issues of race, ethnicity, and gender. Educators finally recognized how they were failing students of color by not creating a conducive, welcoming educational environment.

DRUGS AND ALCOHOL USE AMONG ATHLETES

A common stereotype depicts athletes as abusing drugs and alcohol. Some athletes do use drugs. *CNN Headline News* broadcasts stories about famous athletes caught with drugs. Repeated exposure to such reports inflates the size of the problem, but the facts do not reveal widespread abuse among athletes at the professional, college, or even high school level.

According to an extensive 1995 *Los Angeles Times* survey of athletes and the crimes they committed, a total of 22 professional and college athletes and 3 coaches were accused of drug use or a drug-related crime that year. On average, the media reported a story about a new sport figure with a drug problem every 2 weeks. Center estimates now put the number of sport figures accused of drug-related crimes at 50 per year or one media story per week on average (*Athletes and Crime Fact Sheet: 1998*).

Stories about athletes accused of drug use or a drug-related crime are and should be disturbing. But those stories are rarely, if ever, put in the context of the 1.9 million Americans who use cocaine each month or the

2.1 million who use heroin throughout their lives. A total of 13 million individuals (6% of the American population) use some illicit drug each month, and 17% of men in the 18-to-25 age group are drug users. Whether it is 22 or 50, athletes who use drugs make up a small fraction of a percent of the more than 400,000 athletes who play college and professional sport in America (*Athletes and Crime Fact Sheet: 1998*).

The NBA's drug policy, which leaves open the possibility of a lifetime ban for any athlete who is caught using drugs, is generally recognized as a model for the sports world. The policy may have stopped a substance abuse problem that predated its inception. According to an APBnews.com report, *Crime in the NBA*, released in June 2000, 41 players were charged, booked, or arrested in 82 instances of crimes more serious than traffic tickets over the course of their time on the rosters of the 16 NBA playoff teams. The story noted that "it is perhaps a credit to the NBA's anti-drug policy that none of the eighty-two incidents noted in the APBnews.com study were related to hard drugs." (Marijuana was cited in six cases.) The 41 players put the NBA's arrest rate at 18%. APBnew.com reported that the general population as measured in four different studies ranges from 31% to 50%.

On the subject of alcohol abuse, the same 1995 *Los Angeles Times* survey of athletes and the crimes they committed reported that 28 college and professional athletes and four coaches were charged with alcohol-related infractions. None of these 32 cases were put in the context of the 13 million Americans who engage in binge drinking at least five times per month. Yet we read about a new athlete with an alcohol problem every 11 days (*Athletes and Crime Fact Sheet: 1998*). Such images can fuel an exaggerated sense of crisis in athletics when they are not viewed in full social context.

McPherson remembered being "shocked" when he arrived on Syracuse's campus at how much drinking went on each night among the student body. He felt compelled to call football players he knew on other campuses.

> It was the same everywhere. Now when I go to speak on college campuses I always ask. It is worse today. Athletes are part of that culture, but insist that practice and academics crowd their schedules too much to be in bars as often as other students. (D. McPherson, interview, March 10, 1998)

Student personnel administrators on college campuses acknowledge that abusive drinking is the number 1 issue on college campuses today.

ATHLETES AND VIOLENCE

Media coverage of professional, college, and even high school athletes consistently implies that the violence of sport makes its participants more violent in society.

Are sports any more violent today than they were 20 years ago when no one would have made such an assertion? I don't think so. But streets and schools across America surely are more violent than they were 20 years ago—there are 2,000 assaults in schools across the nation every hour of every day. The number of American children killed by guns in the 1900s has exceeded the total number of soldiers who died in the Vietnam War (*Athletes and Crime Fact Sheet: 1998*). Gun violence obeys no boundaries of race, class, or geography. School shootings occurred in Pearl, Mississippi; Paducah, Kentucky; Jonesboro, Arkansas; and Littleton, Colorado. Violence seems part of the school day.

If one were to put together a lowlights tape of the fights in sports that the public best remembers, I guarantee that most people would list Kermit Washington hitting Rudy Tomjanovich, Latrell Sprewell choking P. J. Carlisiemo, and Roberto Alomar spitting at umpire John Hirschbeck. Fear of men of color attacking Whites in our society is part of the culture. There is no doubt that the treatment afforded to Washington, Sprewell, and Alomar was measurably different from that given to Denver Bronco Bill Romanowski, who is White, after he spit in the face of a Black player in 1999.

Most of the stories written about specific athletes who are violent or gender violent are about African American athletes. Stories about them that appear without the appropriate context of what is going on in society reinforce racial stereotyping.

ATHLETES AND GENDER VIOLENCE

In the wake of the O. J. Simpson case, any incident involving an athlete assaulting a woman has received extraordinary publicity. The individual cases add up to what I consider another stereotype of the new millennium: Athletes, especially basketball and football players, are more inclined to be violent toward women than nonathletes are.

Joyce Williams-Mitchell has worked extensively in this field, most recently as the executive director of the Massachusetts Coalition of Battered Women's Service Groups. As an African American woman, she abhors the image of athletes being more prone to violence against women.

> It is a myth. The facts do not bear this out. All the studies of patterns of batterers defined by occupation point to men who control women through their profession. We hear about police, clergy, dentists, and judges. I only hear about athletes as batterers when I read the paper. They are in the public's eye. Men from every profession have the potential to be batterers. (J. Williams-Mitchell, interview, March 10, 1998)

There have been, of course, too many cases of athletes committing assaults on girls and women. As I wrote this section, I received a voice mail message from a reporter. "Have you heard that Corey Dillion is the latest case of an athlete hitting a woman? I guess that depends on when you pick up the message. There may have already been another case!" (personal communication). His message implied that attacks on women by athletes took place hourly.

However, there has never been a thorough, scientific study conclusively showing that athletes are more inclined to violence. Jeffrey Benedict, Todd Crossett, and Mark McDonald wrote the only study that comes close. It was based on 65 cases of assault against women that took place on 10 Division I campuses over a 3-year period. Thirteen of the cases involved athletes; seven of the athletes were basketball or football players (Benedict, Crossett, & McDonald, 1996).

Despite the authors' acknowledgment of both the small number of cases revealed and the fact that the survey did not control for alcohol and tobacco use or the men's attitudes toward women (the three main predictors of a male's inclination to gender violence), the press regularly quoted their study without qualification. Media reports never stated that the study came up with only 13 abusive athletes over 3 years. They simply said that the study concluded that student-athletes, in particular basketball or football players, committed nearly 20% of all campus assaults. Rosalyn Dunlap pointed out that this is a racially loaded conclusion. When I was a student-athlete at the University of Missouri, I never thought of keeping myself safe from a 260-pound football player any more than any other man on the street. In fact, male athletes on campus protected me. (R. Dunlap, personal communication, March 20, 1998)

The following is a list of data usually missing in the debate about athletes and violence against women.

- In 1994, 1,400 men killed their significant others. In that year, O. J. Simpson was the only athlete accused of murder.
- In 1998, an estimated 3 million women were battered, and close to 1 million were raped. According to various reports in the press in the 5 years between 1995 and 2000, between 70 and 100 athletes and coaches were accused of assault against a woman each year.
- The 1999 *Chronicle of Higher Education*'s annual campus crime survey showed that there were a total of 1,053 forcible sex offenses reported in 1997. Fewer than 35 student-athletes were arrested in conjunction with these crimes (*MVP Fact Sheet*, 1997).

Gender violence is a serious problem among American men. The cost of crime to America is pegged at $500 billion per year, according to a National Institute for Justice research report for the Justice Department released in March 1996. Gender assault and child abuse accounted for $165 billion—more than one third of that total (*MVP Fact Sheet*, 1997.)

Rosalyn Dunlap, who worked with The National Consortium for Academics and Sport to create more awareness about the issue, said,

> There are no men who should be exempted from being educated about the issue of gender violence although many believe they are. It is a problem for naval commanders, daycare providers, fraternities, guys in a bar, in corporations, in halls of higher education and, yes, on athletic teams. But no more so on athletic teams. (R. Dunlap, personal communication, March 20, 1998)

There have been numerous cases in which women brought suits against corporations for harassment or assault. The *Boston Globe* gave extensive coverage in the late 1990s to the case against Astra USA, Inc., a chemical company, where women lodged 16 formal complaints for incidents ranging from sexual harassment to rape. Twenty-nine women brought suit against Mitsubishi for the same reasons. None of the press about Astra suggested that working in a chemical company produced a climate of sexual aggression. At Mitsubishi, no one suggested any relationship between the manufacturing process and gender assault. So why do stories about athletes imply such a linkage to athletics? Does it fit White America's racial imagery? McPherson believes it does:

> Football and basketball mean Black. When the public talks about gender violence and athletes, it talks Black. No one discusses the problems of golfer John Dailey or Braves manager Bobby Cox. Warren Moon was another story altogether. Problems about athletes hit the papers and people think they detect a pattern because of the seeming frequency. But no one else's problems get in the papers. How do we make legitimate comparisons? With Astra and Mitsubishi, we look at the corporate climate and don't generalize about individuals. But with athletes, especially Black athletes, we look at players and look for patterns to add up. (D. McPherson, interview, March 10, 1998)

Some observers say athletes are trained to be violent and that we can expect that training to carry over into their homes. If this is true, then what about the training in lethal force we give to the police, the army, the navy, and the marines? Will these men also come home and kill? McPherson adds, "There is no logic to connect these cases, but we do fit our stereotypes of African-Americans with such images when we carry through the implication for athletes" (interview, March 10, 1998).

With all the recent publicity about the horrors of gender violence, it would be easy to forget that it was America's big, dirty secret until the O. J. Simpson case made it a notorious subject. Before that trial, few Americans were willing to talk about gender violence. The same unwillingness to confront racism diminishes society's ability to eradicate it. But the situation will never change if it remains unconfronted.

Athletes should take a leadership role on this issue, just as they have on drug abuse and educational opportunity. The MVP Program, organized in 1992 by Northeastern University's Center for the Study of Sport in Society and now headed by Jeff O'Brien, a former football player, has worked on more than 65 campuses training male and female athletes to be spokespeople on the issue of gender violence. Each of those schools has become proactive on an issue that has hurt so many women and their families.

Don McPherson insists that

> we have to do more to help our youth survive by including our athletes
> rather than excluding them in helping out youth. The stereotyping of our
> athletes does not help. We need to be ready with facts to dispute the easy la-
> bels. (D. McPherson, interview, March 10, 1998)

McPherson and Tom Sanders both argue vigorously not only that America's athletes don't fit the emerging stereotypes about athletes and crime,
but also that the vast majority of professional athletes are extremely positive roll models. Sanders said,

> When I look at the many NBA players who have their own foundations and
> who are very involved with giving back to the communities where they play
> and where they come from, I know they are hurt by the stereotypes. (T.
> Sanders, interview, February 9, 1998)

McPherson asserts that "most of the players in the NFL are deeply religious, family-centered men who are constantly giving back to their communities with time and money" (interview, March 10, 1998).

Rosalyn Dunlap wonders when the public and the media will stop being cynical about athletes.

> I hear so many people say that if athletes do something in the community
> that they will do it for publicity. Why can't we accept that athletes want to
> help? Sport and those who play it can help educate us, and sensitize us.
> While we can't ignore the bad news, we should also focus on the over-
> whelming good news of what athletes do to make this a better world. (R.
> Dunlap, personal communication, March 20, 1998)

I do not believe the stereotypes. However, I do believe that the high profile of all professional sports makes it incumbent on those involved to call
on sports institutions to demand a higher standard for athletes. Athletes,
once challenged, have played a leading role in the battle to educate our
children, in the life and death fight against alcohol and drug abuse, and in
the attempt to resolve conflicts with reason and not with fists or weapons.
Now it is time to challenge them to fight the long overdue battle against
gender violence.

The challenge to athletes involved a starting point of confronting the behavior of an individual athlete. Some universities had to make star athletes academically ineligible or expel them from school to convince others that they were serious about education and would not tolerate either poor academic records or athletes violating social norms.

After the tragic death of Len Bias, the nation was forced to recognize that cocaine was not "recreational," but lethal. Schools began random drug testing; the NBA promised to uphold a lifetime ban for players who ignored league policies. This ban was necessary to show players as well as their young fans that there could be no tolerance for the use of life-threatening drugs.

The ban will always seem unfair to the player caught with drugs. I am sure Michael Ray Richardson, who was the first NBA player banned for life, still looks in the mirror and asks, "Why me? There were other guys." But the discipline had to start somewhere. What was unfortunate for Richardson was fortunate for the NBA and for society. Action, no matter how symbolic, was critical.

Likewise, when street violence began to invade our rinks, courts, and fields, sport had to take a stand with automatic and serious sanctions that cost players money and cost teams their player services. No commissioner or director of a players association wanted the entire league and all of its athletes branded as thugs because of those who acted out during a game.

The New England Patriots bit the bullet for all professional sports and decided not to sign draftee Christian Peter, the University of Nebraska's highly acclaimed football player, who carried numerous criminal charges on his record. It was a milestone decision. Patriot owner Robert Kraft felt compelled to take a strong stand immediately after they drafted Peter, despite the fact that he would lose dollars in the draft and could have faced lawsuits from Peter's representatives. The importance of his decision was not only that players would see clear consequences for their actions but also that children who idolize those players would see such consequences as relevant to their own choices in life.

Sports figures are in a unique position to affect change. Keith Lee, a 6-year NFL veteran who is now the chief operating officer of the National Consortium for Academics and Sport, works to improve race relations among young people. He states, "We need positive role models who can help young people to believe in what they cannot see. We need them now more than ever" (K. Lee, personal communication, March 10, 1998).

REFERENCES

Athletes and Crime Fact Sheet: 1998. Boston, MA: Center for the Study of Sport in Society, Northeastern University.

Benedict, J., Crossett, T., & McDonald, M. (1996). Male student-athletes and violence against women. *Violence Against Women, 2*(2).

Benedict, J., & Yeager, D. (1998). *Pros and cons: The criminals who play in the NFL*. Clayton, Victoria, Australia: Warner Books.

Blumstein, A., & Benedict, J. (1999). Criminal violence of NFL players compared to the general public. *Chance Magazine, 12*, 393–408.

Crime in the NBA. (2000, June). APBnews.com.

Crime in the NFL. (2000). APBnews.com.

MVP Fact Sheet. (1997). Center for the Study of Sport in Society, Northeastern University.

National Opinion Research Center Survey. (1994). (Sponsored by the National Science Foundation for the University of Chicago.)

NCAA Report of Graduation Rates. (1999). www.ncaa.org/grad_rates/1999/index .html. (The NCAA website publishes graduation rates annually.)

www.acenet.edu/. (1999, June). American Council on Education. (Data collected annually by ACE's Center for Advancement of Racial and Ethnic Equity.)

www.nabj.org. (1998, May). National Association of Black Journalists.

www.nabj.org. (2000, August). National Association of Black Journalists.

10

Exploring Race with Secondary Students: Developing Critical Media Literacy

Brian Lampman
Saline Middle School

THE HISTORICAL HURDLE: RACE

Racism still alive, they just be consealin' it.

(Kanye West, "Never Let Me Down," 2004)

This is America, and although we may have come here in different boats, we're all in the same boat now. If part of the boat sinks, eventually the rest will go down, too. (Carson, 1999)

As a White male secondary educator I have worked hard to learn about historical and contemporary images of race, gender, and social class. While exploring Black culture and history in my own social studies classroom, I have always considered real-world applications of teaching history critical to student success. Successful social studies pedagogy must make history come alive for students and help them to understand the correlation between historical and contemporary issues. The teaching of American history has undergone important transformations, led by scholars such as Howard Zinn and James Loewen. Both authors make it a point to expose students to more multiracial accounts of history, and further, to expose the hypocrisy of past pedagogical tools. For example, Eurocentric versions of Columbus as conquering hero have given way to graphic accounts of cruelty toward the indigenous peoples of the Caribbean. In the process, the teaching of history has become a far more inclusive bastion of learning.

While the construction of history content has evolved, my concerns lie in powerful media representations of minority groups that have been slow to follow suit, and, most alarmingly, the influence these representations can have on impressionable White students whose own race shapes the dominant cultural ideology. As a cultural critic of sports in society, I am particularly troubled by images of minorities in the media, particularly Black male athletes. The focus of this chapter is to highlight my experience as a secondary educator teaching a predominantly White student population to combat the narrow media representations of Black males in sport. The chapter highlights the importance of teaching critical media literacy skills, particularly in homogeneous communities, to disarm rampant, hostile, and disingenuous representations of athletic Black males in our society.

BATTLIN' THE MEDIA: SEEIN' ISN'T BELIEVIN'

Images of Black male athletes saturate television screens daily, and as an educator, I am privy to how my White students respond. I observe my students' desire to cross-over dribble like Allen Iverson of the Philadelphia 76ers, to throw like Michael Vick of the Atlanta Falcons, and to run like Shaun Alexander of the Seattle Seahawks. I witness my White students' interest in the latest NBA jerseys sported by Cleveland Cavaliers basketball phenom LeBron James or high-flying Denver Nuggets forward Carmelo Anthony. Class political cartoon assignments make reference to Detroit Pistons center Ben Wallace as the Minister of Defense and Miami Heat center Shaquille O'Neal as the Man of Steel. Students watch as Tiger Woods endorses everything from Nike golf balls to Buick cars and, most likely, have their first exposure to Julius Erving in a Walt Disney *Wide World of Sports* commercial. My observations of the White student (particularly males) fascination with Black male athletic icons are anecdotal, but I believe they are representative of this fascination of White students as a whole, particularly males. Factors such as politics, social class, and geography play a role in how White students are exposed to and influenced by media representations of Black males; however, I cannot imagine that the White students that I teach are far from the norm in their exposure and response to media representations of Black male athletes.

Noted sociologist Jackson Katz argues that the technology age has ushered in countless media representations of minority men mired in narrowly constructed stereotypes (Katz, 1999). Disproportionate representations of American Indians as noble savages, Latinos as gang members and criminals, Asians as violent or mysterious, men of Middle Eastern descent as terrorists or religious fanatics have exacerbated stereotypes of these minority groups. Black males are traditionally cast as athletes consumed with showmanship on the playing field, court, or diamond. Off the field, the media often highlight their supposed preoccupation with and out-of-hand accumulation of symbols of wealth and power. Far too frequently, the dominant cultural ideologies that provide the framework for cultural norms in our society fuel racist and inaccurate representations of minorities. The popularity of sport in our country makes these biased and exploitative representations dangerous and difficult to undo.

Critical media literacy skills teach students to analyze the plethora of media outlets readily available to them, with critical attention to content, point of view, and historical framework. Without these skills, many students may fall victim to the toxic popular cultural images of minorities, many of which portray African Americans in a particularly insidious light. Research by the Harvard Civil Rights Project demonstrates that our nation's schools are still tragically devoid of a rich racial balance (NAACP Legal Defense and Education Fund, Civil Rights Project at Harvard University, & Center for the Study of Race and Law, 2005). One product of this sobering study is that students are not afforded diverse interactions with other races in the classroom. The lack of direct interaction between Whites and Blacks creates a problem when media images of Black athletes are grounded in misrepresentations, and further, characterizations of Blackness are rooted in fallacies. At the same time, representations of Whiteness are framed by dominant cultural ideologies that hold a great deal of power and privilege in our country; these ideologies are often readily accepted and not always questioned by the mass media.

Teaching critical media literacy strategies is imperative to White students' understanding and appreciation of the rich and varied cultural traditions and experiences of Blacks. White students must be taught skills to situate and resist the media representations and recognize them for what they are: contrived images, not accurate or reliable reflections of Blacks in our country.

For many White suburban schoolchildren, the media become the lens into African American culture; athletics often serve as the portal. Sports sociologist Jay Coakley eloquently addresses how problematic these consequences can be in his highly acclaimed work *Sport in Society: Issues and Controversies*. He examines research into the near exclusive representation of Black males in major newspapers and television programs as entertainers, athletes, and criminals. He explores research examining the coverage of Black athletes in television and print ads as violent and angry—characters to be feared. Coakley speculates about the possibility that violent White male athletes do not cause Whites to view all White males as violent— Whites are afforded such enormous societal interaction with other Whites (and countless positive media representations of White males geared toward a dominant White consumer audience) so as not to believe such ludicrous generalizations. Yet when Whites who have little or no social contact with Blacks see negative constructions of Black athletes in the media, this can easily become their stereotype of all Black males. In contrast, rarely are violent White men viewed as the voice or face of the White race. The actions of a handful of White men are not seen as emblematic of the White race as a whole; the polar opposite can be true for Black males (Coakley, 2001).

The consistent barrage of media representations fuels White perceptions of Black males' cognitive ability and creates a fabricated rationale for athletic success. In 1987, Los Angeles Dodgers executive Al Campanis told Ted Koppel of ABC's *Nightline* that the lack of representation by Blacks in managerial, front-office, and ownership positions was due to their deficiency in the "necessities" for those positions (Shropshire, 1996, p. 21). The implication behind Campanis's comments was clear: Blacks lacked the mental capacities to manage a team or oversee an organization. Campanis's comments led to his firing but further fueled racist ideology in regard to Black male athletes. Evidence of this point can be seen in positional stacking in the NFL. It was well into the 1990s before many teams gave Blacks the opportunity to hold the ultimate "thinking" position on the field: the quarterback (Lapchick, 1991, p. 229). Black quarterbacks currently starting in the NFL, such as Donovan McNabb of the Philadelphia Eagles, Michael Vick of the Atlanta Falcons, and Daunte Culpepper of the Minnesota Vikings, have laid waste to the stereotype that Black athletes cannot play the role of coach on the field. Yet it is still quite common for sports announcers to cite the "athleticism" of African American athletes and the "cerebral" qualities of their White counterparts during the play-by-play commentary of a game.

In 1988, another prominent example of racist Black male representations in sport occurred when CBS announcer Jimmy "the Greek" Snyder offered his comments about Black players in professional football. Snyder summed up the success of Black players in the NFL as due to the careful breeding of Blacks by White slave owners for physical labor dating back to the Civil War. Snyder further stated that all the players in the NFL were Black and the only positions left for Whites to control were the coaching jobs (Shropshire, 1996). Snyder's comments illustrated the historical White fascination with and fear of the Black male body. He gave further credence to racist dominant cultural ideology that Black males are genetically predisposed for success in athletics. In other words, Black males got the jumping genes and White males got the thinking genes.

My students were not born when Campanis and Snyder made their comments about Black athletes. Their media frame of reference is influenced by more recent events splashed across newspapers and played repeatedly by major sport and news organizations. Clearly some progress has been made since Snyder and Campanis offered their conjecture on Black cognitive ability. Yet the media continue to offer dubious examples that leave little doubt that representations of Black male athletes still course with racist ideology. In July of 2004, former Irish football star turned radio commentator Paul Hornung lamented the need for more quality Black players at the University of Notre Dame. To get them, he reasoned, Notre Dame would need to lower academic standards in hopes of attracting more Black athletes. Hornung immediately provoked a firestorm of controversy in response to his remarks from University of Notre Dame officials, fans, and even then-coach Tyrone Willingham. Hornung quickly backpedaled from his initial remarks, making every attempt to qualify his statements with the assertion that it was not just Black athletes that the University of Notre Dame would have to lower its standards for, but all exceptional athletes. While Hornung further fueled the notion that an athlete (of any race) cannot be a great student, his initial remarks reinforced still other stereotypical profiling that defines a Black athlete as a prized performer on the field and an academic liability in the classroom.

The infamous Piston-Pacers basketball game of November 2004 serves as another intriguing example into how the media frames Black athletes.

When Ron Artest charged into the stands to confront the fan who he believed threw water on him, he became the epitome of everything that many thought was wrong with the largely Black National Basketball Association. Artest's indiscretions captured the attention of the nation as footage from the Palace brawl was played over and over again. Artest's actions were certainly one of the precipitating factors in this year's NBA image makeover. In stark contrast, the National Hockey League is by a wide margin composed largely of White males. While violence is a more accepted part of the game of hockey, it is legitimate to question why Vancouver Canucks forward Todd Bertuzzi's vicious on-ice attack of Steve Moore in 2004 (both White males) did not provoke greater outrage against the violent characteristics of White males in the NHL. Media coverage of Artest's actions fed into representations of Black males as violent, while media coverage of Bertuzzi's actions fed into the image of the NHL, not White males, as violent.

In October of 2005 following a loss to Texas Christian University, Air Force football coach Fisher DeBerry was reprimanded for his statements about Black athletes. Coach DeBerry stated that "Afro-American kids can run very well," and his opponent on that day had "more Afro-American kids than we did and they ran a lot faster than we did" (Pells, 2005). Stereotypical race logic illustrated by DeBerry reinforces the notion that Black males on college campuses must be at institutions of higher education because of their brawn, not their brains. Images of White males as athletes and entertainers are certainly present in the media but are always complemented with images of alternative professions for White males such as doctor, lawyer, businessperson, and teacher. As DeBerry's comments illustrate, media representations of viable professions for Black males are almost always very limited to athletics and entertainment.

TOWARD A MORE INCLUSIVE SCHOOL ENVIRONMENT

I am cognizant that my many White students are enamored with images of Blackness and consider it to be the epitome of hip and cool (Boyd, 2004, p. 14) yet devalue its importance beyond popular media icons. I do not want my White students to be merely tourists in Blackness: to appropriate Black culture but do little to appreciate its roots, the legacy of its struggles, or visions for its future. I do not want them to invite Blacks into their homes on television, but not to a seat at the dinner table. I do not want their frame of reference into Black culture to be constructed solely by media bytes from outspoken former Philadelphia Eagles wide receiver Terrell Owens, or a punch thrown by Indiana Pacers forward Ron Artest against unruly fans in last year's Detroit Pistons–Indiana Pacers basketball debacle, or by comments from Paul Hornung.

I do not want my students to explore Blackness only during the month of February. I do not want my students to get their images and ideas about Blackness predominantly from the media, and I rarely investigate those images and their sources. I do not want my students to watch without questioning the depictions of Muslims of Middle Eastern descent on the hit show *24*, the characterizations of Italians on HBO's *The Sopranos*, or the violent, savage portrayal of American Indians as mascots at major sporting events. And I do not want my students to frame their portrait of Blacks solely through news releases of crimes reportedly committed by "young Black males." I do not want their exposure to Blacks to be based entirely on the "bling-bling" lifestyle portrayed in some hip-hop videos. And I do not want my students to limit their understanding of Black males to what they view on the playing field.

There is trouble brewing when impressions of a race of people are based largely on media constructions and not direct personal human interactions. White students must challenge biased media constructions. When White students are not afforded the opportunity to interact with Black students (or students of other racial or ethnic backgrounds), they become even more vulnerable to media imagery. White students must learn to engage in critical media literacy; they must question the source of information. They must probe into the validity of claims. They must consider alternative points of view.

The Benefits

I recognize the popularity of many mainstream media representations of Blacks (beyond athletic images) and their influence on White students. I want White youth to continue to enjoy hip-hop, watch athletics, and rock the Sean John sweats; however, I want their knowledge of Blackness to extend far beyond embracing the music, sport, and fashion commonly associated with Black culture. I want them to understand the rich cultural traditions and contributions made to our society by the Black community. I want them to understand why Chuck D of the rap group Public Enemy said, "Most of my heroes don't appear on no stamp!" (Public Enemy, "Fight the Power," 1990) highlighting the absence of Black history in our school's textbooks. I want White students to feel rage at the inadequate representation of Blacks in Division I athletic and administrative positions. I want White students to recognize the contradiction that a country with the immense resources such as ours could continue to have problems such as AIDS, illiteracy, poverty, and crime that hit minorities (in many cases, the Black community) the hardest. And I want them to remember the tragic images of thousands of Blacks displaced by Hurricane Katrina's wrath to understand the confluence of race, class, power, and privilege in our country and how these factors influence the interaction of various sectors of society following such crises. I want White students to critically assess the manner in which race, gender, and class are framed in our country, and then, most importantly, I want them to be challenged into working for social change.

Teaching White students the skills to resist narrowly constructed representations of race in the media has benefits for all of society. Cross-racial understanding leads to greater tolerance of others; in an increasingly diverse world, this is essential for effective communication and meaningful work environments. Debunking narrowly constructed media representations fosters greater appreciation and understanding among students. Teaching critical media literacy skills enables students to have a broader cultural, historical, and social context for their learning; it further allows students more information to fill in omissions created by the media.

Race is still a very touchy subject in the United States. Politicians, the media, even major universities still grapple with a subject that has created deep divisions in our country. Teaching about race can be equally problematic for teachers, so much so that some educators would rather not tackle this slippery slope on our educational landscape. Some educators would rather stick to a carefully crafted curriculum: Read the textbook and promote the time honored Eurocentric, whitewashed, xenophobic version of history. Other educators tackle the vexing issue of race with a passion for understanding, acceptance, and the importance of working for social change. We must recognize that ours is not a history with separate threads but a fabric of interwoven stories and lives, a fabric that cannot be truly understood by teaching about "other" groups during only one special month (or week) of the year. We must expose incomplete pedagogical approaches that do not challenge dominant cultural ideologies. Imagine if teachers stressed the importance of critical media literacy skills as much as rote memorization of facts!

The efforts of educators to teach critical media literacy skills can be undone by peer groups or resistance from parents at home. Therefore educators, students, and parents must partner in attempts to explore and understand narrow media constructions. White parents must not dismiss or disapprove of their White students' interest in Black athletes but instead partner in their child's education and understanding of Black culture. Imagine if White parents looked past the braids and tattoos of some Black athletes in much the same manner that they asked their own parents to look past Elvis's gyrating hips in their own youth!

Authentic Black male representations in the media are rare and often reduced to visceral images of Black male athletes as the norm. The media must offer alternative positive representations of Black athletes. Imagine if the first thing sportswriters had done after University of Southern California star tailback Reggie Bush's Heisman award was to write about the 3.8 GPA he carried in high school. Or the fact that Bush is on pace to graduate with a degree in political science in less than four years!

As a veteran secondary educator, I consider myself experienced in meeting the educational needs of my homogeneous district. As a White male, I consider myself actively engaged in my understanding of the power and privilege that my Whiteness affords me in our society. And as a coach I have an appreciation for the confluence of race and sport in our culture. I teach in a wonderful community with incredibly supportive parents and eager, creative, and imaginative students. I feel that the majority of parents and students are very committed to teaching and practicing tolerance toward all races. Open acts of racism are uncommon in my district; however, we must not let our guard down as educators, students, and community members—now is the time for continued persistence in the face of intolerance. Subtle forms of racism must be attacked with the same vigilance as overt acts of racism. While it is a losing battle to attempt to control the media images most students consume, encouraging aggressively stimulating classroom discourse and teaching effective critical media literacy strategies to deconstruct these images will lead to a better understanding of all cultures and races. Ultimately, as Ben Carson is quoted as saying earlier in this chapter, we must learn to look out for all our brothers and sisters, regardless of skin color.

REFERENCES

Boyd, T. (2004). *Young, Black, rich and famous*. New York: New York University Press.

Carson, B. (1999). *The big picture*. Grand Rapids, MI: Zondervan Press.

Coakley, J. (2001). *Sport in society: Issues and controversies*. New York: McGraw-Hill.

Katz, J. (1999). *Tough guise: Violence, media and the crisis in masculinity*. Northampton, MA: Media Education Foundation.

Lapchick, R. (1991). *Smashing barriers: Race and sport in the new millennium*. Lanham, MD: Madison Books.

NAACP Legal Defense and Education Fund, Civil Rights Project at Harvard University, & Center for the Study of Race and Law at the University of Virginia School of Law. (2005). *Looking to the future: Voluntary K–12 school integration*. Retrieved from www.civilrightsproject.harvard.edu/resources/manual/manual.pdf.

Pells, E. (2005, October 26). Retrieved from http://famulus.msnbc.com/famulusgen/ap10-26-144452.asp?t=APNEW.

Shropshire, K. (1996). *In Black and White: Race and sports in America*. New York: New York University Press.

11

Unexpected, Undeserved, Unrewarded . . . and Undeniable: Sport and Transformation

Bill Curry
ESPN

The National Football League is a tough place to grow up. Many of us who experienced life in the NFL had to mature in a hurry, usually in a state best described as a stew of fear, fatigue, and wonder. We are afraid, not because we think we will be injured, but because we are terrified of failure—we might be sent home to sports page headlines that scream, "CURRY CUT BY PACKERS!" We are exhausted because of the weeks of physical, emotional, and intellectual strain of training camp. We live in shock and awe at the speed, power, and athleticism of our new teammates.

One thing that adds to our early confusion is the language we hear. Our new NFL coaches speak in a football parlance that is strange, idiomatic, and filled with subtleties we had not known existed. Trying to understand, digest, and respond to this new language is like participating in forced marches responding to orders in Lithuanian.

While we are competing in an arena we have watched all our lives, it is not at all what we had imagined, magnified by veteran creatures from our worst football nightmares. Once we get into the locker room there they are: some stunning specimens, huge, beautiful, and symmetrical. A few are old, bald, and fat. Many talk with strange accents, or not at all. They are from every corner of the United States and some foreign countries. For all their differences, they have one thing in common—the most shocking aspect of all—*they can run like the wind.*

Another fear in this new arena revolves around the competition involved with other rookies. The newcomers, who might be one's friends, are competing for the same jobs, creating a wariness that increases our sense of alienation. It feels as if it is virtually complete. There are a limited number of roster spots available, and from day 1 everybody knows there will be casualties. Any red-blooded American kid who ever watched a war movie knows better than to get too close to folks in the foxhole.

My rookie experience came in 1965 with the Green Bay Packers. Vince Lombardi was at the midpoint of his Green Bay dynasty, with much yet to prove to the world. Our country was at the height of the civil rights movement. Cities were burning and race relations were tense. I grew up in College Park, Georgia, and attended college at Georgia Tech. Prior to going to college, I had never been in a huddle with or across the line from an African American player. Our team at Tech played in the Gator Bowl against Penn State in 1961 and performed against David Robinson, the lone African American player for the Nittany Lions. David was the dominant force on the field for his victorious team and became the subject of much of the postgame talk. He became larger than life in our recollection of him.

Robinson was on that Packer team, 1 of 10 future Hall of Famers on that 40-man roster. The defensive captain was Willie Davis, another Hall of Famer, who was a graduate of Grambling State University, and who was working on his MBA at the University of Chicago. He shattered all the stereotypes from my racist background. Virtually every African American I had ever known had been forced into a subservient role. That was simply an overriding fact of life in most segments of our culture. I wondered, why wouldn't those guys notice my Southern accent, injure me, and send me home? Who could have blamed them? They chose not to do that, deciding to respond in a remarkable manner, one that even changed my life.

I could only practice hard and wait for the moment of truth. While Coach Lombardi would decide if I would play, it was the other men on the team who would decide whether or not I could belong in their very special huddle. Under Davis's leadership the African Americans accepted me and allowed me into their space. While quarterback Bart Starr would be the first veteran to make overt efforts to bring me into the fold, it would be the African American men who took me aside to encourage and admonish me. I could not have been more stunned or chastened. I was getting a cram course in community, acceptance, and the huddle as defined in the NFL. I was learning the magic of team.

As time has allowed for reflection, I have come to understand that Davis, Robinson, Herb Adderley, Elijah Pitts, and the others did not just help a terrified rookie to play in the NFL. They changed my life. I could never again look at other human beings the same way. I could never again judge a person by factors other than his or her individual merits—never. That training camp became the singular epiphany for the remainder of my years on earth. I learned one reason America loves the crazy sport of football so much: I learned about the huddle. Unexpected, undeserved, unrewarded acts of kindness change human lives. When they occur in as unlikely a place as a football field, their impact is exponentially multiplied. I am eternally thankful to those great men.

After September 11, 2001, much was made over whether or not we should play the week's schedule of football games. Some speculated about why the subject should have even been contemplated. Here is one reason: The huddle is a metaphor for our culture. Yes, imperfect like all metaphors, but nonetheless a microcosm. In that huddle is a bunch of folks who are Black, Brown, White, Red, Yellow, liberal, conservative, Muslim, Jewish, Christian, Buddhist, and Hindu. We are slim, fat, short, and tall. We are analytical folks and impulsive folks. We have some of the finest men on earth, and heaven knows we have a few characters. Many of us have been through the fires of coaches like Vince Lombardi, Don Shula, or others who know exactly how to extract every ounce of our energy. Americans see all of that, and they resonate with it. They crave it. They take it, and us, into their hearts.

The men who earn a place in the huddle have experienced the miracle of being a part of a team. The training camp experience is unbelievable. It is day after day, week after week, two-a-day, three-a-day practices in the heat, often in 14 pounds of equipment. Many drop out, are waived or injured. Numbers thin, and everybody thinks about quitting—trust me, everybody. For those who stay, there is the opportunity to participate in the greatest team sport ever devised. It is the only sport in which every player needs every teammate on every play just to survive. The very fact that someone of my limited ability could be a part of this, could hike the ball to Bart Starr and John Unitas, get in some monster's way for 3 seconds and be accepted as part of the team speaks volumes to the common man.

We learn, ever so slowly, that our differences do not matter in the huddle. When we trudge in after each interminable workout, we sense that the sweat smells the same on everybody's T-shirt. When we get busted in the mouth, the blood that trickles is the same color. Everybody is tired. Everybody is hurt. It is in this process that the miracle occurs. Men who have been raised to hate each other's guts become brothers. I have seen racists reformed. I have seen the most unlikely hugs after victories—or losses. I have seen inner-city kids invite country boys from the mountains to go home with them for Thanksgiving dinner. I have seen the invitations accepted, and reciprocated, thus changing parents' lives. Our players become brothers—for life. It is what America is supposed to be, could be, might be, in our best dreams.

12

Making Sense of the American Indian Mascot Issue

Ellen J. Staurowsky
Department of Sport Management
& Media, Ithaca College

Since the civil rights era of the 1960s and 1970s, an increasing number of American Indians across a spectrum of tribal affiliations and from all walks of life, including educators, psychologists, lawyers, scholars, writers, politicians, artists, actors, journalists, government officials, veterans of the armed forces, and tribal leaders, have challenged the use of American Indian imagery by corporations, government agencies, schools, the entertainment industry, and sports teams. American Indians question why racially offensive images like Chief Wahoo, the mascot for the Cleveland Indians, receive widespread public support while similar caricatures of other racial groups, such as Amos and Andy and the Frito Bandito, have long since disappeared from the American landscape. Opponents of American Indian imagery argue that its continued misappropriation is an extension of long-standing practices of mistreatment directed toward American Indian people that date back before the founding of the United States as a nation. The cartoon below begs the question. Why is Chief Wahoo still so popular and acceptable while the caricatures of Asians, Africans, and Hispanics as shown in the cartoon are intolerable today?

Forty years of steady and persistent opposition to American Indian sport imagery have resulted in some organizations choosing new mascots and nicknames. Relatively speaking, schools have been more inclined to change mascots in recognition of the need to reassess the educational value of images that routinely stereotype American Indians and the harms they cause. As American Indian leader Vernon Bellecourt has stated,

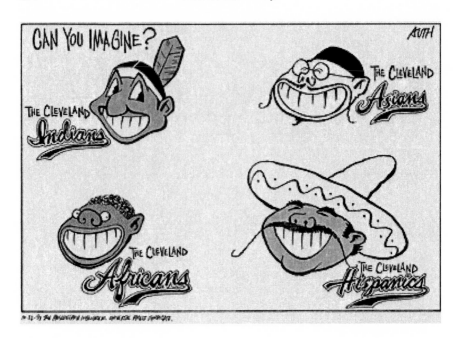

"We've made considerable gains. Many colleges, universities and high schools have either changed or are in the midst of a dialogue of change" (Lesnick, 2004, n.p.). Mr. Bellecourt's point is demonstrated in the decisions reached throughout the spring and summer of 2004. Southeast Missouri University, Ottawa Hills High School in Michigan, and Rice Memorial High School in Vermont have chosen to stop using Indians as nicknames for their athletic teams (Associated Press, 2004; "High school to change," 2004; Murray, 2004). In January, the Guilford County School District in North Carolina agreed to create a policy that would prohibit the use of such mascots (Fernandez, 2004). Similarly, in June of 2004, the California Senate Education Committee passed a bill that would prohibit schools in that state from using the term "Redskins" as their nickname.

According to Suzan Shown Harjo (Muscogee), Director of the Morning Star Institute and columnist of *Indian Country Today*, an estimated 1,500 mascots have been retired or modified since 1970 (as cited in King, 2002). In professional baseball, minor league clubs have demonstrated more responsiveness to requests to eliminate these images than their major league counterparts. As a case in point, the Akron Aeros, Buffalo Bisons, and Mahoning Valley Scrappers have all parted company on the mascot issue with the major league club with which they are affiliated, the Cleveland baseball franchise.

Despite the changes that have occurred, American Indian sociologist Darius Smith (2003) points out that "there remains profound resistance to letting go of Indian mascots or acknowledging the current impact on Indian identity and cross-cultural relationships" (p. 2). In point of fact, for every step forward on this issue there are several steps back. While the schools in Missouri, Michigan, North Carolina, and Vermont were reaching the conclusion that they needed to stop stereotyping American Indians, students and alumni at the University of Illinois continued to defend the invented "Indian" figure that dances at their half-time shows, "Chief Illiniwek." In May of 2004, the vice chair of Marquette University's board of trustees, Wayne Sanders, offered to join a fellow alumnus in donating $2 million to the university on the condition that it reverse a decision made 12 years previously to replace its "warrior" mascot with the "golden eagles." Although Marquette's president, the Reverend Robert Wild, SJ, declined to accept the gift, a decision by the board of trustees as to whether the university will reconsider the name change issue remains pending.

The purpose of this chapter is to equip you with basic analytical tools and background for studying this issue and deciding where you stand on it. Because American sport and consumer culture are saturated with American Indian imagery and symbols, I begin with a reflection on how our views are shaped by what is called the *dominant culture* and why the influence of the dominant culture makes an *objective* examination of this issue problematic. I proceed to look briefly at the history behind this imagery, move on to consider two of the most common misperceptions about American Indian mascots, and conclude with the negative impact this imagery has on American Indians and non–American Indians.

AMERICAN INDIAN SPORT IMAGERY AS PART OF THE DOMINANT CULTURE

To test the idea that American Indian sport imagery is interwoven into the dominant culture, let's start with a quick exercise. Can you pinpoint when you first became aware that teams had American Indian mascots and nicknames?

The question appears simple but the answer is complicated. Living in a society where daily reports about the Cleveland Indians, Atlanta Braves, Kansas City Chiefs, and Chicago Blackhawks are broadcast around the globe, where children put on feathered headdresses and mark their faces with "war paint" at Halloween, and where popular movies like *Pocahontas* and the *Indian in the Cupboard* are shown over and over and over again, locating a specific moment in time when you knew these images existed and were accepted is nearly impossible. This illustrates the influence society, and the culture in which we live, has on our behavior. On the one hand, we are encouraged to think of ourselves as individuals, people who have our own ideas and perceptions. And yet when we are repeatedly exposed to certain ways of behaving, acting, and thinking, we adopt those behaviors, actions, and modes of thinking without consciously deciding to do so.

In schools, these images have historically served as a powerful means of building what is called *community* or *team identity*. To illustrate, here is a song that is sung at a school that has a "warrior" as a mascot. If you go to a game, you will hear students, parents, athletes, school officials, and teachers, all singing:

> We are the warriors,
> The mighty, mighty warriors.
> Everywhere we go-o,
> People want to know-o,
> Who we are-re,
> So we tell them,
> We are the warriors,
> The mighty, mighty warriors.
>
> (Anonymous, n.d.)

Similarly, identification with this imagery begins for many American children at very young ages. As one graduate of the University of Illinois explains, "I listen to friends of mine tell their children about the Chief and what he stands for and the children are hanging on every word, eventually saying that when they grow up they want to be like the Chief" (Farnell, 2004, p. 36).

Spanning every age group and regardless of social and economic standing, athletes play on teams with American Indian names from Little

League to the Big Leagues. Whether one is following sports the old-fashioned way on the printed sports pages of daily newspapers or the trendier modes offered by sports television and the Internet, American Indian imagery is displayed millions of times in a given day to numerous audiences and consumers. From computer games to fantasy leagues to merchandise catalogs, from team stores to gift shops to outlet centers to fine stores at the mall, from wall posters to lighting fixtures to furniture to barbecue grills, from food items to beverages to games for the kids and license plates for the adults, as well as clothes for both humans and pets, representations associated with American Indians in the form of symbols, words, and images compose a prominent part of American consumer and sport culture.

Developing an awareness of the prevalence of American Indian imagery is critical to better understanding why the issue of American Indian sport imagery and mascots draws debate and sometimes provokes controversy. Because this imagery appears so frequently, and permission to use it is supported by the people most entrusted with the welfare of children, including parents, teachers, coaches, team owners, and government officials, it is no wonder that when American Indians and their allies protest the practice of using American Indian imagery in this way, the protests are experienced by those in the majority as confusing, out of place, strange, or annoying. What this also illustrates, however, is the inherent or *hidden bias* toward American Indians that exists within the society at large.

The fact that many of us cannot definitely recall when we knew that American Indian imagery was used for the purpose of naming sport teams and marketing them provides a lesson in how a *dominant culture* works. We are usually not aware of many of the forces that shape our attitudes and beliefs, including attitudes and beliefs about members of various racial and ethnic groups. This explains how racial stereotyping of American Indians can become an accepted part of everyday life.

This is the reason why studying sport from a *sociological perspective* is so helpful and important. It gives us a chance to examine more closely ideas and perspectives we often take for granted without questioning. The reason names like the Indians, Braves, Warriors, and Chiefs are so familiar and appear so often is because they represent shared meanings for many people. In other words, they form part of the *dominant culture* in which we live. At the same time, when groups like the National Congress of American Indians, National Coalition for Racism in Sport, Native American Journalists Association (NAJA), Society of Indian Psychologists of the Americas, and other American Indian organizations advise that these images are harmful and should be eliminated, opportunities arise to learn more about how these images came to play such a prominent role in the creation of school identity and fan loyalty and to rethink whether they are appropriate now.

A sincere discussion of the American Indian mascot issue must include a consideration of the imbalances that exist surrounding the issue. Especially for those of us who are athletes or sports fans, we understand the idea of competitive balance and an even playing field. One of the most central lessons we learn in sport, which mirrors our most sacred democratic values, is that Americans strive to be fair, just, and equitable. Given the fact that American Indians compose approximately 2% of the population, the likelihood of our discussions being distorted in a way that might not favor the interests of American Indians needs to be given careful consideration.

Further, several questions can be raised. What effect has the sheer number of these stereotypes had on our curiosity about them? Why do these images look so much alike? Why do they emphasize war and fighting? Why is it that the population of American Indians is so small while the expanse and availability of this imagery is so great? Perhaps, most importantly, why are the recommendations to eliminate these images by many American Indians dismissed and the requests of so many American Indians ignored?

Some insight into these questions can be gained by looking at the forces that contributed to the creation of these images over time.

A BRIEF HISTORY OF AMERICAN INDIAN SPORT IMAGERY

Whereas many communities regard the American Indian imagery and symbols they use in conjunction with their athletic teams as unique to their particular community and region, American Indians have been stereotyped in stories since before the time European explorers made their way to the North American continent. As Dr. Gretchen Bataille, vice president for academic affairs at the University of North Carolina, pointed out,

"Travel narratives as early as the 1500s depicted the American Indian as a fierce cannibalistic creature, and the woodcuts accompanying the stories portrayed the Indian as less than human—naked, violent, warlike, and frequently, more animalistic than human" (2001, p. 2). Such characters proved to be adaptable to many forms of political activism, entertainment, and advertising over the years. They also provided the rationale for viewing American Indians as threats to progress and civilization, a rationale that contributed to the dispossession of Indians from their land and removal from their homes.

What we see as so familiar today in the figure of Chief Illiniwek dancing at halftime during football games at the University of Illinois or Chief Osceola riding in on his horse Renegade at Florida State football games is the most recent version of a long-standing practice of playing Indian that extends back before the American Revolution. In 1773, Boston patriots who objected to taxation without the right to vote sought to express their opposition to King George III by donning Mohawk disguises and throwing tea into Boston Harbor (Deloria, 1998).

Over the years, the American fascination with fantasy Indians would change in form but not at its core. In the late 1800s and early 1900s, on the heels of the Indian Wars in the western United States, battle scenes pitting the U.S. Calvary against troupes of Plains Indians were reenacted in Wild West shows and sold to the public as a form of entertainment. The simplistic script of these battle scenes, with the U.S. Calvary riding in to the stirring sound of a bugle (a sound familiar to us in ballparks today that leads to fans yelling "charge") and fighting a group of painted, feathered, whooping, tomahawk-wielding Indians would eventually become the substance for the classic Western movie, popularized in the 1950s (Moses, 1996). From the music to the buckskins to the face paint and feathers, the elements found in those early images constitute the essential formula for the American Indian "mascot look" of the early 21st century.

As a matter of significance to discussions about American Indian mascots, the moment when American Indian military resistance disappeared and U.S. government efforts to render American Indians extinct increased in the form of forced assimilation, representations of American Indians in advertising proliferated. This displacement of real Indians with imaginary Indians established a legacy of habits of mind and ways of viewing American Indians that remains intact in American Indian mascots (Farnell, 2004).

Postcards featuring portraits of Plains Indians printed between 1898 and 1918 show how this displacement occurred. As researcher Patricia Albers (1998) explains, "In creating suitable and saleable visual images, postcard manufacturers followed several different strategies to select, stage, and even alter American Indian photographs to fit popular conventions" (p. 67). Seventy percent of the postcard portraits in Dr. Albers's research collection are of "chiefs" or "warriors."

Not surprisingly, savvy owners of professional teams and coaches of college football programs at the turn of the 20th century well understood the public's fascination with Indian spectacles and learned early to capitalize on it. Many of the American Indian images associated with athletic teams today have direct and indirect connections to the racially charged American Indian stereotypes that served as a staple of the sport writer's repertoire in the late 1800s and early 1900s. As professor Jeff Powers-Beck (2001) writes in his work on the American Indian integration of the major leagues,

Starting with [Louis Francis] Sockalexis in 1897, many native players in professional baseball, especially those with clear affiliations with tribes and ties to reservations, were nicknamed "Chief." . . . In the early decades of the century, indeed, it appears virtually impossible for a baseball player of admitted native origin to be known popularly as anything but "Chief." (p. 510)

On the surface, referring to someone as "Chief" doesn't seem to be harmful. After all, nicknames can be signs of affection or appreciation. However, they can also be signs of disrespect as well. As Dr. Joseph Oxendine (Lumbee), former provost of the University of North Carolina, Pembroke, and a minor league baseball player who was called "Chief" in the 1950 explained:

It is really used by non-Indians to say, "Hey, you're an Indian. Therefore, that's how I can define you and keep you in your place." . . . They used to call me "Chief" because I was the only Indian in school. . . . Nobody believed you were chief of a tribe. . . . Most Indians do not want to be called "Chief" because it demeans the significance of the [tribal] chief, and it's a constant reminder, like saying "Hey, Indian." (Powers-Beck, 2001, p. 510).

Importantly, this stereotype of the Indian, connected as it was to the rollicking, shoot-'em-up aura of the Wild West show, became an integral part of the marketing of professional sports in the United States. The National Football League, whose first president was the great Sac and Fox athlete Jim Thorpe, benefited from marketing campaigns that emphasized the uniqueness of Indian athletes. When Thorpe coached and played for the Oorang Indians in 1923, the only all-Indian team ever to play in professional football, the players performed "war dances" at halftime, thus increasing the appeal of the league at a time when creating what we would call today buzz and excitement was important to a new league. The theme of the Indians on the warpath provided the substance of pregame publicity. A cartoon published in the December 6 edition of the *Baltimore News* featured "wild Indians" coming to town in headdresses and tomahawks, with fierce expressions on their faces, while their opponents cowered in the trees, saying "Gosh, they are the real Indians" (Whitman, 2002).

George Preston Marshall, the owner of the Washington football franchise when it was originally located in Boston, had a similar mindset. Following a mediocre season in which Marshall's three partners decided to invest their money elsewhere, Marshall decided he needed something that would draw crowds to the stadium. Exploiting what he called the "Indian motif" and calling himself the "Big Chief," Marshall hired William "Lone Star" Dietz, a Sioux Indian, to coach the team along with several other American Indian players. Whereas the franchise today says that the name "Redskins" was adopted to honor Coach Dietz, it is significant that Marshall had players wear feathers and put on war paint while Dietz appeared in full headdress. According to Cliff Battles, a star rusher on the team, the players would "at the urging of George [Preston Marshall], put on war paint before a game and do a little Indian dance to entertain the paying customers. None of us liked that very much" (Whittingham, 2001, p. 11). One must wonder why, if Coach Dietz and the other Indian players he brought with him from the Carlisle Indian School were really so valued by the franchise, they were released within 1 or 2 years of being hired.

Thus, the practice of using American Indians to sell sports to the American public and to create community and team identity is deeply rooted in the ways the dominant culture has treated American Indians over the span of a century and more. Exploiting the "Indian motif," to use George Preston Marshall's words, is part of the larger picture of exploitation that these images represent. The vast amount of this imagery has been created by Whites for social, economic, and political reasons. The adoption of this imagery by schools reflects the larger culture, where this imagery has received widespread acceptance. A balanced review of the American Indian mascot issue must include a consideration of the history of these images and the forces that created them.

COMMON MISCONCEPTIONS
ABOUT AMERICAN INDIAN MASCOTS

In this section, two common misconceptions about American Indian mascots are discussed in light of the history of these images. The first is the misconception that all mascots are alike and can be compared on an equal basis. The second misconception is that American Indian mascots honor American Indians.

In response to an editorial decision by the *Lincoln Journal Star* in 2003 to stop publishing racially offensive American Indian imagery on its sports pages, the paper received over 500 letters and e-mail messages from readers complaining about the decision. According to the editor, almost all the complaints asked the same question, "Hey, what about the 'Fighting Irish' of Notre Dame?" (Fitzgerald, 2003). This reaction is typical of what occurs around the country when challenges are made to American Indian mascots.

The underlying logic behind the question suggests that all mascots and images have similar meanings. This, however, is a misconception. Because these images derive from different social contexts, they cannot be compared on an equal basis, one to one. Whereas the Fighting Irish of Notre Dame is a direct reference to Irish resistance against forces that would oppress them, American Indian imagery was taken by Whites for their own purposes without consultation with American Indians.

Further, in the early years of its existence, the University of Notre Dame provided an educational haven for men from various European national and religious backgrounds (German, Polish, Irish) who were denied access by other educational institutions. The University of Notre Dame empowered students from disenfranchised backgrounds (Sperber, 1993). At the same time, American Indians were being forced into boarding schools with the goal of stripping them of their languages, religious practices, customs, manner of dress, social behaviors, living arrangements, and value system (Bloom, 2000). The effect is important here. Whereas those of Irish descent, who adhered to their Catholic faith, achieved upward mobility in the United States, as evidenced in the U.S. presidential election of 2004 in which the Democratic nominee was the Irish Catholic senator from Massachusetts, John Kerry, American Indian imagery has not helped to advance the economic and political interests of American Indians in any way that can be considered comparable.

Rather than asking the question "What about the Fighting Irish?" the more significant question is why is there only *one* Fighting Irish at the college and university level and only a handful around the country, when there are thousands of American Indian images? To ask this question shifts the focus on where a legitimate comparison of these images should be made. As Gavin Clarkson (2003), Native American Fellow at Harvard University, found when he built a preliminary dataset of 18,000 records documenting high school mascots using a web crawler, 10.6% of the high schools across the country had Indian mascots, with Indians and Warriors being two of the top seven. Of the top nine mascots, all were either carnivorous animals or Indians. As he concluded, of the Indian mascots identified, Indians, Redskins, Warriors, and Braves all refer to Indians in a racially monolithic way.

Why do Indians and Warriors appear alongside tigers, cougars, wildcats, bears, eagles, bulldogs, panthers, and lions? As psychology professor David Rider (1991) points out, all of these groups represent species whose numbers have declined dramatically during the past 500 years and are on the verge of extinction. He also points out that American Indians have historically been portrayed as "barbaric," "wild," "bestial," and "savage."

This leads into the second misconception about American Indian mascots honoring American Indians. Supporters cite the bravery and courage of American Indians as reasons to keep these mascots. The rhetoric associated with their support is, at times, persuasive. An intention to memorialize something out of respect and admiration is difficult to challenge. However, is that what these images really do? Based on the degree to which American Indians do not feel honored by this imagery, the intention falls far short of the mark.

As Comanche/Kiowa educator Cornel Pewewardy (1999) points out, "Native Americans would never have associated the sacred practices of becoming a warrior with the hoopla of a high school pep rally, half-time entertainment, being a sidekick to cheerleaders, or royalty in homecoming pageants" (p. 342). Similarly, Barbara Munson (1997), a woman of the Oneida Nation, explains,

> We experience it [the imagery and behavior] as no less than a mockery of our cultures. We see objects sacred to us—such as the drum, eagle feathers, face painting and traditional dress—being used, not in sacred ceremony, or in any cultural setting, but in another culture's game. (n.p.)

In an attempt to interpret the offense American Indians experience, author Sherman Alexis (Spokane/Coeur d'Alene) suggests that for people who don't understand the objections of American Indians,

> Don't think about it in terms of race. Think about it in terms of religion. Those are our religious imagery up there. Feather, the paint, the sun—that's our religious imagery. You couldn't have a Catholic priest running around the floor with a basketball throwing communion wafers. (interview with CBSNews.com, March 20, 2001)

Rob Schmidt, who publishes a multicultural comic book featuring American Indians, approaches the perception of honor from a different perspective, asking, "should Native people feel honored by the association with athletes?" (Schmidt, 2001). He goes on to point out that, contrary to American Indian stereotypes, the constant conflict inherent in sport as it is played in the United States and the attitudes of animosity toward opponents are not things that most American Indians would want to be associated with. As a matter of logic, why would any group of people wish to be depicted solely as warring, fighting people?

IMPACT THIS IMAGERY HAS ON
AMERICAN INDIANS AND NON–AMERICAN INDIANS

A well-known outcome of negative stereotyping of racial groups is the systematic diminishment of self-esteem of those groups that have been targeted as inferior. According to the Society of Indian Psychologists of the Americas (1999), the stereotyping of American Indians is a form of dehumanization that has serious consequences for American Indians who struggle in the United States for the very dignity and respect these mascots are supposed to convey. As an educator in Indian schools for many years, Pewewardy (2000) concludes that these negative stereotypes "play a crucial role in distorting and warping Native American children's cultural perceptions of themselves as well as non-Indian children's attitudes toward Native Americans" (B5). Researchers and educators have cautioned that American Indian imagery as represented in mascots and team names and symbols is detrimental to the self-identity, self-concept, and self-esteem of Indian people (Fryberg, 2001; Huff, 1997; Pewewardy, 1999, 2000, 2004; Society for Indian Psychologists, 1999). In schools, these images have created a hostile learning environment for American Indian children, making it more difficult for them to have equal access to the same educational resources as other students (Baca, 2004; Munson, 1997).

Despite claims that American Indian mascots honor American Indians, the reality is that American Indians are among the most at-risk in our society. In schools, American Indian children struggle and experience dropout rates that are among the highest in the United States (Huff, 1997). Similarly, according to statistics provided by the United States Justice Department, American Indians and Alaska Natives are victims of violent crimes at rates that exceed those for members of other racial minority groups. In 1998, American Indians were victims of violent crime at about twice the rate of Blacks, Whites, or Asians, and they are 3 1/2 times more likely to be victims of violent crimes directed at them by other racial groups (Rennison, 2001). In practical reality, based on these statistics, that American Indians are clearly not honored in this society and are held up to contempt, harassment, and harm (Staurowsky, 2004).

The negative impact these stereotypes have is not restricted just to American Indians. Most Americans have had greater exposure to American Indian mascots than they have to substantive and meaningful education about the history of White-Indian relations in the United States. This gap in education leads to the acceptance of imagery like that used by the Washington football franchise without an awareness that the term "redskins" is described in the dictionary as a racial slur and is considered as offensive in some circles as the "n" word is in the African American community. Further, why has the general population forgotten that the term "redskins" comes from a time when American Indians were killed for bounty by the United States government? Regardless of how "nice" the image looks on a football helmet, ought not all students, both Indian and non-Indian alike, be educated about what these words mean before being encouraged to use them so freely?

CONCLUSION

Discussions about American Indian mascots provide an opportunity to learn about American Indian culture, traditions, and life, both in a historical and contemporary sense. As you continue to grapple with the question of whether American Indian imagery should be eliminated, here is a final question to ponder. Is the sports environment the best place in schools to teach students about American Indians?

REFERENCES

Albers, P. (1998). Symbols, souvenirs, and sentiments: Postcard imagery of Plains Indians, 1898–1918. In C. Geary & V. L. Webb (Eds.), *Delivering views: Distant cultures in early postcards* (pp. 65–90). Washington, DC: Smithsonian Institution Press.

Associated Press (2004, April 30). *Settle the Chief issue.* Retrieved May 4, 2004, from www.dailyherald.com.

Baca, L. (2004). Native images in schools and the racially hostile environment. *Journal of Sport & Social Issues, 28*(1), 71–78.

Bataille, G. (Ed.). (2001). *Native American representations: First encounters, distorted images, and literary appropriations.* Lincoln: University of Nebraska Press.

Bloom, J. (2000). *To show what an Indian can do: Sports in Native American boarding schools.* Minneapolis: University of Minnesota Press.

Clarkson, G. (2003). Racial imagery and Native Americans: A first look at the empirical evidence behind the Indian mascot controversy. *Cardozo Journal of International and Comparative Law, 2*, 393–408.

Deloria, P. (1998). *Playing Indian.* New Haven, CT: Yale University Press.

Farnell, B. (2004). The fancy dance of racializing discourse. *Journal of Sport and Social Issues, 28*(1), 30–55.

Fernandez, J. (2004, January 14). Guilford schools board forbids Indian mascots. *News & Record.* Retrieved December 13, 2004, from http://www.main.nc.us/ wncceib/NewsRecordGuilford11404.htm.

Fitzgerald, M. (2003, February 13). Is Lee too politically correct? *Editor & Publisher.* Retrieved December 13, 2005, from www.editorandpublisher.com/eandp/ news/article_display.jsp?vnu_content_id=18.

Fryberg, S. (2001). *Really! You don't look like an American Indian.* Unpublished dissertation. Palo Alto, CA: Stanford University.

High school to change Little Indian mascot. (2004, July 8). Retrieved December 13, 2005, from www.boston.com/news/education/k_12/articles/2004/07/08/ high_school_to_change.

Huff, D. (1997). *To live heroically: Institutional racism and American Indian education.* Albany: State University of New York Press.

King, R. (2002, February). Defensive dialogues: Native American mascots, anti-Indianness, and educational institutions. *Studies in Media & Information Literacy Education, 2*(1).

Lesnick, G. (2004, June 30). Activist groups rally for removal of "racist" mascots, nicknames. *The East Carolinian.* Retrieved from www.theeastcarolinian.com/ vnews/display.v/ART/2004/06/30/40e1dfe5a93de.

Moses, L. G. (1996). *Wild west shows and the images of American Indians: 1883–1933.* Albuquerque: University of New Mexico Press.

Munson, B. (1997). *"Indian" mascot and logo taskforce: Common themes and questions about the use of "Indian" logos.* Retrieved from http://pages .prodigy.net/munson/newpage1.htm.

Murray, D. (2004). Ottawa Hills looks to lose its Indians nickname. *The Grand Rapids Press.* Retrieved December 13, 2005, from www.aistm.org/2004mascot .articles.htm.

Pewewardy, C. (1999). The deculturalization of indigenous mascots in U.S. sports culture. *The Educational Forum, 63,* 342–347.

Pewewardy, C. (2000). Will another school year bring insult or honor? The usage of Indian mascots in school-related events. *Oklahoma Indian Times, VI*(9), B5.

Pewewardy, C. (2004). Playing Indian at halftime: The controversy over American Indian mascots, logos, and nicknames in school-related events. *The Clearing House, 77*(5), 180–186.

Powers-Beck, J. (2001). "Chief": The American Indian integration of baseball, 1897–1945. *American Indian Quarterly, 25*(4), 508–538.

Rennison, C. (2001). *Violent victimization and race report, 1993–1998.* Retrieved from www.ojp.usdoj.gov/bjs/pub/ascii/vvr98.txt.

Rider, D. P. (1991). *"Indians" and animals: A comparative essay.* Retrieved from http://aistm.org/david_rider_essay.htm.

Schmidt, R. (2001, October 31). Smashing people: The "honor" of being an athlete. *San Diego Moon Online*. Retrieved on November 27, 2005 from www.bluecorn comics.com/athletes.htm.

Smith, D. (2003). *American Indian mascots: Hype, insult, or ignorance*. Denver, CO: The Alma Curriculum and Teacher Training Project, Denver Public Schools.

Society of Indian Psychologists of the Americas. (1999, January). *American Indian sports teams mascots, tokens, nicknames, logos and associated symbols: Psychological considerations*. Position paper. Retrieved from http://aistm.org/1psychpage.html.

Sperber, M. (1993). *Shake down the thunder: The creation of Notre Dame football*. New York: Henry Holt.

Staurowsky, E. J. (2004). On the legal and social fictions that sustain American Indian sport imagery. *Journal of Sport & Social Issues, 28*(1), 11–29.

Whitman, R. (2002). *Jim Thorpe: Athlete of the century*. Defiance, OH: The Hubbard Company.

Whittingham, R. (2001). *Hail Redskins: Celebration of the greatest players, teams, and coaches*. Chicago: Triumph Books.

IV

SPORT AND THE MEDIA

13

Songs Sung Red, White, and Blue: Music, Sports, and the Rhetoric of Patriotism

Stephen D. Mosher
Ithaca College

Apologia

Trumpets are sounding,
War-steeds are bounding,
Stand to your arms then, and march in good order;
England shall many a day
Tell of the bloody fray,
When the Blue Bonnets came over the Border.

—Sir Walter Scott

Monday, December 1, 1969, was my lucky day. The first selective service draft lottery during the Vietnam War was held that night. As a teenager I had already been witness to four traumatic assassinations that had sent America spinning out of control . . . and now, this. I was walking to my dormitory after my creative writing class at the University of Massachusetts, Amherst, when I saw my roommate stick his head out our window and screamed, "Mosher, you ^%^*&^*@!!!" I found out soon enough that my number had come up 345 and I was "safe." His was 16 and he was not. Thus were lives changed in a blink of an eye. Today, 36 years later, I have no idea what I would have done if my number had been below the cutoff . . . but I think about that often.

Music helps us define our lives. Our memory for pop songs is a powerful force, and it can bring us back immediately to a time and a place that may be good, bad, hot, cold, romantic, funereal, sweaty, or fresh with fallen snow. This chapter considers the role of pop music and flags as they intersect with the world of sport, especially in the wake of September 11, 2001. It is not meant to be encyclopedic or even objective. It is meant to be as accurate as possible, but it is emotional and personal. For me, almost all the songs mentioned in this essay are dominated by one emotion, whether out in the open or buried deep in a private place, and that emotion is — terror.

1968—THE WHOLE WORLD IS WATCHING

In the spring of 1968, that terrible, awful, tumultuous year, Eric Burdon and the Animals released "Sky Pilot," the first overtly antiwar song of the Vietnam era to gain significant playing time in the United States. At over 7 minutes long, the complete song was relegated to FM radio, but the abridged version was regularly played on AM radio too. The English establishment was outraged at Burdon's audacious, ironic "sampling" of a bagpipe version of the Scottish war anthem "When the Blue Bonnets Came Over the Border."

On Monday, October 7, 1968, before game 5 of the World Series between the Detroit Tigers and St. Louis Cardinals, at the invitation of Ernie Harwell (broadcaster for the Tigers), Jose Feliciano performed a soulful version of the National Anthem, setting off an almost universal firestorm of criticism against him, the Detroit Tigers, and anyone else who was not quick to condemn such an untraditional rendition of the song (Zang, 2001). Just days later, Tommie Smith and John Carlos raised their gloved fists and bowed their heads during the playing of the National Anthem at the Mexico City Olympic Games. They were suspended from the U.S. team and expelled from the Olympic Village in a highly visible move. Perhaps their actions were considered especially injurious given that they occurred during the playing of the National Anthem and the raising of the U.S. flag. Their actions were thus seen as political statement, and they were condemned for utilizing a sporting event for their expression. However, days before, on October 2, the slaughter of hundreds of student protesters by the Mexican police and military at the Plaza of the Three Cultures went unnoticed. Ever since the revival of the Olympic Games after World War II, the International Olympic Committee (IOC) and host countries had diligently worked together to prevent any politicization of the Olympic Games such as occurred in during the notorious 1936 "Hitler Games" in Berlin. Political protesters, on the other hand, saw the Olympic Games as a grand public platform where they could be seen and heard by the entire world. Unless a protest was staged within the Games themselves (Smith and Carlos), however, most, if not all, protests were ignored or even covered up by the media, the host nation, and the IOC itself. The slaughter at the Plaza of the Three Cultures was effectively suppressed by the Mexican authorities, and it would be decades before the world learned of this great tragedy.

In response to events like those at the Plaza of the Three Cultures, the movement against the Vietnam War and for civil rights reached a crescendo in the next few years. During this time, popular music functioned as a sounding board for and about these movements in a way never seen before. Aretha Franklin's "Respect," The Beatles' "Revolution," Country Joe McDonald and the Fish's "The Feel Like I'm Fixin' To Die Rag," and Crosby, Stills, Nash, and Young's "Four Dead in Ohio" are just a few of the pop songs that dominated the airwaves.

One of the angriest songs came from John Fogerty and Creedence Clearwater Revival in 1968. "Fortunate Son" was a modest hit for the group, rising to #14 on the American pop charts, but it carried a much stronger sense of moral validity given that Fogerty, while not seeing action in Vietnam, had served in the U.S. army reserves. The song is short (under 3 minutes long), easily sung, and quite direct in its indictment of a military draft system that exempts the privileged and targets the others.

In an interview for VH1's program *Behind the Music: 1968* (2001) Fogerty said, "I believed I would be drafted, I believed I would go to Vietnam, and I most certainly believed that I would be killed." The song, because its author carried the credibility of having served in the army, posed a great threat to military morale, especially when soldiers serving in Vietnam itself began singing it out loud. In 1968, it seemed that popular culture, especially music, would be one of the most significant forces in bringing about an end to the war. Of course, rock and roll may be a powerful aesthetic expression, but it does not change the world; and it would be 7 more bloody years before the United States would be able to extract itself from this awful war, when, on April 30, 1975, the last soldiers evacuated the country and the South surrendered unconditionally to the Communist forces.

1978—A GREAT CATHARSIS

God Bless America,
Land that I love.
Stand beside her, and guide her
Through the night with a light from above.
From the mountains, to the prairies,
To the oceans, white with foam.
God bless America, My home sweet home.

—Irving Berlin

At the end of Michael Cimino's masterpiece, *The Deer Hunter*, after Michael has failed to save his friend Nick, after the funeral in that western Pennsylvania steel town, after the friends retreat to John's bar, after John rescues himself from weeping over the scrambled eggs by humming "God Bless America," Linda quietly but firmly begins singing the words to the song. The entire group joins her, desperately seeking comfort in the words. This version of Irving Berlin's call to arms on the eve of World-War II is not jingoistic or self-righteous, but rather the only way these people know how to convey their emotions at that moment. These aren't superpatriots whooping a war cry, but rather ordinary people simply trying to find a way to continue. What makes *The Deer Hunter* great is that it takes no position on war and offers no easy answers. There is no doubt that war has destroyed at least one life and changed all of their lives, but there is absolutely no irony in Michael's voice when he raises his glass and ends the story with "Here's to Nick."

Theater managers across America were forced to separate showings of *The Deer Hunter* by up to half an hour and leave the house lights dim so that audiences could have the time to collect themselves, to dry their eyes, to quiet the weeping. Clearly, the movie, and its depiction of war, affected the public. John Fogerty remembers that Vietnam

was one of the stupidest exercises America ever went through. Regardless of your politics, I think by the end of the Vietnam War, almost everybody was saying, "Wow, this should have been over a long time ago." . . . I remember clearly saying in 1974, let's don't ever do this again. . . ." (Hebert, 2004)

While then is not now and Vietnam was not Iraq, Fogerty, now a 59-year-old father, sees war, whatever the cause, as a destructive and futile endeavor. Memories of these songs, movies, and events pervade my own memory as more current events unfold.

1991—ONE VICTIM OF DESERT STORM

On Wednesday, January 16, 1991, the liberation of Kuwait was said to have begun. On January 27, 1991, while the war raged half a world away, the New York Giants beat the Buffalo Bills 20–19 in Super Bowl XXV. Before the game, Whitney Houston provided the stirring rendition of "The Star-Spangled Banner" that has become a defining moment in United States sport history. On the helmets of all of the football players in that game were small decals of the U.S. flag. This was not a recent development, for professional athletes in the United States had been wearing small flags on their uniforms since at least the previous fall. But these flags spoke to a more alarming development. Not only were professional sport teams adding flags to their athletes' uniforms, but flags were being attached to the uniforms of college, high school, and even youth league athletes as well. Flags were sprouting up everywhere.

On January 18, 1991, Henry O. Nichols and Marcy Weston (chairs of their respective NCAA rules committees) wrote a letter to the supervisors of men's and women's basketball officials and conference commissioners regarding the wearing of the American flag on game uniforms. It said, "The magnitude of the events in the Persian Gulf has led to interest in wearing the American flag on basketball uniform jerseys. Because this gesture is patriotic in nature, the American flag may be worn on the game jersey. The flag shall not obscure the number or make the number difficult to read" (Nichols & Weston, 1991).

Nichols and Weston were addressing a concern raised by officials that the flags that had appeared on many, but not all, NCAA basketball team uniforms were a technical violation of the rules and warranted a two-shot foul to be called every time a player entered the game. The overt reference to the American flag as a patriotic symbol, however, raises serious questions about the institutionalization of a practice that is fraught with problems of free speech. Certainly free speech, even unpopular speech, is a protected right in the United States; but the practice of expecting all athletes on a sports team, even athletes who may be opposed to the war or are noncitizens, to wear a symbol that endorses the war serves to squelch any other opinion. Additionally, the teams that adopted the application of flags on their uniforms were explicitly violating the United States of America Flag Code. It should be pointed out that the Flag Code is not law, and it is not criminal to violate the Code (Corcoran, 2002, p. 139; United States Code, 2005), but it is intended to advise citizens and organizations as to the proper and respectful treatment of this national symbol.

Among its functions, the Flag Code, in section 175, regulates the position and manner of display of the flag, and paragraph (j) specifically states, "No part of the flag should ever be used as a costume or athletic uniform" (United States Code, 2005). In other words, in their attempts to offer patriotic support, the NCAA, MLB, NFL, NHL, and NBA, as well as many public school and community sports organizations, adopted a practice that is considered disrespectful to the flag and the country it symbolizes. But at least these organizations are not violating game rules. Professional sports leagues in North America are all regulated by contractual agreements, and individual players are represented by their own unions; thus free speech issues over wearing a uniform that has a United States flag attached to it do not present a particularly vexing problem even if a significant number of players in each league do not support the symbolic meaning of the flag or are not even citizens of the United States of America. However, the same cannot be said for college, high school, and elementary students.

Consider the case of Marco Lokar. Until January 15, 1991, Lokar had been an anonymous substitute sophomore guard for the Seton Hall basketball team. On that day, the Pirates players began wearing flags on their uniforms. Lokar did not. Coming from a Slovenian-Italian family living in Trieste, Italy, caught in the Yugoslavian war, now studying philosophy at a Catholic university in the United States, Lokar did not make his decision lightly. However, by March 1, Lokar had withdrawn from Seton Hall and left the United States. In less than a month, this simple act of exercising his right to free speech had resulted in crowds booing him every time he entered a game or touched the ball, in addition to death threats to him and his pregnant wife.

On February 13, 1991, the day he withdrew from Seton Hall, Lokar made the following statement: "From a Christian standpoint, I cannot support any war, with no exception for the Persian Gulf war" (Shulman,

1991). In between, as the booing and death threats mounted, several compromises were considered, including Lokar wearing a yellow ribbon to indicate that while he opposed the war he supported the troops. In a conversation with his wife, Lara, Lokar recalled her saying, "The troops are there to *fight* the war, Marco. You must be a man and make a true choice" (Toperoff, 1991, p. 53). P. J. Carlisiemo, coach of the Seton Hall team, said, "We talked to Marco about various possibilities. . . . Maybe we could send Lara home. Or they could both leave and come back the next year after Lara had the baby. The thing would have blown over eventually" (Toperoff, p. 54). Of course, Carlisiemo could not have been more wrong. The harassment continued, and within a month Lokar and his family had returned to Trieste, a casualty of refusing to compromise his personal ethics in the face of overwhelming persecution and a lack of support from those who had sworn to support him.

In an editorial titled "Misusing the Flag, Again," the *New York Times* (1991) opined,

> It is saddening when even a few Americans use the flag as a license for persecution. . . . The dark patriotism to which Mr. Lokar was subjected is a troubling reminder of the efforts to extort conformity in a nation built on free speech and diversity. Though Mr. Lokar was persecuted by a rabid few, he is due an apology from all Americans who love freedom.

The apology never came. Lokar's teammates disappointed him the most: "When you're someone's teammate, you make a commitment to them. . . . It's like you're brothers—at least that's how I feel about it. But not one of them came to me, not even to ask me why I was doing what I was" (Toperoff, 1991, p. 54). Seton Hall, as an institution, said nothing. A half year later, Carlisiemo stated, "Yes, I'm embarrassed for Seton Hall. I'm embarrassed for our country. Would I do things the same way again? I'd be a moron if I did" (Toperoff, p. 56). It is difficult to imagine Carlisiemo's explanation as rising to the level of an apology. With Lokar now out of the country and the political distraction having been eliminated, the flags remained on the uniforms, the discussion about the appropriateness of them on the uniforms stopped, and the basketball season was free to hurtle on to its culmination during March Madness.

On April 4, 1991, with the war won, CBS opened its coverage of the men's NCAA Championship basketball game between Duke and Kansas with President George H. W. Bush greeting the country and saying, "Let us pause to pay tribute to some other American heroes, the men and women of our armed forces, who . . . liberated a country abroad" (*NCAA Men's Basketball*, 1991). As the president's final words asking for God's blessing faded, the opening chords of John Mellencamp's "Small Town" began. For the next several minutes viewers were shown pictures of soldiers and sailors, along with their wives and children. Pictures also appeared of Kuwaiti men, women, and children, as well as pictures of basketball players like Christian Laettner and Bobby Hurley and basketball coaches Dean Smith, Roy Williams, and Mike Krzyzewski. We were also shown farms and dirt roads, churches and egg and bacon breakfasts, basketball hoops on garage roofs and on blighted urban walls. All of this was intercut with the actual music video of Mellencamp and his band performing the song for the first Farm Aid concert to raise money and awareness for the independent farmers in small-town America. The song is bitterly ironic and suggests that America has not lived up to its promise to middle America. In one scene in the music video, it was almost impossible not to see the huge poster of Woody Guthrie serving as a backdrop for Mellencamp's stage performance. It was almost impossible to avoid Guthrie's ghost singing "This Land is Your Land," the classic folk song that simultaneously celebrates America's natural wonder and condemns the failure of its government to help its most downtrodden citizens. What is more difficult to remember is that Guthrie was more than just a troublemaker and union former, but a socialist to his core. Mellencamp's song is infectious and ultimately optimistic, but not in any official way. Its patriotism stems from the routines of daily life, small communities and families persisting in the face of corporate greed.

The great irony is that CBS and the NCAA as well as the president of the United States of America felt secure enough in their version of patriotism that they could take a song of resistance to the status quo and turn it into a propaganda piece that affirms a war that many citizens questioned, a war that many citizens claimed was illegal, and under the protection of sport could persuade an uncritical audience that it's appropriate and patriotic to employ basketball players as billboards. The great irony is that these institutions understood that the viewers would not complain about 3 minutes of television that reified a status quo version of patriotism because they considered the music video as nothing more than a warmup tape. Let the game begin! These 3 minutes seemed clearly to be saying, "As for you, Marco Lokar, and the people who sympathize with you, love it or leave it!"

The flags have remained on the uniforms. They are still there today, continuing to violate the carefully negotiated and codified rules of respect for the most important symbol of America and democracy. It seems more convenient, therefore, to conduct the war through song, symbols, and emotion than diplomacy and reason.

2001—ANOTHER LOSS OF INNOCENCE

In the summer of 2001, Wrangler Jeans introduced a 30-second commercial using John Fogerty's "Fortunate Son" to sell its pants. The commercial takes only the first two lines from the song, which refer to unreflective flag waving superpatriots while showing pictures of healthy Americans, all wearing jeans, at work and play. The commercial ends with a voice-over about comfortable jeans. The spot enjoyed the typical 6- to 8-week run, appearing countless times in sports programming, but by the end of August it was gone. If Fogerty was outraged at the use of this blatantly antiwar anthem being used to sell pants and a middle-American way of life, it hardly mattered, since he lost the fair trade and property rights to his own words decades ago. Like so many young professional musicians, Fogerty was taken advantage of by clever businesspeople, and his words could be used for any purpose the owners wished.

Then came the terrible events of September 11, 2001. That day, according to many, the world changed forever. Within a week, the Wrangler Jeans commercial came back with a vengeance and played continuously for well over another year. This time it was selling first and foremost the American way of life, and only secondarily, pants. Clearly, even in the face of protests from consumers concerned about the misappropriation of Fogerty's song, the Wrangler Jeans Company decided that its version of patriotic expression was the one that mattered most and the one that Americans would buy.

Choosing not to engage the country in political discourse, President George W. Bush made public appearances at "ground zero," the Pentagon, and the field in western Pennsylvania to promote his campaign against

El Qaeda, against the "evildoers." But even these public appearances pale in comparison to appearances at the World Series, the Army-Navy football game, the Super Bowl, and the Winter Olympic Games in Salt Lake City. On Friday, February 8, 2002, President Bush looked on as the now famous tattered flag that had flown over the World Trade Center was reverently carried in by a team of United States Olympians and New York City police and firefighter heroes. He seemed to be deliberately exploiting the fact that a worldwide audience of over 600 million people were watching these opening ceremonies. It should be noted that the flag was carried in to all these sporting events horizontally, also violating the U.S. Flag Code, which states that "The flag should never be carried flat or horizontally, but always aloft and free" (Corcoran, 2002, p. 139; United States Code, 2005).

Then, as the first national leader to break from IOC protocol, President Bush departed from the Olympic Charter when he put in the words "On behalf of a proud, determined and grateful nation" in front of the official line "I declare open the Games of Salt Lake City" (Mackay, 2002, p. 3).

He spoke this, not from center stage, but standing in the midst of the United States Olympic team, thereby signifying that the president is no more important than any individual and that a "team" that is "united" in its cause can never be defeated. President Bush even admitted that he had closed his private remarks to the U.S. team with the now famous phrase, "Let's roll!" The Olympic Games, however, are a special circumstance, highly visible but isolated and temporary. Each specific Olympic Games lasts but 16 days. They may dominate a certain segment of the television landscape for 2 weeks, but they are no match for a medium that is everywhere and always on. It was ordinary television programming that most effectively used popular music to comfort a shaken nation and to carry it on toward a future of retribution and warfare.

Popular music artists made countless appearances in the months immediately following the attacks, signifying their support in the effort against terrorism. The first televised concert to raise funds for the victims of the terrorist attacks opened with a silent scene of a tugboat on the Hudson River in front of where the World Trade Center towers had stood and then faded to a quiet Bruce Springsteen, who introduced "My City of Ruins." The choice of Springsteen to open the concert, arguably America's pop music poet laureate, was a bit odd given that hardly a year had passed since the furor over his 2000 concert at Madison Square Garden. This concert ended with "41 Shots (American Skin)." Springsteen's powerful indictment of a racist and overzealous New York City Police Department in the notorious Amadu Dialo shooting resulted in the police force working that night's concert to walk out in protest. Clearly, in 2001, Springsteen was no friend of the NYPD.

But in the days immediately after September 11, comfort and healing seemed the only essential thing. Creed's singing of "My Sacrifice" at the halftime of a Thanksgiving football game evokes a religious (Christian) endorsement of American patriotism. R. Kelley's "The World's Greatest," written for Michael Mann's film about Muhammad Ali, was transformed into a gospel song at the opening ceremonies of the Salt Lake City Olympic Games to suggest that all Americans, even the most disenfranchised of its citizens, wanted to let the world know we are united. Bruce Springsteen's "Promised Land" was used to open a Fox telecast of the World Series. And Ray Charles's version of "America the Beautiful" was used many times, including game 2 of the World Series. Perhaps the most striking moment of all occurred at the halftime of the Super Bowl in New Orleans, when U2 sang "Where the Streets Have No Name" as the names of the nearly 3,000 victims of September 11 were projected on a giant translucent sheet, rising to the heavens. An anomaly in all of this overt grieving was the wordless, somber, and almost silent harmonica version of "This Land is Your Land" that opened the first *Monday Night Football* telecast after the attacks.

Above all the popular music, however, stood one song. Barely 10 days passed before the world of sport rose from its grief to take the lead in healing the nation. Within a week "God Bless America" became our second National Anthem, being played at the seventh-inning stretch of every major league baseball game. The song was most poignant, moreover, when sung in New York City, particularly Yankee Stadium. It is a song, however, that carries with it historical problems. The seldom-sung prelude speaks volumes about the politics of the individual who wrote it.

> While the storm clouds gather far across the sea,
> Let us swear allegiance to a land that's free,
> Let us all be grateful for a land so fair,
> As we raise our voices in a solemn prayer.
>
> —Irving Berlin

Written in 1938, it was intended by Berlin, perhaps the most influential songwriter of his time, to encourage a reluctant nation to pay attention to the "storm clouds" gathering over Europe on the eve of World War II. Berlin's friend Kate Smith introduced the song on her weekly radio show, and before long the song dominated American radio. It is a militant and, perhaps, jingoistic song and quite directly suggests that God endorses one country above all others. As a response to Berlin, Woody Guthrie wrote "This Land is Your Land" (originally titled "God Blessed America"), a song that celebrates the bounty of America but asks, in the wake of the Great Depression, whether the nation has the courage to save its own ruined citizenry.

The duel between these songs, written over half a century and several wars ago, suggests that there can be competing ideas of what constitutes patriotism. Interestingly enough "The Star-Spangled Banner" became the official National Anthem in 1931. (Since then, "America the Beautiful," "God Bless America," and "This Land is Your Land" have all been nominated as replacements for Francis Scott Key's unsingable song.) The attacks of September 11, 2001, did not occur in a political vacuum or without well–thought out reasons. The government's persistent claim that the terrorists are "pure evil" mitigates against an understanding that many of the world's citizens view the United States as an oppressor nation. Once again, it seems easier, therefore, to conduct the war through song and emotion than through diplomacy and reason. And if the battle is to be waged through song, "God Bless America" becomes one that does more than comfort and ease pain, as it did when sung in *The Deer Hunter* a generation before. It moves from seeking solace to seeking vengeance. Woody Guthrie never stood a chance.

2003—YOU'VE GOTTA STAND FOR SOMETHING

Until she was caught in the cross fire of patriotic debate, Toni Smith was an anonymous student athlete playing basketball at Manhattanville College. Entering her senior year, the sociology major from New York City decided that she could not, in good conscience, continue to face the United States flag during the playing of the National Anthem before her team's games. For most of the season her silent protest went unnoticed, but then, as with Marco Lokar a decade earlier, someone noticed.

In the furor that followed, Smith was harassed on the court and became the subject of much passionate debate. The coach of the women's basketball team at the University of Oklahoma, Sherri Coale, spoke for many when, on the ESPN show *Outside the Lines*, she said,

> I think it would be very difficult for her teammates to be able to put the team first, which I think is the essence of this issue. When you commit to be a part of a team you make the commitment to have your own selfish desires come secondary. I think whatever she wants to do on her own time in street clothes, when she is on campus, wherever she is, that is certainly her constitutional right. I think the moment that she slips that uniform on she becomes a representative of more than just herself. And to disrespect the flag is to disrespect her teammates. (*Outside the Lines*, 2003)

Smith's reasons for her protest were deeper and more nuanced than simply opposition to the war in Iraq. Her public statement, in part, said,

> For some time now, the inequalities that are embedded into the American system have bothered me. As they are becoming progressively worse and it is clear that the government's priorities are not bettering the quality of life for all of its people . . . I can no longer, in good conscience, salute the flag. . . . It does not bother me that so many Americans oppose me. . . . Patriotism can be shown in many ways, but those who choose to do so by saluting the flag, should recognize that the American flag stands for individuality and freedom. Therefore, any true patriot must acknowledge and respect my right to be different. (*Outside the Lines*, 2003)

Such a well-constructed statement by one so young suggests that Smith had thought this problem out. After all, she was raised in Manhattan, in the shadows of the twin towers, by a single mother, and she was in her senior year of college preparing for a career in social work. This was a young woman committed to helping others, and it was her hometown that had been attacked. However, perhaps the most revealing clue to the reasoning behind Smith's actions can be found in the Manhattanville College *Women's Basketball Media Guide*, where in her student profile Smith listed some her favorite quotes. They include, "If you don't stand for something, you will fall for anything," and "It will be a great day when our schools get all the money they need and the military has to hold a bake sale to buy a bomber" (Toni Smith).

Perhaps the most ironic development of this incident was a poll taken by ESPN. The poll revealed, among other things, that 60% of respondents maintained that "sporting events are not the proper place for political protests." The poll of 601 adults, conducted on March 3, 2003, had a 5% margin of error, quite good for ESPN, thus revealing where the public stood on this issue (*Not even one in four*, 2003). This response, of course, begs the question of exactly what songs like "The Star-Spangled Banner" or "God Bless America" or "America the Beautiful," along with patches and decals of the United States flag on uniforms, are for if they do not serve as political statements. Exactly why do we play these songs before and during sporting events, but typically not before or during concerts or plays or movies or even church services?

2004—IT'S DÉJÀ VU (ALL OVER AGAIN)

She's lost her precious child

—John Fogerty

Pat Tillman was dead. America finally had its athlete-warrior hero. In the frenzy that followed the news on April 22, 2004, America once again came to an understanding that sport and war are inextricably linked. The myth that sports build character had its latest poster child. A week later, in its haste to exploit the moment, the army awarded Tillman a posthumous Silver Star before a complete investigation had been conducted. In the middle of May it was declared that Tillman had died from friendly fire. By the end of the year the story had become even more confusing and sad.

> The records show that Tillman fought bravely and honorably until his last breath. They also show that his superiors exaggerated his actions and invented details as they burnished his legend in public, at the same time suppressing details that might tarnish Tillman's commanders. (Coll, 2004, p. A1)

Both the *London Times* and the *Washington Post* ran feature length stories exposing this fiasco.

And John Fogerty heard a voice inside his head leading him to a place he would rather not go. But this time, Fogerty is 59 years old, and war means something different to him. After all, he has children of his own now. "It's more about war's personal toll—the pain felt by the mothers he saw interviewed on TV after their sons and daughters had died in the early days of the Iraq war" (Hebert, 2004). Fogerty was about to join Bruce Springsteen, REM, and others on the nationwide Vote For Change tour in support of John Kerry, the Democratic presidential nominee. For weeks they would sing "Fortunate Son" together. And they would fail in their attempt to change the political landscape. They would be overwhelmed by the likes of Lee Greenwood's "Proud to Be an American," Toby Keith's "Courtesy of the Red, White and Blue," Darryl Worley's "Have You Forgotten?" and Martina McBride's "Independence Day."

FEBRUARY 5, 2005: EPILOGUE

John Fogerty is in Tampa, Florida. He is about to take the stage in the early afternoon, hours before Super Bowl XXVI between the New England Patriots and Philadelphia Eagles. In the official Super Bowl telecast, just before kickoff, the Florida School for the Blind choir will accompany the now dead Ray Charles in singing "America the Beautiful." Shortly after, Michael Douglas will introduce veteran soldiers from America's wars including women (Waves) and Black (the Tuskegee Airmen) veterans from World War II, that "greatest generation." Finally, Beyonce Knowles will sing a reverent "Star-Spangled Banner."

I'm surprised that Fogerty has been invited to this year's televised pregame party. Haven't the powers that be been listening to his latest record? While Fogerty isn't Incubus (the funk-rap-metal group that stepped outside its previous comfort zone to produce the stunning *Megalomaniac* video, complete with American eagles eating the country's citizens and the citizens drinking oil, while cardboard Hitlers with angel wings fall from the sky) or even Green Day (the aged punk band that reenergized itself with a new rock opera, *American Idiot*, suggesting that contemporary suburban America has produced a generation of comfortable numb and apolitical robots), he hasn't exactly gone completely country, even if he is performing with Keith Urban and singing little ditties like "Sugar, Sugar" and "Honey Do" that revel in marriage and family. After all, Fogerty is 59, comfortable with a solid marriage and loved children; and he is thrilled to have again found his poet's voice after a long dry spell.

I'm hoping Fogerty will sing "Déjà Vu (All Over Again)," but I'm afraid it will be something less confrontational like "Down on the Corner" or "I Will Walk with You." I'm shocked to hear him immediately blast into "Fortunate Son."

For a few moments I'm 19 again—angry and full of terror. But I too am a father. And I have immediate family members risking their lives in the military. At least one member has seen duty in Afghanistan and Iraq over the past 2 years, and he will be going back in just a few days. And all I can hear as Fogerty moves on to "Bad Moon Rising" are the words from his latest lament for the seeming endlessness of war.

What I want is for America to wake up and respond to the wars being waged in its name. What I want is for our nation to commit to a democracy that respects all people. What I want is for our media to stop equating war and sport, to stop using a wonderful cultural product for the most base purpose. What I want is for our citizens to consider the possibility that artists and prophets, who may seem insignificant and are suggesting that we are on the "eve of destruction," just might be right. What I want is to join Bruce Springsteen in singing "Land of Hope and Dreams," to celebrate a nation that has the potential to be the best there ever was and to hear bells of freedom ringing. But all I can hear in my head is Fogerty's last line, and I become even more convinced than ever that the game, as we currently play it, is not much fun.

REFERENCES

Behind the Music: 1968. (2001). [Television broadcast]. VH1.

Cimino, M. (Director). (1978). *The Deer Hunter* [Motion picture]. Universal.

Coll, S. (2004, December 5). Barrage of bullets drowned out cries of comrades; communication breakdown, split platoon among the factors contributing to "friendly fire." *The Washington Post*, p. A1.

Corcoran, M. (2002). *For which it stands: An anecdotal biography of the American flag.* New York: Simon & Schuster.

Eric Burdon and the Animals. (1991). Sky pilot. On *The Best of Eric Burdon and the Animals: 1966–1968* [CD]. Polygram.

Fogerty, J. (2004). Déjà vu (All over again). On *Déjà Vu (All Over Again)* [CD]. Geffen.

Hebert, J. (2004, September 24). Painful memories: War brings John Fogerty back in song and soul to a sad place. *San Diego Union Tribune*, p. E3.

Mackay, D. (2002, February 15). Chariots of ire: Is US jingoism tarnishing the Olympic ideal? *The Guardian*, p. 3.

Misusing the flag, again. (1991, February 20). *The New York Times*, p. A26.

NCAA Men's Basketball Championship Game. (1991). [Television broadcast]. Columbia Broadcasting System.

Nichols, H. O., & Weston, M. (1991, January 18). A letter to the supervisors of men's and women's basketball officials and conference commissioners. Unpublished raw data.

Not even one in four support Smith's protests. (2003). Retrieved November 1, 2004, from http://espn.go.com/ncw/news/2003/0303/1517193.html.

Outside the Lines: Personal Protest. (2003, March 10). Retrieved November 1, 2004, from http://sports.espn.go.com/espn/print?id=1517404&type=page2Story.

Shulman, K. (1991, March 3). A man of principle pays the price. *The New York Times*, 8: pp. 1, 8.

Smith, T. (2002). Retrieved January 5, 2005, from www.manhattanville.edu/ athletics/sports/wbask/02-03_season/02-03_roster/Toni_Smith.htm.

Toperoff, S. (1991, November 4). In pursuit of peace. *Sports Illustrated*, 44–56.

United States Code. (2005, February 10). Retrieved December 14, 2004, from www.usflag.org/uscode36.html.

Zang, D. (2001). *Sports wars: Athletes in the age of aquarius.* Fayetteville, AR: University of Arkansas Press.

•

14

Reconsidering Girl Power: Examining Media Images of Female Athletes

Maureen Smith
California State University, Sacramento

After the gold medal victories of the United States women's soccer, soft-ball, basketball, and gymnastic teams at the 1996 Atlanta Olympic Games, along with a number of other individual medal performances by American female athletes, there was a noticeable, albeit momentary, shift in the me-dia coverage of women in athletics. Momentum for this shift began in the year prior to the 1996 Games, as the women's U.S. basketball and soccer teams played in exhibition games before thousands of fans. In the years following the 1996 Olympic Games, new professional leagues for women athletes in softball, basketball, and soccer were created. Female athletes were hired to endorse sneakers, sport drinks, and other products. Girls across the country were celebrating these victories, finally able to enjoy the athletic exploits of their heroes during non-Olympic years, but also able to enjoy their own athletic abilities without rebuke. Fathers attended the women's soccer 1999 FIFA World Cup with their daughters in tow, girls played sport with a renewed purpose hoping for a college scholar-ship, and female Olympians posed for revealing photos. When Brandi Chastain scored the game-winning shot against China in the 1999 World Cup, little girls had another powerful image of "the athletic woman." Over the course of the tournament, the U.S. soccer team had become synony-mous with the spirit of "girl power," and the image of Chastain down on her knees with her shirt in hand and ripped abdominal muscles glistening in the California sun confirmed that "girl power" was alive and well in America as the photo spread across the globe (Cole, 2000).

Over the last several years, in newspapers and magazines and television, there appears to have been a decline in the "increased" coverage of women in sport, as well as the favorable athletic images of these women. This suspicion is confirmed by several recent studies (Amateur Athletic Foundation of Los Angeles [AAFLA], 2000; Bishop, 2003; George, 2001; Messner, Duncan, & Cooky, 2003). What had been a celebration of female athletes has quickly returned to old form. In many forms of media, the images of women in society and in sport have returned to the era when a greater emphasis was placed on the femininity of the subject, rather than her athleticism. A good example of this type of coverage is how former tennis player Anna Kournikova was hired to endorse several products unrelated to sport due to her attractive looks, not her athletic skills. In fact, she failed to win a major tennis tournament and yet made more money (and continues to make more money in her retirement) than a majority of female tennis players as a result of her endorsement contracts. Another noteworthy example is of a recent ABC television show, *All American Girl*. Contestants competed in activities that tested their "athletic ability, mental agility, and performance in the popular arts and beauty" (2003). While the show's inclusion of athletic ability indicates that for a girl to be considered all-American she should be athletic, the girl's performance in athletics had little bearing on her winning the title—which was ultimately determined by a popular vote of viewers. Bear in mind that these "girls" were actually women.

This chapter explores media images of female athletes into the 21st century and argues that despite noticeable changes in the amount and type of media coverage every so often, significant inequities continue to exist, as do the types of images presented. Additionally, images of athletic females in advertisements represent girls and women who do not play an organized sport but exercise or engage in physical activities that allow them to appear to be athletic, as well as identified as being physically fit without being identified as athletes. Girl power refers to an attitude that supports and celebrates girls' involvement in sport, but also an empowered sense of self for girls in society, by using the images of the females in athletics and the meanings attached to their athleticism.

Many societal factors have combined to create many opportunities for girls and women to be more active in sport and physical activity. The women's rights movement, legislation such as Title IX, and the health and fitness movement of the 1980s have all contributed to the increased participation of girls and women in sport and physical activity. Girls who are not interested in competing in traditional sport have a number of opportunities to be physically active and are encouraged to be active for health benefits. The success of female athletes has also promoted a greater acceptance of girls being more active in sports and physical activity.

CURRENT TRENDS IN MEDIA COVERAGE OF FEMALE ATHLETES

Media coverage of sport is critical to our consumption of sport. The media provide powerful visible images of female athletes, and as such shape consumer ideas of who female athletes are, what they look like, and the sports they play. If women are not depicted in the media or are represented in a way that is inaccurate, it has damaging effects on current and future female athletes. If women athletes are not seen in the media, it serves to reinforce the nonimportance of their sporting participation. Thomsen, Bower, and Barnes (2004) found that adolescent female athletes use photographic images of female athletes in magazines in the construction of their physical ability and body image. While the self-evaluations of physical ability tended to be positive, evaluations of body image were frequently negative and were "exacerbated by photographic poses that emphasize an athlete's aesthetic beauty rather than her athletic prowess" (p. 266). Clearly, the images of female athletes in the media have an impact on the young girls consuming those images, as well as the general public, who often support the sports and athletes they see represented in the media.

Numerous scholars have documented both the quantity and type of media coverage of female athletes in newspapers, magazines, and television (Bishop, 2003; Eastman & Billings, 2000; Higgs, Weiller, & Martin, 2003; Messner et al., 2003). In 1989, newspaper stories focusing on female athletes accounted for only 3.5% of all sport stories in a study of four newspapers: *USA Today*, the *Boston Globe*, the *Orange County Register*, and the *Dallas Morning News*. By a ratio of 23 to 1, men's sport stories outnumbered women's sports coverage (AAFLA, 1990). Television coverage was similar. Of local television news sports coverage, women's sports received 5%, men's sports 94%, and gender-neutral coverage accounted for 1% (AAFLA, 1994). In analyzing the type of coverage, gender was "verbally, visually and graphically marked" over 100 times a game in women's basketball, which was close to twice the rate of similar gender marking in women's basketball games 5 years previous, and was nearly nonexistent in men's basketball games (AAFLA, 1994). Gender marking is when the gender of the athletes is indicated in the title of a league, the name of a tournament, or in discussion of the sport. An example of gender marking is the Final Four and the Women's Final Four. By 1999, this type of gender marking was still occurring; in NCAA women's basketball games it remained high, occurring 57.2 times a game compared to men's games being described in gender-neutral terms (AAFLA, 2000).

In a year-long study of *Sports Illustrated* covers (from 1993 and 1994), the issues in 6 of 52 weeks had females on the cover, though only three of these were female athletes. The swimsuit issue accounted for the first woman, with two other issues having the widows of baseball players on the cover. The three female athletes to grace the cover were Monica Seles after she was stabbed; fellow tennis player Mary Pierce, who discussed her fear of her father; and lastly, Nancy Kerrigan after she was clubbed on the knee prior to the 1994 Olympics (Women's Sports Foundation [WSF], 2005); all three were featured for reasons having nothing to do with their athletic accomplishments. Davis addresses the heterosexism that is implicit in the annual swimsuit issue (Davis, 1997). In a more recent analysis of the coverage of female athletes in *Sports Illustrated*, Bishop (2003) found that despite a slight increase in feature coverage in the early 1990s, the overall coverage during the time period examined (1980 to present) did not show a significant change in the percentage of articles about women and the percentage of pages devoted to coverage of women. An examination of the photographs shows that the percentage of photos of female athletes "dropped dramatically" from 1994 to 1996. A number of studies have examined the portrayal of female athletes in *Sports Illustrated for Kids*, which targets a young audience of males and females (Duncan, 1988; Duncan & Sayaovong, 1991; Hardin, Lynn, Walsdorf, & Hardin, 2002; Hardin, Walsdorf, Lynn, & Hardin, 2003; Lynn, Walsdorf, Hardin, & Hardin, 2002; Rintala & Birrell, 1984). It was found that there are twice as many photos of boys, and boys are on the covers five times more often than girls.

In addition to studies that have documented the quantity of coverage of female athletes, scholars have also examined the types of images of female athletes (Duncan, 1990; Hardin et al., 2002; Kane, 1988; Kane & Lenskyj,

1998; Kane & Parks, 1992; Lee, 1992). Heterosexism and homophobia play powerful roles in how the media depict female athletes. Despite the success of American female athletes and the growing acceptance by society of girls and women in sport, images of girls and women in sport in the mainstream media have gone from hyperfeminization to hypersexualization. Experts suggest that men find "high-performing women athletes a threat to their male sports bastion," and as a result media images of female athletes appear as trivial, romantic, or hypersexualized (Holste, 2000). Professor Pat Griffin stated, "The hypersexualized images of women athletes function to normalize women athletes for men in the sports culture. . . . When it once was enough to feminize women athletes, now it is necessary to sexualize them for men" (Holste, 2000). Some female athletes go along with such depictions by posing in magazines that focus on their femininity and heterosexuality rather than their athleticism. Examples of these types of images are what Professor Mary Jo Kane, director of the Tucker Center for Research on Girls & Women in Sport at the University of Minnesota, refers to as "soft porn shots" (Holste, 2000). Two examples Kane noted were when World Cup hero Brandi Chastain posed naked in *Gear* magazine, holding two soccer balls in front of her, and a *Sports Illustrated* photo of Olympic swimmer Jenny Thompson wearing red boots, boxer trunks, and holding her hands across her naked chest in a Wonder Woman pose. Unfortunately, these opportunities to pose sometimes offer more money than their actual playing contracts, and it is one more way for female athletes to make money, though their endorsement deals still fall short of those of their male counterparts, who rarely remove their clothing.

According to Kane, female athletes are "routinely shown off court, out of uniform and in highly sexualized poses" (Holste, 2000). Twenty years ago it was routine to have a women's team pose in a "sorority shot" for the media guide. The group poses are no longer a practice, though media guides still rarely show female athletes in action shots. Thus, they remain to be seen in the same ways as their male counterparts, who are shown in action shots representative of their athleticism (Holste, 2000). Kane categorized the coverage of female athletes into groups she called "wives and mothers," where the photos reinforce the heterosexuality of the female athlete, another category she called "ambiguous," where the female athlete is pictured doing things away from her sport and in clothing that does not refer to her athleticism, and lastly, images that "dehumanize and fragment," in which the photos do not show the whole image of the female athlete (Holste, 2000).

Current images of female athletes depict them in a number of ways consistent with Kane's categories. In a classic "wives and mothers" type of image, WNBA player Sheryl Swoopes, several months pregnant, graced the inaugural cover of *Sports Illustrated for Women*. Photos continue to show female athletes in "ambiguous" images, such as an image of Olympic softball pitcher Jennie Finch in a gown with her boyfriend at an awards show. In the most recent *Sports Illustrated* swimsuit issue (February 2005), three female Olympians (Amanda Beard, U.S., swimming; Finch, U.S., softball; Lauren Thompson, Australia, basketball) modeled bathing suits, and unless you knew who the athletes were and what sport they played, you could easily assume that the bathing beauties were models rather than female athletes at the top of their respective sports. In the same issue, tennis player Venus Williams was photographed in a nonfunctional silver swimsuit and high-heeled shoes; the reader could easily overlook that she is among the world's best tennis players. Photos of female athletes in sporting magazines frequently show them in nonaction shots, so instead of Serena Williams's backhand, you see her raising the winner's cup in the awards ceremony or shaking hands after a match.

Tennis players Serena Williams and Maria Sharapova receive a great deal of media attention for their athletic talent, but also their feminine appearance. When Sharapova won Wimbledon in 2004, she was adamant in differentiating herself from her fellow Russian and former tennis player Anna Kournikova by emphasizing that she (Sharapova) would be recognized for her beauty, but also her tennis skills. She reminded the press that she had won a Grand Slam tournament, something Kournikova had never accomplished. That she was also beautiful was helpful in earning her numerous endorsements. Similar to Sharapova, Serena Williams, winner of seven Grand Slam titles, signed an endorsement contract with Reebok worth $40 million, though a majority of her media coverage focuses on the clothing she wears for her matches. She warms up in fashion ensembles that include boots that go up to her knee, which are zipped off before the match begins, and one of her outfits was called a "cat suit." Williams attended fashion school and in interviews discusses her desires to be viewed on the tennis court as an entertainer rather than an athlete. Several American female Olympians were featured in magazines, both sporting and nonsporting, in images that showed them partially clothed and in sexy poses rather than with any emphasis on their athleticism. A few posed nude for magazines. Though she has said she would not pose in uncompromising positions, Jennie Finch, a pitcher on the Olympic softball team, thinks that the coverage of female athletes is terrific because it is sending the message to girls that being athletic is sexy (Igoe, 2004).

More recently, the Amateur Athletic Foundation conducted a study to determine how media coverage of female athletes has changed and compared results from 1989, 1993, and 1999. In 1999, newspaper coverage of female athletes in Los Angeles newspapers had increased from 5.1% to 8.7%. One of the more significant improvements was in the quality of news coverage for female athletes. In 1993, only 7% of news stories on female athletes included an interview with the athlete or her coach. By 1999, 21% interviewed the athlete or her coach or both; the same practice was used in 25% of news stories on male athletes. Serious concerns remain for televised coverage of women's sports. ESPN's *Sports Center* had no lead stories dealing with female athletes, local news coverage often sexualized the female athletes to get viewers more interested, and commentators still referred to female athletes by their first name three times more often than they did with male athletes.

Partly in response to the increased attention given to female athletes in Olympic years and in anticipation of the upcoming 2000 Olympic Games, *Sports Illustrated for Women* (note the gender marking) published its first issue in spring 1999 and began publishing bimonthly issues a year later. The magazine didn't last as its circulation failed to garner the large audience it needed to survive. Criticisms of the magazine included its penchant for making women's sports try to fit into a *Vogue* or *Cosmopolitan* type magazine rather than focusing on features of females as athletes in the same way its counterpart *Sports Illustrated* covers male athletes. The female version of the sporting weekly consistently offered images of girls and women as athletic rather than as athletes. Features dealt with pregnancy and exercise, fashion for movement, as well as the occasional recognition of athletic accomplishments by females at the college and professional level. The last issue was published in December 2002.

Besides female athletes receiving "increased attention" in the media, more women are working as broadcasters on television, such as ESPN and during NFL games, though the number is still very small and their roles are often minimal, not being central in discussing the actual game. As part of its NFL Sunday pregame coverage, Fox TV has a weather "girl" whose main function besides forecasting game conditions is to look good for the primarily male audience. According to the Associated Press Sports Editors, 10% of sports reporters are female (Skwar, 1999). *USA Today* sports columnist Christine Brennan states that part of the lack of coverage of women's sports is related to the reporters being predominantly men, and that these men do not like covering women's sports. She states, "It's not cool to cover women's sports" (Skwar). What is perhaps the greatest disappointment is Brennan's claim to be gender-blind when she stated, "I don't consider myself an advocate of women's sports. We are journalists; we're advocates for good stories. And women's sports are becoming good stories" (Skwar). While it is a nice sentiment that women's sports are becoming "more worthy" of attention from journalists, Brennan's disclaimer would be more appropriate and acceptable if coverage and reporting positions were more equitable.

The sports reporter plays a significant role in the type of coverage the female athlete receives. In a study of female athletes participating in 14 different sports, as well as coaches and media specialists, Monica L. Heppel, research director of the Inter-American Institute on Migration and Labor in Washington, DC, (as cited in Policinski, 1998) found that half of the female athletes interviewed faulted the reporters with whom they had spoken and felt that the reporters were unfamiliar with the sport, uncomfortable interviewing women athletes, and sometimes dismissive of the women's athletic accomplishments. Eighty-four percent of those interviewed felt that the coverage of female athletics had improved over the last 5 years, though they argued that there was still not enough coverage. Athletes reported that broadcasters seemed to focus more on skill and less on appearance. Of all levels of the media, local media were rated as doing the "best job on reporting on women athletes and sports for women," with the exception of radio coverage (Policinski, 1998). Athletes rated local newspapers the highest.

History shows us that media coverage of female athletes enjoys cycles of popularity that typically occur in Olympic years. For example, every four summers, there is a focus on the female Olympians of the Summer Games, and every four winters, there is a focus on the female Olympians of the Winter Games. Every March, ESPN2 showcases the women's basketball tournament. These are patterns we can now expect and count on. Though there is often a temporary increase in the coverage during these time periods, the type of coverage continues to represent female athletes in sexualized ways (Daddario, 1994; Duncan, 1990; Higgs et al., 2003). Other coverage sources are developing, such as Lifetime and Oxygen's coverage of the WNBA and ESPN2's coverage of the NCAA playoff and championship games for women's sports such as soccer and volleyball. Network coverage of sports such as figure skating remains popular, and cheerleading is becoming increasingly more frequently covered and more popular on ESPN channels. The demise of *Sports Illustrated for Women*, besides being disappointing, leaves a gap in the magazine coverage of women's sports, though mainstream magazines occasionally cover women's sports, and sport-specific publications are also including more coverage of the females in their sport (sometimes as much as one to two pages). Newspaper coverage of women's sports is steadily increasing, though it still pales in comparison to the coverage men's sports receive.

STRATEGIES FOR IMPROVING
MEDIA COVERAGE OF GIRLS AND WOMEN IN SPORT

A number of strategies have been offered to help improve the coverage of girls and women in sport that address the structure of the media. The most recent AAFLA report (2000) concluded with a number of policy recommendations to help guide the media in the necessary changes in future coverage. The AAFLA recommended that television sport news should provide more coverage of existing women's sports and suggested that "coverage should be devoted to respectful, in-depth reporting, on serious, established women's sports." Media were encouraged to include "more than token coverage of women's sports in every broadcast" and to educate themselves concerning the ways that humorous putdowns of women athletes contribute to a "climate of disrespect for women athletes." It was recommended that the media "adopt standard usage of first and last name" for male and female athletes of all races. Gender marking should be done symmetrically for men and women's events when it is needed for clarity. There should be an effort toward more equal technical quality of coverage of women's events, and amounts of resources should be equivalent for men and women. Lastly, a call was issued to desegregate the announcer's booth by including more women and people of color in central roles (news anchors, play-by-play, and color commentary) (p. 9). Imagine turning on the television, opening *Sports Illustrated*, turning to the sports page if all these recommendations were acted upon. How would consumers, both male and female, view female athletes if they saw them in athletic images on a daily basis? The Women's Sports Foundation encourages fans of women's sports to call and write letters to their networks asking for more coverage and state that "watching women's sports on television is a practice in activism. The more you view this programming, the more likely we are to see increases in media coverage of women's sports" (WSF, 2005).

While it seems clear that the popularity of television and the Internet has surpassed that of books, there are an increasing number of books being published that focus on the participation of girls and women in a number of sports (Betancourt, 2001; Blais, 1996; Bradford, 2002; Buren, 2004; Macy, 1999; Sandoz & Winans, 1999; Silby, 2001; Smith, Burton Nelson, & Danzinger, 1999; Summitt, 1999; Zimmerman, 1999). Ranging from autobiographies to chronicles of a season to collections of essays, the popularity of books related to girls and women in sports is undeniable. One publication is taking the written word one step further with a traveling exhibition of photographs that make up the book *Game Face* (Gottesman, 2001). According to the website, the concept of "Game Face" "explores not only what a female athlete looks like, but what makes her tick" (Game Face). The book of photographs "documents the tremendous impact that sports has on the daily lives of millions of girls and women" (Game Face). The photos include females in a variety of activities, "on playing fields and street corners, in backyards and gyms," and depicts athletes as well as active girls and women. The book explores "the physical and emotional pleasures of competition and play," and seeks to answer the question, "What do girls and women look like, freed from traditional feminine constraints, using their bodies in joyful and empowering ways?" (Gottesman, 2001, book jacket). As part of the Game Face movement, the organization has worked with Girl Scouts to issue a Game Face patch for Girl Scouts who participate in Game Face–related activities. There is also an education outreach program designed to "promote a positive body-image and to help students achieve a balance between elite achievement in sports and playing for the simple joy of participation" (The Concept). The collection of photos offers powerful visual images of females across the life span being active and physical, and enjoying that freedom, and serves as a counternarrative to the messages in mainstream media coverage.

The increased participation of girls and women in sport and physical activity is undeniable, as is the growing popularity of women's athletics. While television ratings and the front page of sports sections may not reflect these trends, at the grassroots level of girls and women in sports, it is clear that the playing fields of America are ever-expanding to include everyone. Despite this increased participation, numerous studies have documented the lack of coverage of girls and women in sports. Consumers who are concerned with social justice should demand to see a wider variety of images of female athletes in the media that include representations of them as capable, strong, and athletic. With an increased vigilance and a sporting public, both male and female, willing to hold the media accountable, we should demand to and expect to see the expanding coverage of girls and women in all forms of media 365 days a year rather than only during the Olympiad or a championship event. "Girl Power" unite!

REFERENCES

All American Girl. (2003). Television Series. American Broadcasting Company, New York.

Amateur Athletic Foundation of Los Angeles. (1990). *Gender stereotyping in televised sports*. Los Angeles: Author.

Amateur Athletic Foundation of Los Angeles. (1994). *Gender stereotyping in televised sports: A follow-up to the 1989 study*. Los Angeles: Author.

Amateur Athletic Foundation of Los Angeles. (2000). *Gender stereotyping in televised sports: 1989, 1993 and 1999*. Los Angeles: Author.

Betancourt, M. (2001). *Playing like a girl: Transforming our lives through team sports*. New York: McGraw-Hill.

Bishop, R. (2003). Missing in action: Feature coverage of women's sports in *Sports Illustrated*. *Journal of Sport & Social Issues, 27*(2), 184–194.

Blais, M. (1996). *In these girls, hope is a muscle*. New York: Warner Books.

Bradford, M. (2002). *Nice girls finish first: The remarkable story of Notre Dame's rise to the top of women's college basketball*. Lanham, MD: Diamond Communications.

Buren, J. (2004). *Superwomen: 100 women—100 sports*. New York: Bulfinch Press.

Cole, C. L. (2000). The year that girls ruled. *Journal of Sport & Social Issues, 24*(1), 3–7.

Daddario, G. (1994). Chilly scenes of the 1992 Winter Games: The mass media and the marginalization of female athletes. *Sociology of Sport Journal, 11,* 275–288.

Davis, L. (1997). *The swimsuit issue and sport: hegemonic masculinity in* Sports Illustrated. Albany: State University of New York Press.

Duncan, M. C. (1988). Denial of power in televised women's sports. *Sociology of Sport Journal, 5*(1), 1–21.

Duncan, M. C. (1990). Sports photographs and sexual difference: Images of women and men in the 1984 and 1988 Olympic Games. *Sociology of Sport Journal, 7,* 22–43.

Duncan, M. C., & Sayaovong, A. (1991). Photographic images and gender in *Sports Illustrated for Kids. Play and Culture, 3,* 91–116.

Eastman, S. T., & Billings, A. C. (2000). Sportscasting and sports reporting: The power of gender bias. *Journal of Sport and Social Issues, 24,* 192–213.

Game Face. *The Book.* (n.d.). http://gamefaceonline.org/2_0_book.htm.

Game Face. *The Concept.* (n.d.). http://gamefaceonline.org/3_0_concept.htm.

George, J. J. (2001, August 24). Lack of news coverage for women's athletics: A questionable practice of newspaper priorities. Retrieved October 22, 2005, from www.womenssportsfoundation.org/cgi-bin/iowa/issues/media/article.html? record+807.

Gottesman, J. (2001). *Game face: What does a female athlete look like?* New York: Random House.

Hardin, M., Lynn, S., Walsdorf, K., & Hardin, B. (2002). The framing of sexual difference in *Sports Illustrated for Kids* editorial photos. *Mass Communication and Society, 5*(3), 341–359.

Hardin, M., Walsdorf, K., Lynn, S., & Hardin, B. (2003). Gender and sport media: Sexual difference and *Sports Illustrated for Kids.* In R.A. Lind (Ed.), *Race/gender/media: Considering diversity across audiences, content, and producers.* Boston: Allyn & Bacon.

Higgs, C. T., Weiller, K. H., & Martin, S. B. (2003). Gender bias in the 1996 Olympic Games: A comparative analysis. *Journal of Sport & Social Issues, 27*(1), 52–64.

Holste, G. C. (2000, October 17). Women athletes often debased by media images. *Women's eNews.* Retrieved October 22, 2005, from www.womensenews .org/article.cfm?aid=310.

Igoe, S. (2004, October 18). Jennie Finch throws fans a curveball. http://sports .espn.go.com/espn/page3/story?page=10bqs/finch.

Kane, M. J. (1988). Media coverage of the female athlete in the media before, during, and after Title IX: *Sports Illustrated* revisited. *Journal of Sport Management, 2,* 87–99.

Kane, M. J., & Lenskyj, H. J. (1998). Media treatment of female athletes: Issues of gender and sexualities. In L. A. Wenner (Ed.), *MediaSport* (pp. 186–201). New York & London: Routledge.

Kane, M. J., & Parks, J. B. (1992). The social construction of gender difference and hierarchy in sport journalism: Few new twists on very old themes. *Women in Sport & Physical Activity Journal 1*(1), 54.

Lee, J. (1992). Media portrayals of male and female Olympic athletes: Analyses of newspaper accounts of the 1984 and the 1988 summer Games, *International Review of Sociology of Sport, 23*(3), 197–219.

Lynn, S., Walsdorf, K., Hardin, M., & Hardin, B. (2002). Selling girls short: Advertising gender images in *Sports Illustrated for Kids*. *Women in Sport & Physical Activity Journal, 11*(2), 77–100.

Macy, S. (1999). *Play like a girl: A celebration of women in sports*. New York: Henry Holt.

Messner, M., Duncan, M. C., & Cooky, C. A. (2003). Silence, sports bras, and wrestling porn: Women in televised sport news and highlights shows. *Journal of Sport & Social Issues, 27*(1), 38–51.

Policinski, G. (1998, November 13). Study finds media still fail in quality, quantity of women's sports coverage. Retrieved October 22, 2005, from www.freedom forum.org/templates/document.asp?documentID=7597&printerfriendly=1.

Rintala, J., & Birrell, S. (1984). Fair treatment for the active female: A content analysis of *Young Athlete* magazine. *Sociology of Sport Journal, 1,* 231–250.

Sandoz, J., & Winans, J. (Eds.). (1999). *Whatever it takes : Women on women's sport*. New York: Farrar, Straus and Giroux.

Silby, C. (2001). *Games girls play: Understanding and guiding young female athletes*. New York: St. Martin's Press.

Skwar, D. (1999). Women's sports gain the spotlight. Associated Press Sports Editors. Retrieved October 22, 2005, from http://apse.dallasnews.com/aug1999/14skwar.html.

Smith, L., Burton Nelson, M., & Danzinger, L. (1999). *Nike is a goddess: The history of women in sports*. New York: Atlantic Monthly Press.

Summitt, P. (1999). *Reach for the summit*. New York: Broadway.

Thomsen, S. R., Bower, D. W., & Barnes, M. D. (2004). Photographic images in women's health, fitness, and sports magazines and the physical self-concept of a group of adolescent female volleyball players. *Journal of Sport & Social Issues, 28*(3), 266–283.

Women's Sports Foundation. (2005). *Q & A: Media Coverage of Women's Sports.* Retrieved October 22, 2005, from www.womenssportsfoundation.org/cgi-bin/iowa/issues/media/article.html?record=965.

Zimmerman, J. (1999). *Raising our athletic daughters: How sports can build self-esteem and save girls' lives.* New York: Main Street Books.

15

Why Be A "Jackass"?: Media Images of Young White Men In and Out of Sport in New Millennium America

Kyle W. Kusz
University of Rhode Island

WHITE MALE ANGER IN 1990s AMERICA

Below is an online rant by Ben, a sophomore at New Canaan High School, after he watched Jackson Katz's antisexist video, *Tough Guise*, which critically examines the narrow image of masculinity offered in contemporary media culture:

> Jackson Katz claims to be an anti-sexist. Yeah, they got another word for that, you castrated pile of discharge. It's "feminist." And there's nothing worst than a feminist. . . . Katz is one of those guys that likes to blame men on everything. He doesn't want to change the definition of masculinity, he wants to eliminate masculinity altogether. He wants us [men] all reduced to whiny girls. He wants to MAKE US WOMEN. . . . And we men have to band together, and fight this growing movement. A woman today is one penis short of being a man, and they want us trading parts. It has got to stop. (*Tough Guise My Ass*, 2004)

Clearly, Ben is more than a little bit angry at Katz's effort to have young men question the limited messages about masculinity shown through the media. But make no mistake, Ben is not alone in his thoughts. In the past decade, many cultural observers have commented that there has been a growing sense of anger, discontentment, and resentment in many White men of all ages. Some have labeled this sentiment a "generational thing," specific to the under-30 crowd, while others identify it as a feeling shared by White men of all ages.

We have seen White men go on killing sprees and commit large-scale violent and destructive acts in real life (Timothy McVeigh—Oklahoma City bombing, Benjamin Smith—killing spree in Illinois in the summer of 1997, David Koresh—Waco, and Dylan Klebold and Eric Harris—Columbine) and on the big screen (*Falling Down*, *Fight Club*). Some young, angry White men have followed the example set forth in the film *Fight Club* to create their own "real-life" fight clubs. During this same time period, new sporting practices like World Wrestling Entertainment (WWE), the Ultimate Fighting Championship, and extreme sports have not only found a place in the American mainstream sports media but have become very popular with young White male audiences. Interestingly, these sporting activities feature White men enduring pain, demonstrating their superiority over others, or dominating and punishing opponents (in the case of WWE and Ultimate Fighting).

The feelings of anger and resentment experienced by some White men do not occur in a vacuum, and they are often expressed in ways that are not always obvious at first glance. These feelings of anger and resentment in some White men are also not innate personality traits or character flaws. They are learned responses to the social, cultural, and economic changes that have taken place in American society over the past 30 years. Job losses, declining and stagnating wages, and the erosion of benefits have hurt the American workforce. The nature of work has changed. Manufacturing and industrial jobs performed mainly by men that had afforded them (and their families) comfortable middle-class lifestyles in the past have been moved to cheaper labor markets overseas. They have been replaced by low-paying service industry jobs that can be performed by women as well as, if not better than, men. Additionally, much work in our information age involves pushing papers and sitting at a desk working on a computer. These are not the types of jobs that enable the men who perform them to feel like "real men." Finally, the civil rights and women's movements changed the landscape of American society and culture by exposing the racial and gender inequalities that still mean discrimination against millions of Americans. Their messages still reverberate and shape the stories that circulate in our culture today: stories of empowering women, promoting a multicultural vision of America, and criticizing White male privilege.

While these changes were embraced by many Americans, they also caused fear, anger, and anxiety in others. Today, some White men are resentful and angry about the progress (limited as it might be) that women and racial minorities have made since the 1960s, feeling as though it has come at their expense. These White men often express their discontent with these social changes, not by mentioning how they challenge and threaten White male privilege, but by alleging that they have eroded "traditional American values." But when they talk of traditional American values, these men are not talking about foundational American values like fairness, true meritocracy, and equal opportunities for all. Instead, it is a code phrase that hides the true intent of their stand: They want to protect the social power and authority that go along with being White and male in American society.

Ironically, it was the much-ballyhooed book by Susan Faludi (1999), *Stiffed: The Betrayal of the American Man*, that made the American public aware of this growing feeling of anger, anxiety, and resentment in contemporary American men. Shortly thereafter, the film *Fight Club* reinforced this message. Immensely popular with young White males, the film starred Brad Pitt and Ed Norton Jr. and showed many men who were discontent with their lives, for many of the reasons mentioned above. In an effort to once again feel like men, they choose to join underground fight clubs and brutally beat up one another. Interestingly, many young American White men were so enamored with the film that they created their own secret fight clubs in real life. Finally, the pervasiveness of these feelings became apparent when Comedy Central aired *The Man Show*, a show that unabashedly and unapologetically celebrates the ability of White men to objectify women, act crudely, and defy those who have made them feel guilty for basking in their privileged social position.

That many American White male youths would copycat the street fighting of *Fight Club* or find pleasure in watching the sophomoric antics of *The Man Show* should not come as a surprise. These cultural texts, like Ultimate Fighting and WWE, offer a rather traditional model of White masculinity as tough, masochistic, authoritarian, and superior to all others. They have made a comeback in American popular culture since the late 1990s and now pervade the media that young White males consume daily. They get a sampling of it when they watch the films mentioned above or television shows, listen to the music of Limp Bizkit or Eminem, play video games like *Grand Theft Auto*, or watch the stunts and pranks performed by the *Jackass* crew first seen on MTV and later in the film:

Jackass: The Movie (or even the more recent MTV spin-off: *Viva La Bam* or *Wild Boys*).

In this chapter, I take a closer look at the characteristics of this type of White masculinity that circulates in the American media culture where the lines between sport, music, television, and film have become blurred. To do this, I examine two contemporary media texts that are popular with White male youth and promote this type of White masculinity: the *Jackass* phenomenon and the performance of the White rapper Eminem in the semiautobiographical film *8 Mile*. My discussion shows how the antics and performances of the *Jackass* crew and Eminem display a distinct contemporary trend of White men wishing to recover a privileged social position that most importantly marks them as different from and superior to women and seeks to mask or deny any thought of White racial privilege. Finally, I conclude by urging young White males to consciously think about the social consequences of performing this type of masculinity.

What's Wrong with Being a "*Jackass*"?

The *Jackass* television show and feature film of the same name showcase an all-White male group of skateboarders who perform various daring stunts and gross pranks on one another, such as crashing themselves in shopping carts into curbs and bushes, putting drops of hot sauce in each other's eyes, or getting shot with a paintball gun from close range. The common feature of virtually all of their stunts is the infliction of pain on themselves and their buddies.

Some people dismiss the *Jackass* crew as an abnormal group of wayward young men who have an irrational death wish. End of story. For those who take this position, there is no reason to study the antics of these boys any further. They are simply the latest version of an age-old pattern of teen male aggression, rebellion, angst, and boredom. However, such an interpretation of the *Jackass* phenomenon prevents one from seeing their behaviors as exemplifying broader desires and feelings held by many White men in American society at the turn of the century. Namely, the *Jackass* crew represents a social trend of White men finding pleasure in experiencing pain, desiring exclusive all-male spaces, creating social hierarchies, and trying to appear as different and unprivileged White folk (not wealthy or socially advantaged).

No Pain, No Gain

So why do Johnny Knoxville, Bam Margera, Steve-O, and the rest of the *Jackass* boys enjoy inflicting pain on themselves and one another? Some people think they do it just because it is funny. But scholars who have studied masculinity have noted that men have long participated in activities that involve enduring pain as a means of proving to themselves and others that they are adequately masculine. This point is especially true when men willingly choose to inflict pain on themselves or have it inflicted upon them. These sorts of masochistic physical activities become popular with men at specific times in history, like today, when women's social power increases and men feel uncertain about their own authority and masculine adequacy at work and in their home lives. During these times in history, men often create leisure activities where they can "prove" their masculinity by enduring and inflicting pain and competing with other men.

Clearly, the *Jackass* crew regularly perform risky stunts and ridiculous dares that often involve enduring pain or risking painful injuries. Also, the pain and injuries that these White men incur are not often downplayed or hidden. Rather they are prominently displayed and embraced in *Jackass* episodes and by their audiences. Like the injuries these men suffer when performing these stunts, the images of dramatic and painful crashes are highlighted as badges of honor that are meant to demonstrate the toughness and masculinity of these men. This unapologetic and even proud display of the ability to withstand pain and serious injury exhibited by the members of the *Jackass* crew is also apparent in mainstream television shows and videos featuring extreme sports such as skateboarding, BMX dirt jumping, street luge, and, more recently, motocross dirt jumping. On one level, then, some White boys and men find extreme sport performers and the *Jackass* crew appealing because they demonstrate the return of a traditional form of masculinity. This form of masculinity relishes taking risks, defies those who tell men to be careful and cautious, and enjoys the infliction of pain because these things allow them to demonstrate to themselves and others that they are adequately masculine.

It's a Man's World

Historically, fraternal orders that include only, or even mainly, Whites have long helped to divide social groups (men and women; Whites and

Blacks) and maintain a privileged position for White men in society. So their growing reappearance on television and in film should be disturbing. The social Darwinist "battles of the sexes," where only "the fittest" are said to survive, are once again popular in contemporary American culture, particularly in television shows like *Fear Factor, Survivor, The Apprentice, and The Real World–Road Rules Challenge*, which are marketed toward younger Americans. Central to many of these shows are regular athletic contests and competitions that not only often pit men against women, but frequently include the recirculation of very sexist ideas about gender (men and women as essentially different and men as naturally superior to women) that are the foundations upon which gender inequalities are built. It's important to interpret the *Jackass* crew as a fraternal order as well. Like the underground all-male fight clubs glamorized in *Fight Club* or the technologically created fraternity of *The Man Show*, *Jackass* is part of a growing desire in many White boys and men to re-create exclusive social spaces for men only. This exclusive, gendered space is one reminiscent of sports, which were originally constructed to serve such a purpose.

So why would White men and boys be interested in creating these exclusive, all-male spaces? In an era when the cultural authority of women and racial minorities has grown and White men perceive that their every action in public is being scrutinized to determine whether they act or think like "overprivileged oppressors," "Whitey," or "The Man," perhaps it is no wonder that some White men have sought out private, exclusive spaces where they feel they can freely express a traditional White masculinity that celebrates male authority and gives them a sense of superiority over women and people of color.

Although you may not think of it when you sit down to watch *Jackass* programs, it quickly becomes apparent that the main players in this group are White men. Women and people of color are just not a part of this crew. Interestingly, the exclusion of women and people of color appears to be random. The home movie look of the show and film creates the impression that the racial and gender exclusivity of the group is not intentional— it is just a bunch of good friends getting together to play pranks on one another. When women do appear on the show, they rarely participate in the daredevil antics and largely endorse the values of the crew. There is little room for dissent within the *Jackass* fraternity. You either find these guys hilarious and cool or you're discounted by them as too square and uncool to be allowed in their club.

On the rare occasions when people of color do appear in *Jackass* (rarely African Americans), they are usually portrayed only in a stereotypical manner and made to be the brunt of the crew's jokes. In such scenarios, the person of color is usually portrayed as powerless to stop the members of the *Jackass* crew from wreaking havoc on them or breaking social norms. Subtly, through these vignettes, we see White male privilege restored. These man-boys prove to themselves and others that they will not be constrained by the authority of others (especially people of color). They will do as they please, and if you really get upset at them and criticize them for their actions, they'll simply undercut your criticism by proclaiming, "Loosen up, it's just a joke!" In the name of having a good time, they become immune from public criticism. And although their antics seem juvenile and unimportant, they represent a subtle and complex strategy of restoring a sense of superiority and sovereignty in White men.

Also, because women and people of color rarely appear in their shows, the sexist and racist aspects of the fraternal order they create are often hard for people to see at first. But in a world that is becoming more racially diverse and where women are gaining more social power, we should be suspicious of emergent "hip and edgy" cultural activities that include only White men or that blatantly stereotype women and people of color in the few instances in which they do appear. We've made some good progress in chipping away at racial inequalities and blatant forms of discrimination, but racism and sexism are resilient, and today they take on more disguised forms that, on the face of things, often do not appear as racist or sexist.

Finally, the actions of the *Jackass* fraternity should not be easily dismissed or ignored because they are symptomatic of broader efforts in contemporary American society to re-create sex-segregated schools, to undercut the power of Title IX in providing opportunities for girls and women in sports, and to revive old sexist ideas that men and women are essentially different (biologically, socially, and psychologically). History has shown us that such notions of natural difference between genders or races, and social arrangements that divide the sexes and races, are what lead to and sustain social inequalities, preserving the power and privilege of White men.

PRETTY FLY FOR A WHITE GUY

It is also important to more closely examine the look and lifestyle displayed by the *Jackass* crew. Frequently, they display a downtrodden, unkempt, and seemingly impoverished appearance. Some of their stunts are performed in their apartments where viewers see them living like slobs in cramped quarters. In fact, their living spaces differ dramatically from the opulent homes of celebrities and sport stars glamorized in another popular MTV show, *Cribs*. Their impoverished look and lifestyle symbolize a more prevalent effort on the part of White people during the 1990s to distance themselves from the idea that White people are inherently wealthy, privileged, and oppressive that emerged out of the civil rights movement years earlier. Although White people are often not aware of, nor upfront about, these efforts, the emergence and popularity of everything "alternative" (especially grunge music and extreme sports, which prominently provided images of disheveled and seemingly unprivileged White men who came from the social margins), as well as America's fascination with "White trash" during the 1990s, demonstrate how widespread this desire to be seen as different and unprivileged was for many White people during this time period.

Of course, you might think that the grunge look of the *Jackass* crew is just a meaningless style. But in an era when many Whites are making irrational claims about being victims of affirmative action programs and reverse racism, and when *Sports Illustrated* produced a cover story in 1997 proclaiming the White male athlete as the new "minority" and "second class citizen" in sport (Price, 1997), the faux impoverished style of the *Jackass* crew takes on additional meaning as another example of contemporary White people denying the fact that White racism against people of color is alive and well, even today.

8 Mile

Perhaps it is also no surprise that *8 Mile* was created during this moment in history (Grazer, Hanson, & Iovine, 2002). Like *Jackass*, it also taps into the feelings of anger, discontent, and resentment being felt by a sizable number of young White men, especially those from urban, working-class backgrounds who are not only finding it difficult to find meaningful and adequately paid work in today's service economy, but are increasingly living in places where being White means you're the racial minority. But *8 Mile* does so in a slightly different way than *Jackass* does. Whereas proving one's masculinity is the key aspect of the *Jackass* phenomenon, the salient feature of *8 Mile* is what it teaches us about race.

8 Mile offers the seemingly authentic story of a White male rapper, Rabbit (played by Eminem), who is economically disadvantaged and socially unprivileged. This image of White masculinity is one that White America craves at this time in history. In an era when most Whites and Blacks have divergent views on the existence of White racism and White privilege, *8 Mile* counters the popular notion that all Whites are automatically privileged and wealthy through its portrayal of Eminem's character, Rabbit. The similarities between the story of Rabbit in *8 Mile* and Eminem's own biography blur the line between fiction and reality and help authenticate the idea that what the film represents is "reality." Put most simply, the film allows White people an opportunity to say, "See, White people can also be social victims and economically and socially disadvantaged!"

The effort to find authentic stories of White people who are poor or in a position of being the racial minority is prevalent in late 1990s American society. An excellent example of this effort within the realm of sport that mirrors the story of *8 Mile* is Ira Berkow's (2001) award-winning *New York Times* piece titled "Minority Quarterback." The article featured the story of Marcus Jacoby, a White quarterback who always dreamed of earning a scholarship to play college football. But after completing his senior football season in high school, he was passed over for a scholarship by White universities. The only school to offer him a football scholarship was the historically Black university, Southern University. After a difficult and disappointing first season, Jacoby led Southern to its first-ever Black college football championship in his sophomore year. Just one year later, Jacoby quit school, later citing the feelings of extreme isolation, stress, and anxiety that he experienced (in his opinion) due to the racial prejudices of the Black members of the Southern University community. Written as part of the *New York Times* special report on race in America, the tone of this story was sympathy for Jacoby's plight as a White racial minority. Yet the story failed to note that Jacoby's story is the exception rather than the rule for White college athletes, most of whom play at predominantly White universities. No mention was made of how Jacoby's experience of being a member of the racial minority group on a college campus is the common experience that thousands of African American athletes go through every day. It begs the question: Why isn't anyone telling you about their story?

This theme of a White male athlete who is unfairly disadvantaged and stereotyped because of his race is also repeated in the 1997 *Sports Illustrated* cover story mentioned earlier through the story of White male sprinter Kevin Little (Price, 1997). Little's story is employed in the article to attempt to authenticate the article's main thesis that White (male) athletes are being systematically disadvantaged and discriminated against in the world of sport. Although the article's thesis of White men's disadvantage and discrimination in sport can be easily criticized for failing to consider who is represented in the ranks of coaches, general managers, team presidents, team owners, league officials, and so on, Little's story, like Rabbit's in *8 Mile*, is remarkably effective in seducing White audiences into believing this idea that White men are the new disadvantaged social group in contemporary American society.

Stories such as the ones above try to create the impression that the playing field between Whites and Blacks in American society is level and equal, or if it is slanted in any way, it is against White men. The logic at work in media texts like *8 Mile* and "The Minority Quarterback" is that if examples of Black prejudice against Whites (however exceptional or isolated those examples might be) or Black overrepresentation/white underrepresentation in lucrative occupations (such as professional athletics) can be found, then White racism can be said not to exist; if impoverished or disadvantaged Whites exist, then the notion of White privilege can be dismissed. Stories of poor and unprivileged Whites such as *8 Mile* get made into Hollywood feature films because they paint a picture of race that serves the collective interests of White people. Thus, this seemingly unimportant Hollywood film can have far-reaching political implications if it's used by White people as credible "evidence" to deny the existence of White racism or White privilege.

Anti-"Whitey" I: White Male as Economically Unprivileged

As mentioned earlier, one of the outcomes of the civil rights movement of the 1960s is the production and circulation of an image of White people as evil oppressors who deny equal opportunities to African Americans due to their racist beliefs about Blacks. Since then, White America has worked to counter this image of all White people as evil, arrogant, oppressive, and privileged. Popular culture (films, television, sport, and pop music in particular) has been a prominent place where this image of White people has been challenged. *8 Mile* is part of this cultural effort. But how does it do this?

First, the film goes to great lengths to portray Rabbit as economically unprivileged. For example, when we first meet Rabbit, he is homeless after having been kicked out of the apartment where he and his former girlfriend lived. With nothing but a trash bag full of clothes, he returns to the trailer park where his mother and younger sister live. Then we discover that his mother and sister are a month away from being evicted. Nonetheless, his mother surprises Rabbit by generously giving him an early birthday present of her car. Any glimmer of hope and optimism he feels quickly dissipates the next morning when he learns that the car does not run anymore. Rabbit is eventually able to fix the car, but it constantly breaks down on him. In addition, throughout the film, Rabbit wears filthy, no-name T-shirts and jeans. He is also shown working on an unglamorous assembly line, constantly asking his boss if he can work extra shifts to make more money. Clearly, these scenes in the film drive home the idea that this White male is anything but economically privileged.

Anti-"Whitey" II: White Male as Racial Minority

The film also portrays Rabbit as a White male who is a member of a socially unprivileged racial minority. He is constantly shown living in a social world surrounded by Black people. Three of the four members of his crew are Black. The club where the weekly rap battles take place is dominated by Black participants and an overwhelmingly Black audience. At work, all his coworkers and his boss are Black. Even in the trailer park where he lives (which is stereotypically imagined as a White space in contemporary American culture), the only neighbor we see and meet is Black. Indeed, the film goes to great lengths to portray the White male Rabbit as a racial minority surrounded by African Americans.

The negative consequences of being a racial minority for Rabbit are implied in one of the first scenes of the film. A large Black bouncer denies Rabbit access to the backstage area where the rappers who are slated to perform that night are supposed to meet. Very subtly, the scene dramatizes the idea that Whites can be discriminated against by Black people due to their racial identity. Shortly thereafter, we see Rabbit choke onstage in front of the all-Black audience, who thoroughly enjoy seeing him freeze in his first rap battle. Later, we see Rabbit feeling as though his Black shift boss is subtly discriminating against him because he is not being given extra shifts at work. Finally, one of the Black friends Rabbit grew up with, who promised to get him a record deal, ends up double-crossing him when he has sex with Rabbit's girl and fails to deliver the recording deal.

Such scenes of subtle discrimination and poor treatment against Rabbit by various Black people can evoke feelings of sympathy for Rabbit from White male viewers who imagine the difficulty he must be experiencing living in this virtual all-Black world. These scenes not only imply that Rabbit is a victim of reverse racism, but they suggest that such racism against Whites would be the inevitable outcome of a social world where Whites were the racial minority. Considering that some demographers project that Whites will be the racial minority by the middle of this century, this storyline is one that could provoke racial anxiety and even hatred in Whites stricken by what the famous MC Chuck D. once called "the fear of a black planet" (Sadler, Shocklee, & Ridenhour, 1990).

Yet it is also important to note that although Rabbit seems to encounter some prejudice because of his race during the film, it never prevents him from taking advantage of any social opportunities. Rabbit is always (miraculously!) able to easily overcome any apparent social barriers. For example, after initially being denied backstage access, Rabbit's Black friend, who emcees the rap battles, clears up the misunderstanding with the bouncer so he is able to perform. His Black male shift boss eventually sees that Rabbit is a reliable, hard worker and gives him the extra work shifts he wants. And by film's end, Rabbit's White identity does not prevent him from winning over the overwhelmingly Black audience in his battle with the members of the all-Black "Free World" crew.

So then, the image of White masculinity that is offered by the film through Rabbit is one that always serves the interests of White people in contemporary America in a variety of ways. On the one hand, it provides viewers with a White male who is seemingly authentically portrayed as a racial minority and a disadvantaged social victim. Yet, amazingly, Rabbit never experiences any sort of material discrimination or disadvantage due to his race. Here, White masculinity masquerades as a disadvantaged minority but never has to suffer any injury or injustice.

Restoring "Whitey": Reproducing White Masculinity as a Superior,
Rugged Individualist

Lastly, the final scenes of the film, like many throughout it, show Rabbit portrayed as a very traditional example of White masculinity. Despite his minority status, Rabbit displays his verbal "genius" by winning the final rap battles and amazingly winning the support of the Black crowd. Rabbit's climactic victory at the end of the film thereby reestablishes the very traditional image of White male superiority relative to African Americans. Also, the final scene portrays Rabbit in a very traditional manner as a White male rugged individualist when it shows him leaving behind his crew and walking off alone, victorious as a cowboy in a Western.

The final scene of Rabbit walking off into the proverbial sunset also implies that Rabbit has found success by winning the rap battle that will enable him to earn a record deal and transcend his impoverished condition in the near future. By glamorizing Rabbit as a rugged individualist, *8 Mile*, like so many Hollywood films, also reinforces the myth that any social barrier can be easily overcome by the strong will, determination, and hard work of any individual. At the same time, Rabbit's strong work ethic, desire for upward mobility, and self-reliance uphold and reinforce the American myth of meritocracy held dear by so many White American males. The myth of meritocracy, of course, makes sense as a "truth" about the world only to those who have never known what it feels like to have their race, gender, or social class limit the merits of their efforts.

CONCLUSION: MEDIA MESSAGES ABOUT WHITE MASCULINITY AND PERSONAL RESPONSIBILITY

Clearly, television shows and films involving physical activity and competitions of various sorts such as *Jackass* and *8 Mile* are important cultural sites where we learn ideas about various social groups and our society. In this chapter, I have examined some of the subtle lessons about what it means to be White and male in new millennium America that young White males learn from watching media productions such as *Jackass* and *8 Mile*. I have also mentioned how some of the themes about White masculinity evident in *Jackass* and *8 Mile* can also be seen in more obvious sport examples such as WWE, Ultimate Fighting, and extreme sports, as well as some interesting pieces of sport journalism during this same time period. We might also use the lessons learned from this chapter to better understand more recent sport phenomena. For example, the rise in popularity of NASCAR, a racial and gender exclusive sport where Confederate flags—a symbol of the South's racist past to many African Americans—are still displayed proudly, could be critically examined for the messages embedded in it. Or the popularity of poker on television, with its Wild West imagery and rhetoric that advertise the program on ESPN, could be interrogated.

The *Jackass* fraternity offers a model of White masculinity that values inflicting pain on oneself and others, performing risky and dangerous stunts, and creating a White-exclusive fraternity. These sophomoric activities help the *Jackass* fraternity to re-create a place where they can confirm that they are adequately men and that they are the undoubted rulers of their own domain. The portrayal of popular White male rapper Eminem in the film *8 Mile* provides an image of White masculinity as economically unprivileged and socially disadvantaged that serves the interests of Whites in an era when the privileges of being White and male are being criticized publicly. As they are embraced by the American White mainstream, such images of Whites as unprivileged and disadvantaged work subtly to deny the existence of White racism and White privilege in American society today.

In this age when most of us are bombarded daily with hundreds of messages and ideas from the increasingly pervasive American media, it is important that youth develop a critical awareness of the ideas being promoted through these programs. Although simply watching television or a film seems to be little more than something we do for fun and leisure, our opinions about such things as men's and women's "proper" roles in society or the state of race relations in American society are often heavily influenced by what we watch on television and the big screen. The actions and attitudes of the people we watch on the screen often shape our own actions and attitudes even if we are not fully conscious of this influence. That is why films or television programs that resist social norms in one way or another create social controversies; the powers that be fear that such shows will teach large numbers of people to resist and challenge social norms in their own lives.

Finally, it is important to emphasize that although the media play a significant, even if often overlooked, role in shaping the thoughts and actions of individuals in our society, by no means are we cultural dupes who, like zombies, must blindly adopt and follow the ideas presented to us by the media. We all have the ability to draw on different models of behavior to define for ourselves what it means to be a man or woman, Black or White. And we all should consider the social consequences of the gender and racial identities that we perform daily.

I want to remind us of our ability to act in this process because I am concerned about the ideas and messages being taught to young White males today through television programs and films such as *Jackass* and *8 Mile*. It seems that there are far too many young White males like Ben, whom we met at the beginning of the chapter, who seem to have swallowed these media messages about White men without questioning them. Yet far too many of us will suffer negative consequences of the seemingly unimportant desire to be like the *Jackass* crew, Tyler Durden, or Eminem.

REFERENCES

Berkow, I. (2001). Minority quarterback. In J. Lelyveld (Ed.), *How race is lived in America* (pp. 189–210). New York: Times Books.

Ehrman, J. L. (Producer). (1999). *The Man Show*. [Television series]. Comedy Central.

Faludi, S. (1999). *Stiffed: The Betrayal of the American Man*. New York: William Morrow & Company.

Grazer, B., Hanson, C., & Iovine, J. (Producers), & Hanson, C. (Director). (2002). *8 Mile* [Film]. Universal City, CA: Universal Studios.

Jonze, S., Knoxville, J., & Tremaine, J. (Producers), & Tremaine, J. (Director). (2002). *Jackass: The Movie* [Film]. Hollywood, CA: Paramount Picture & MTV Films.

Linson, A., Grayson Bell, R., & Chaffin, C. (Producers), & Fincher, D. (Director). (1999). *Fight Club* [Film]. Hollywood, CA: Twentieth Century Fox Home Entertainment.

Price, S. (1997, December 6). Whatever happened to the white athlete? *Sports Illustrated, 87*, 32–51.

Sadler, E., Shocklee, K., & Ridenhour, C. (1990). [Recorded by Public Enemy]. On *Fear of a Black Planet* [cassette tape]. New York: Def Jam.

Tough Guise My Ass. (2004, March 22). Retrieved March 20, 2003, from www.ubersite.com/m/28288.

16

Education, Sport, and Hip-Hop through the "Mic" of Stuart Scott

*C. Keith Harrison, Arizona State University, and
Quaylan Allen, Arizona State University*

Bring your A game.

—Contemporary cultural slogan

My people be projects and jail
never Harvard and Yale.

—Jones, *Book of Rhymes*, 2004

While the occupational identities of African Americans are diverse, mainstream media continue to illuminate primarily three representations: athlete, entertainer, and criminal. Historically this has presented a very limited view of African American cultural talents. This short chapter examines one media personality, Stuart Scott (cited as one of the top minorities in sport), who has helped to mainstream urban culture and hip-hop through his platform as a sportscaster. Stuart Scott is a graduate of the University of North Carolina and a leader for social change for the globalization of urban American culture. Through his work and passion for academics, Scott presents an alternative image to the dominant portrayals of African American males in mainstream media.

STUART SCOTT: THE POWER OF WORDS

A graduate of North Carolina and former high school student-athlete, Stuart Scott has influenced the mainstream culture of broadcasting and sport announcing like few in the game. Since 1995, Scott has integrated the most recent phrases, songs, and slang from urban culture into the booth. This is significant, considering the assimilation patterns of his predecessor. Beginning with Bryant Gumbel, representations of African Americans as sportscasters originated from the model of hyperassimilation rather than hyperacculturation. In other words, urban language, street vernacular, and hip-hop music were excluded from the tongues of all sportscasters. As hip-hop became more and more popular, so did the occupational opportunities of former African American athletes and entertainers and in general cultural expressions of popular culture that extended beyond mainstream "White" perspectives.

Stuart Scott has been largely responsible for the shift in sports commentating. The hip-hop and rap lyrics that he includes in his reporting lexicon and verbiage have spread like wildfire among his sportscaster colleagues. Scott's intentional pedagogical technique and cultural expression has led ESPN to continuously infuse hip-hop culture into many of the programs and has led to the hiring of more urban and hip-hop writers for *ESPN The Magazine*. It is not uncommon for *Sportscenter* to play hip-hop music in the background of the many video montages of sports highlights as a means of emphasizing the intensity of the games that are played and the plays that are made.

In fact, during the summer of 2004, ESPN presented a weeklong segment on how music and sports are intertwined. It is evident that music is a part of our human makeup and that certain genres of music have been able to transcend various cultures and generations. Hip-hop's infusion into mainstream sports entertainment has created an avenue and platform for the dissemination of knowledge about Black culture to society. As universal as sport is, anything that passes through the realms of sport and athletic competition indubitably becomes a staple in mainstream culture. Thus, we can argue that hip-hop, and more specifically African American culture, has become globally mainstreamed. The intersection of hip-hop and sport can be found through a multitude of visual images, and the interaction is two-way. Multiple hip-hop artists wear athletic jerseys, and athletes use hip-hop as background music in their athletic events. For example, at the NBA All-Star game, hip-hop artists were the entertainment. Commercials for the soft drink Sprite use LeBron James at a party with hip-hop music in the background, which is not a new ploy by the Coca-Cola Company. In the early 1990s they used the same format with Anfernee Hardaway and Grant Hill as spokesmen, and hip-hop music played in the background.

THE NEXT LEVEL

Scott began conducting his *Poetry Corner* as a segment of the *Sportscenter* show. In this segment, Scott summarizes the highlights of a particular game set to a melancholy mood of jazz in the background. He eloquently and rhythmically comments on the sport highlights while "spitting" ill (superior lyrics and stellar oration) rhymes and verses that walk the line between Phat Cat, night club, jazz poetry, and thought-provoking, lyrically masterminded, socially conscious rap lyric, all while talking about sports. Stuart Scott has even taken the lexicon of hip-hop into the academic realm by choosing to infuse hip-hop slang and sport stories into his 2001 commencement address at his alma mater, the University of North Carolina, Chapel Hill. In doing this, Stuart Scott has become one of the poster children for the concept of scholar-baller; he is a true icon of hip-hop and athletic verbal expression through his educational prowess (see chapter 19).

The next level for hip-hop culture is to bring to education the passion and energy that many global citizens have for hip-hop and sport—a scholar-baller mentality. The potential for social change when education becomes aligned with sport and entertainment may be best summed up by Def Jam artist Ludacris in a recent *ESPN the Magazine* article: "In rap it's about competition, and in the NBA it's about competition. Hip hop is about confidence and boldness, so when a player has a hip hop mentality it means he shows confidence and is creative" (ESPN, 2005, p. 31).

In the final analysis, how might a universal scholar-baller mentality influence American culture specifically? Kids would walk to school each day "rocking" their laptops. Student-athletes at universities would take pictures of their performances in the classroom and celebrate academic achievement with chest bumps and high fives. When someone asks, "Are you balling or falling?" the meaning of success would involve more than music and sports but also include life—especially the classroom. In other words, life and knowledge would be woven and embedded into the culture of entertainment, athletics, and the arts. This is the foundation and true spirit of hip-hop, "edutainment," and self-empowerment. Stuart Scott displays this alternative paradigm for education woven through hip-hop and sport and has even influenced another ESPN cultural creation with urban and hip-hop energy, *Quite Frankly* with NBA commentator Steven A. Smith. Smith's access to mainstream media is but one outcome of Stuart Scott's influence and legacy. This legacy of hip-hop expression is best described by the executive vice president of the Warner Music Group:

> We are all about overcoming the odds and making success happen for ourselves by being ourselves, only better. You could be a firefighter, a rapper, a banker, an athlete or a nurse. If you fight against the odds to realize a dream and be the best that you can be at whatever industry you choose, you are doing it the hip-hop way. (Liles & Marshall, 2005)

REFERENCES

ESPN (2005, February 21). Hip hop and sport. *ESPN the Magazine*, 45.

Jones, N. (2004). *God's Son*. New York: Sony.

Liles, K., & Marshall, S. (2005). *Make it happen: The hip-hop generation guide to success*. New York: Atria Books.

V

SPORT AND VIOLENCE

17

In the Name of Obedience: Overcoming the Damaging Myths about Hazing

Joe Gervais
University of Vermont

I knew something big was up the moment I saw Coach's face. As I entered his office on that fateful Friday afternoon, he was staring blankly out the window with a kind of dazed look on his face, a very unusual posture for him. Usually he is on the phone or busily catching up with correspondence. Now he was staring into space. Then he told me that our season was being canceled. The immediate sensation for me was that of the moment of initial descent in a high-speed elevator. It was a visceral effect that literally made me lightheaded. The season is over? In mid-January, with 15 games left? All the hard work, the hours and weeks and months of preparation down the tubes? Just when the team was coming together on the ice, when we were beginning to click, to feel confident, poised to win games and enter the stretch drive with some authority, in a year when conditions were ripe for success in our league. All for naught. What a waste of talent and effort!

Such was my state of mind at the moment I learned that the University of Vermont ice hockey team I was coaching (and had played for years earlier) had its 1999–2000 season canceled at the halfway point due to a major hazing incident. What began as a team initiation party in early October had led over the course of the ensuing months to graphically detailed allegations of hazing, a media frenzy, two lawsuits, investigations by the university and by Vermont's attorney general, the cancellation of our season, hostility all around, and deep psychic wounds for many.

I wrote the description above nearly 5 years ago, as part of my master's thesis about our lost season and athletic team hazing (Gervais, 2000), yet the echoes of that cold January day still reverberate for me. I recall the dread of seeing our team's fate splashed across newspapers, broadcasts, and Internet chat rooms across the United States and Canada. I can still see the embarrassment and shame etched on our players' faces as they plodded through the rest of that school year. I remember the anger and frustration and helplessness I felt as the situation spiraled out of control.

It was not until later that spring that I began to understand what had happened, what forces were at work to put us in that awful place. I had never experienced hazing or any other form of team initiation in high school or in college and did not have a clear sense of the dynamics driving it. I couldn't understand why our team members, the vast majority of whom I still consider to be upstanding individuals of sound moral character, would demean their teammates to such a degree and then blithely deny the seriousness of their actions. Through writing about our experience and researching the issue of hazing I began to sort through and understand some of the psychological, social, and cultural forces at work.

As I reread my thesis now, I hear echoes of what I have come to expect when I read or hear about other hazing incidents around the country. I see elements of defensiveness and denial, born out of a lack of understanding of what hazing is and how it works. I see a sharp focus on the complainant and his or her motives. I see a tendency in many parties to attribute blame as opposed to seeking understanding. I see young people who are so desperate to belong that they willingly submit to degrading and dangerous acts. I see many in our communities who defend or tolerate hazing as a time-honored rite of passage. After 5 years of reading, writing, and presenting on the issue of hazing to a variety of audiences, I have come to understand better the insidious nature of hazing and its lasting effects.

The journalist and academic Hank Nuwer (1990, 1999), one of the foremost experts on hazing in the United States, traces the origins of hazing—in the form of servitude, forced consumption of alcohol and other substances, and mean-spirited stunts and practical jokes—all the way back to ancient Greece. The earliest critics of hazing include Plato in ancient Greece, Augustine in fourth-century Carthage, and Justinian I, the sixth-century Byzantine emperor who outlawed the practice. Says Nuwer (1999),

During the twelfth century and for hundreds of years afterward, hazing was a common scourge that universities failed to eradicate. . . . University documents from the Middle Ages contain so many references to hazing and alcohol misuse among students that then, as now, the case can be made that the two practices were among the most serious social problems facing administrators and faculty on university campuses. (p. 93)

In 17th- and 18th-century America, personal servitude (or "fagging"—the term "hazing" would not come into common use on college campuses until after the Civil War, according to Nuwer) was a part of life at many college campuses. During this period, when the general purpose of higher education was to prepare leaders, there was an educational justification of these practices: the instillation of obedience. Before one can lead, went the thinking, one must learn to obey. With the rise of student organizations and societies at American colleges in the late 18th and early 19th centuries, there was a corresponding rise in hazing activity. Despite college administrators' efforts to curb these behaviors, hazing seems to have flourished. Today hazing remains a widespread and persistent problem. In fact, in what is perhaps the most compelling aspect of his research, Nuwer (1999) documents that in every year since 1970 hazing and alcohol have claimed the lives of at least one sorority or fraternity member in the United States. At the end of *Wrongs of Passage*, he includes a timeline of these tragedies, with the names of the deceased and details surrounding their deaths. Considering this tragic loss of life, Nuwer and many others wonder why these activities have not received more attention. Recently, however, as a number of hazing incidents (including ours) have become widely publicized, there has been a sharper focus on these practices.

Nuwer's work informs the most comprehensive study to date on athletic team hazing, produced by Alfred University with support from the National Collegiate Athletic Association (Hoover, 1999). Alfred's president created an investigative commission in response to an athletic hazing incident on its campus in 1998. When no empirical evidence could be found on athletic hazing, the commission recommended that Alfred conduct a national baseline study. The resulting 40-page report attempts to identify the scope of initiation rites in college athletics, the perceptions about the appropriateness of these activities, and strategies to prevent hazing on college campuses.

The Alfred study defines hazing as

> any activity expected of someone joining a group that humiliates, degrades,
> abuses or endangers, regardless of the person's willingness to participate.
> This does not include activities such as rookies carrying the balls, team par-
> ties with community games, or going out with your teammates, unless an at-
> mosphere of humiliation, degradation, abuse or danger arises. (Hoover,
> 1999, p. 8)

Among the many significant findings of the study are that 45% of the
respondents (2,027 student-athletes, men and women, representing all
NCAA sports and divisions) reported that they knew of, had heard of, or
suspected hazing on their campuses. Moreover, 80% of the student-
athletes reported that they were subjected to *questionable* (humiliating or
degrading), *alcohol-related* (drinking games or other high-risk drinking),
or *unacceptable* (dangerous or illegal activities) initiation behaviors that
would fall under the Alfred report's definition of hazing.

According to the Alfred study, this projects to over 255,000 college
student-athletes engaging in hazing behaviors nationally! Yet only 12% of
these same athletes report being hazed. A similar trend is documented
among high school students in a second national study conducted by Alfred University (Hoover, 2000). Among high school students who belong
to groups—not just sports teams, but music, academic, or social clubs, and
even church groups—nearly half (48%) reported being subjected to hazing activities. Based on this percentage, up to 1.5 million high school students in the United States are being subjected to some form of hazing each
year. Yet only 14% of these high school respondents report being hazed.

The large discrepancy between students' perceptions of hazing and their
behavior during initiations is instructive. One reason that misperceptions
about initiation activities may exist is that the rituals themselves are often
intensely secret affairs. The *last* place a student-athlete is going to talk
about an initiation party is in the presence of coaches or administrators who
have likely warned them against such activity. Nuwer (2000) suggests that
the practices are not only secretive, but deceptive as well. He explains,

> Nearly all acts of hazing involve deception. Hazers lie all the time to new-
> comers. First they lie about the severity of the hazing, which is intended to
> build fear in the initiate. Then as newcomers invest more and as the initia-

tion process nears an end, hazing escalates, always remaining secret. Hazers also lie to one another, to adults, and to themselves to rationalize that the brutal practices build group unity. (p. 26)

Another important reason for the general misunderstanding of hazing rituals has to do with the issue of consent. I find this issue to be a formidable obstacle in attempting to educate students about hazing. When I ask a group of students to define hazing in their own words, usually the very first comment is, "Hazing is when you are forced to do something you don't want to do." While it is true that hazing can involve coercion, it has become clear to me that many, if not most, instances of hazing involve voluntary participation. Many students willingly, even eagerly, take part in these initiations because of their desire to belong to the group and their genuine (but I believe mistaken) belief that these initiations lead to improved group functioning. But just because students agree to take part does not mean they know what they are getting themselves into, nor does it justify the activity. Our university's hazing policy, and those at many other institutions, clearly states that one's willingness to participate in hazing activities, even as an initiate, does not in any way change those activities' status as a banned activity. Increasingly, state laws are explicit about consent not being a valid defense against charges of hazing (*State Anti-Hazing Laws*, 2005). (See www.stophazing.org for a listing of hazing statutes from around the United States.)

What our players, and others who defend hazing practices, had not grasped was that in the context of a highly secretive event (especially one in which alcohol was to play a major role) consent may not be freely or fairly given by the initiates. As Nuwer (2000) explains,

When it comes to hazing, consent is meaningless. Victims give it without getting full disclosure from hazers and without really knowing what the initiations will involve. Hazings are unpredictable. Not even the hazers can say exactly how the initiation rituals will turn out. That's why when someone is hurt, a hazer is sure to respond that no one ever meant for *that* to happen. (p. 44)

Consent is but one of a number of popular *myths* operating to perpetuate hazing among sports teams. Others include the idea that hazing is just a set of harmless pranks, that hazing is an effective way to teach discipline, that as long as there is no ill intent a little hazing is OK, and, perhaps most prevalent of all, that hazing creates positive bonds between team members leading to improved team performance (*Myths & Facts*, 2005). (See www.stophazing.org for more on these myths.)

In my conversations about hazing with students here and elsewhere, most of these beliefs surface early in the discussion. Therefore, I find it useful to talk about the concept of myths with students as a way to begin the conversation about hazing. In particular, I point to the following definitions of *myth*: (1) a popular belief or assumption embodying the ideals and institutions of a society or segment of society, and (2) an unfounded or false notion (Merriam-Webster online). In other words, a myth is a set of beliefs or assumptions that may guide people's behavior, but that may or may not, in fact, be well-founded or true. I emphasize to students that the beliefs and assumptions that exist in regard to athletic initiations are *socially* constructed — that is, the myths are perpetuated over time by the people whose interests they serve. For example, it is in the interest of returning members of a team to have new members believe that hazing contributes to team unity because this makes the new members more willing to endure the initiation. By getting the rookies to submit to hazing, the veterans assert themselves atop the team hierarchy. In this way, beliefs and assumptions about hazing help preserve power relationships within the team that favor the veterans.

I need look no further than our own experience 5 years ago to see that these common beliefs about hazing do not operate in the way that many assume. What many called mere horseplay was, in fact, a very deliberate, demeaning, and potentially dangerous set of activities. While no one intended harm, a great deal of harm was done to a wide range of parties, including the team members themselves, who lost out on opportunities to perform on the ice and struggled to live down their role in the ordeal; coaches and administrators, who had no knowledge of the party yet had their integrity questioned and jobs threatened; our university, which lost income from canceled contests and suffered a severe public relations hit; competitor schools, whose athletes also lost opportunities to play and who lost considerable income due to canceled home events; hotels, restaurants, and bus companies who lost revenue due to canceled travel by various teams; right down to arena staff, who lost overtime wages that they usually earn on game night. An event intended to bring the team together was, in fact, extremely divisive not only for the team but for an entire community.

Why does hazing persist if these initiation practices do not work in the way that the myths suggest they do? When I ask students this question, they often reply that hazing is a tradition and that team members feel compelled to carry on tradition. This was the case with our hockey team. They assumed that hazing had been practiced forever in our program, when in actuality it had been happening in a recognizable form for no more than 6 or 7 years (as best as I can place it, based on conversations with former teammates and alumni). When I told our team members that I had not experienced hazing at Vermont, they didn't believe me. Such was the strength of their association of hazing with tradition.

Some students bring up this common justification for the continuation of initiation practices: "We had to do it as rookies. Now it's their turn." This attitude reflects a primary mechanism for the perpetuation (and, frequently, escalation) of hazing activities. Psychologist Michael Milburn has referred to this process as *emotional displacement*, the denial of emotional consequences of an unpleasant or traumatic experience that can lead to aggressive or punitive behaviors at some future point (Milburn, 2002). This may manifest itself as a team member transferring his or her anger at those who hazed toward new team members the following year. While this is not likely a conscious process, I think it may explain why a seemingly respectful person will deliberately debase a younger teammate when he or she had an unpleasant experience in the same context in the recent past.

Bandura (2002) refers to this willingness by generally moral persons to engage in inhumane behavior as *selective moral disengagement*. He suggests that moral functioning is governed less by abstract reasoning ("hazing is wrong") than by a more complex interplay between one's thoughts and feelings and one's social environment. In other words, our moral judgment can be strongly influenced by a particular social setting. A relatively clear-cut example of this process is that of a soldier at war. It is through the process of moral disengagement that a soldier can prepare himself mentally to kill an enemy. Killing is generally wrong, of course, but is morally justifiable in the soldier's mind in the particular setting of an ongoing war. In this way, seemingly inhumane conduct becomes more benign, acceptable, or even worthy.

You would be hard-pressed to find anyone who would describe joining an athletic team as a life-or-death situation. However, drawing on Bandura (2002), I see mechanisms of moral disengagement at work in hazing practices in the following ways: *Moral justification*—hazing is made socially worthy because it "creates bonds" and "builds unity"; *Euphemistic labeling*—even severe hazing is commonly referred to as "team building" and "initiation"; *Advantageous comparison*—athletes and coaches often make reference to "going to battle," and hazing is merely responsible preparation for this important initiative; *Displacement of responsibility*—the case of athletes saying, "We're just carrying on tradition" or coaches remaining intentionally uninformed; *Diffusion of responsibility*—groupthink, or athletes refusing to single out teammates and taking the punishment "as a team"; *Disregard/distortion of consequences*—athletes are very good at hiding pain, whether physical or emotional; *Dehumanization*—masks, costumes, dehumanizing language (rook, grunt, etc.), perception of "rookies" as less-than, sexist and homophobic attitudes and elements; and *Attribution of blame*—blame the victim! In conscious and unconscious ways, hazers rationalize inhumane behavior by granting it a worthy purpose and downplaying or ignoring its harmful effects. As Bandura suggests, "People suffer from the wrongs done to them regardless of how perpetrators justify their inhumane actions" (Bandura, 2002, p. 101).

Astute students will point to power relationships within the team as a driving force in the perpetuation of hazing. Recent research and commentary speak compellingly about sociocultural issues at work in the athletic environment. Messner and Sabo (1989), Robinson (1998), Allan and DeAngelis (2004), Lenskyj (2004), and others bring gender theory to the conversation about power relationships in athletic contexts. In various ways, these authors speak to the idea that sports culture in North America, from professional leagues right down through youth sport programs, both reflects and contributes to a traditional masculine culture where ideals of strength, physical and emotional endurance, and obedience are highly valued. These traits are not problematic in themselves. However, this "hypermasculine" sports culture also exhibits sexist and homophobic attitudes. According to Allan (2002), this can create "a climate in which violent and demeaning hazing practices are more likely to be tolerated and even considered beneficial" (para. 9). Young men especially are far more likely to acquiesce to aggressive initiations, even if they don't generally agree with them, because the consequences for refusing—being labeled as weak or feminine or gay or being isolated from the rest of the group—are perceived to be more damaging than the actual initiation.

Until the broader sports culture becomes more inclusive and less hostile to dissenting attitudes, changing young people's attitudes about hazing will be difficult. I am gratified that the number of our 1st-year student-athletes at Vermont who report having experienced hazing in high school is lower than it was 3 or 4 years ago. Prevention efforts at secondary schools may be having a positive effect. In addition, it seems that more students and coaches are speaking out against hazing. But there is still a persistent attitude among many students I encounter that some hazing is acceptable, as long as it doesn't "get out of hand." This worries me. Until this attitude changes, hazing will continue to occur, along with the unintended harmful consequences that we read about on a regular basis.

It is widely understood that hazing prevention efforts must be multifaceted. Successful prevention strategies must combine unambiguous policies that are well disseminated, clear mechanisms for anonymous reporting, and strong sanctions for known violations. Johnson and Miller (2004) and others emphasize the importance of replacing hazing rituals with alternative team-building activities such as ropes courses, community service projects, mentoring programs, outdoor recreation, and team meals and outings. Policy initiatives, enforcement, and alternative activities are all invaluable, but this is only the start. Most important, in my view, is to regularly engage students, coaches, and administrators in meaningful conversation about the nature of hazing and the culture that feeds it. Ultimately, only the athletes themselves can prevent hazing within their teams. But I believe that all of us in the world of athletics—coaches and administrators, especially—have a moral responsibility to create the social conditions that will empower the students to resist these insidious initiations.

I don't pretend to have all the answers as to how to do this, but at Vermont we are making an effort. We have implemented a Student-Athlete Code of Conduct that includes an antihazing agreement. We conduct individual team meetings to discuss the issues covered in the code, especially hazing. We offer leadership training for our team captains and other student-athlete leaders that emphasizes not only team dynamics but also mental health issues, communication, and conflict resolution. We also offer a mandatory semester-long Life Skills class for 1st-year student-athletes that addresses not only academic and athletic performance, but also health behaviors. We spend several weeks discussing moral leadership, and we practice decision-making skills in case studies about race, gender, alcohol, hazing, and other contemporary issues in athletics.

The basic appeal I make in regard to hazing to every group possible is this: On a practical level, hazing does not work in the way that the common myths would have us believe. On a moral level, do we really want to be responsible for harming someone else physically or emotionally, even unintentionally? And on a pragmatic level, in nearly all places today hazing is against institutional policy and more than likely illegal. Social condemnation of hazing, while not nearly complete, is growing. Are the perceived benefits, dubious as they are, really worth it?

REFERENCES

Allan, E. J. (2002). *Hazing and the making of men*. Retrieved January 3, 2004, from www.stophazing.org/gender.html.

Allan, E. J., & DeAngelis, G. (2004). Hazing, masculinity, and collision sports: (Un)becoming heroes. In J. Johnson & M. Holman (Eds.), *Making the team: Inside the world of sport initiations and hazing* (pp. 61–82). Toronto: Canadian Scholar's Press.

Bandura, A. (2002). Selective moral disengagement in the exercise of moral agency. *Journal of Moral Education, 32*, 2.

Gervais, J. (2000). *A lost season: The nature, culture, and prevention of athletic team hazing*. Unpublished master's thesis, University of Vermont, Burlington.

Hoover, N. (1999). *Initiation rites and athletics for NCAA sports teams: A national survey*. Retrieved November 8, 2005, from www.alfred.edu/sports_hazing/introduction.html.

Hoover, N. (2000). *Initiation rites in American high schools: A national survey*. Retrieved November 8, 2005, from www.alfred.edu/hs_hazing.html.

Johnson, J., & Miller, P. (2004). Changing the initiation ceremony. In J. Johnson & M. Holman (Eds.), *Making the team: Inside the world of sport initiations and hazing* (pp. 155–175). Toronto: Canadian Scholar's Press.

Lenskyj, H. J. (2004). What's sex got to do with it?: Analysing the sex + violence agenda in sport hazing practices. In J. Johnson & M. Holman (Eds.), *Making the team: Inside the world of sport initiations and hazing* (pp. 83–96). Toronto: Canadian Scholar's Press.

Merriam-Webster Online (2005). Retrieved November 8, 2005, from www.mw.com/dictionary/myth.

Messner, M. A., & Sabo, D. F. (1989). *Sex, violence and power in sports*. Freedom, CA: The Crossing Press.

Milburn, M. (2002, June). *The psychological underpinnings of hazing*. Presented at Hazing in Schools and Youth Groups conference, Chelsea, MA.

Myths & facts about hazing. (2005). Retrieved November 8, 2005, from www.stophazing.org/mythsandfacts.html.

Nuwer, H. (1990). *Broken pledges: The deadly rite of hazing*. Atlanta: Longstreet Press.

Nuwer, H. (1999). *Wrongs of passage: Fraternities, sororities, hazing and binge drinking*. Bloomington: Indiana University Press.

Nuwer, H. (2000). *High school hazing: When rites become wrongs*. New York: Grolier.

Robinson, L. (1998). *Crossing the line: Violence and sexual assault in Canada's national sport*. Toronto: McClelland and Stewart.

State anti-hazing laws. (2005). Retrieved November 8, 2005, from www .stophazing.org/laws.html.

StopHazing.org. (2005). www.stophazing.org.

18

Athletes, Role Models, and Criminals: What Do We Make of This Tripartite Mess?

Earl Smith and Angela Hattery
Wake Forest University

I am not a role model—parents should be role models.

—Charles Barkley, professional basketball player (Smith, 2003)

Charles Barkley, a former collegiate and professional basketball player and currently a color analyst for Fox TV, said in a widely broadcast Nike commercial in 1993 that he should not be seen as a role model for American youth (Smith, 2003). The commercial sparked controversy, for it came at a time when there was widespread consumer opinion that those in American society who are highly visible, including movie stars, athletes, politicians, and even daytime TV actors and actresses, should aspire to high standards of living, thus providing the country with role models. Furthermore, because we have christened them "role models," this sentiment extends to our collective belief that we can scrutinize and evaluate the degree to which these highly visible people meet this high standard. In his book *Wooden: A Lifetime of Observations and Reflections On and Off the Court*, legendary coach John Wooden (1997) argues,

> It's sad to hear someone like Charles Barkley say he's not interested in being a role model for anyone. When you get into a profession that puts you in the limelight you have accepted that responsibility. It comes with the job. (p. 137)

When Barkley made his pronouncement, others soon followed. Bo Jackson, the two-sport superstar (football and baseball), said much the same thing (Jackson, 1990). Quite succinctly, he solemnly warned the audience, "I am not a role model."

This chapter is about role models, athletes, and the perils of leadership in American society today. It is clear that there are confusing messages being sent to sport fans, especially the youth in America, from the athletes themselves and from others about the role of athletes in modern society. Part of that message is that because of their high profiles, athletes can and should be role models for our youth. From Tiger Woods to Mia Hamm to Allen Iverson, the media portray these women and men in a star-studded spotlight—day and night—and their images are often used to send implicit and explicit messages about everything from buying your next pair of Nike shoes to what type of beer to drink to saying No to drugs, sex, and cigarettes.

The problem is that there are mixed messages being sent. Many of the same athletes whose images are used to send messages via their corporate sponsors behave in ways diametrically opposed to those messages, on the playing fields and off. Kobe Bryant is one example of this. Bryant, a 19-year-old post–high school basketball star, entered the adult world of the National Basketball Association (NBA), a world not unfamiliar to him as his father, Joe "Jelly Bean" Bryant, was also a professional player. Until recently, Bryant was viewed by many as a clean-cut, good kid from the "right side of the tracks." He speaks several languages, grew up abroad in Italy (not in a housing project), and despite not going to college (he was drafted to the NBA out of high school) he could have gained admission to elite private institutions based on his SAT scores, not just his basketball skills. He seems an ideal choice for a "role model."

Yet during the summer of 2003 and for the entire next year, Kobe Bryant's personal life began to quickly unravel. He was charged with felony sexual assault, and the criminal justice system prepared for the trial. Bryant's case exemplifies the issues raised in this chapter: While on trial for felony sexual assault, Kobe Bryant continued to run up and down the court, making baskets and flashing his contagious smile. In what other arena than sport would Americans encourage young people to watch and emulate a man on television who was charged with a *serious* crime? Guilty or not, this is a man who had sex with a woman he had known for 45 minutes, and we continue to encourage young people to wear his jersey and emulate him, continuing to believe he could not be guilty because he seems like such a nice guy, a next-door neighbor, a "role model." This is the issue that we explore in this chapter.

The issue raised here is not so much a discussion of whether highly visible people should be christened role models, whether they choose to be or not. Rather, we question the prudence of elevating these mostly young, mostly African American, mostly men to the status of "role model" when in fact many of them live in a world of easy access to sex and drugs and a world where elaborate spending is the norm. Many of them flaunt multimillion-dollar homes, sport cars, and jewelry, a life, if you will, of conspicuous consumption. If that isn't enough to raise concern, many also engage in felonious behavior. When our young men and women watch Kobe and Shaq on television, the athletes look like nice guys playing a game. Yet, in fact, both have been involved in illicit if not illegal sexual behavior. How can we reconcile the "role model" on the court with the man in the mug shot?

Currently, sport may be considered to be in a mode of self-destruction. Self-destruction is not a far-fetched term to use here. After the infamous "basket brawl" in Detroit on November 19, 2004, in a game between the Indiana Pacers and Detroit Pistons, it seems reasonable. In this instance, a fight erupted on the court that then spilled into the stands. Fans and players brawled, and the Pacers' Ron Artest was suspended for the rest of the season. By examining several instances of athletes running afoul of the law, we explore this self-destruction by uncovering the intricacies of the three-part relationship among athletes, role models, and criminals. We begin with a brief review of the literature followed by a nuanced analysis of the events surrounding several troubled athletes. We conclude the chapter with a discussion of ways to provide real role models who are assets rather than deficits. We believe taking these suggestions to heart may begin to save the institution of sport from the type of self-destruction toward which it is heading.

THE CENTRAL PROBLEMATIC OF THE ROLE MODEL THESIS

We believe that the role model concept is pernicious. The role model thesis is a part of the double standard that African Americans are held to when competing against Whites in all aspects of life, and one of the classic sites for this competition, and thus the application of the double standard is the field of sports.

For us, role model as it is used in sport is the belief that a highly visible, well paid, (African American) athlete, because of his or her athletic prowess, can influence the day-to-day behavior of America's youth. The extension of the thesis is that by being on TV, doing a pass-through at a local hospital or soup kitchen, these athletes will provide an aura that will rub off on the less fortunate.

The thesis is applied most often to African American men, for it is they who are seen as lost to the world yet simultaneously dominating the visible world of sport that the American public and American sport fans see. Almost never do you see the thesis applied to White athletes and White youth. Larry Bird was never asked nor expected to be a role model to anyone.

The thesis is false. *Why?* First, these athletes are so far removed from day-to-day reality that they exist in rarefied space; they live in gated communities, far away from the very youth they are supposed to be helping. Second, they are not athletes but athlete-entertainers similar to movie stars who live in surreal communities and live shallow, often broken lives (e.g., Elizabeth Taylor: many, many marriages and just as many divorces). The thesis is also false in that many of the highly visible are criminals, from O. J. Simpson to Allen Iverson to Kobe Bryant. Would a White family want a criminal for a "friend"? Would they admire a criminal even if only in the distant world of TV land? No!

Yet African American youth are sold this lie every day: that their way out of hopelessness and despair is with a ball. However, in reality only about 1,700 African American men make a living playing some type of sport. We believe the role model thesis does not belong anywhere in our class-based society (augmented by gender and race), for Horatio Alger has long been dead.

Perhaps what makes this thesis so compelling to Whites is that it creates an image of the Black man that is diametrically opposed to the images that we are fed in the media. Though few African American men make a living playing sports, that is the only positive image we ever see. In contrast, though only a small percentage of African American men commit violent crimes, that is the only other image we ever see. When Whites, especially men, are depicted in the media, we see the whole continuum from heinous terrorists such as Timothy McVeigh to the president of the United States. Thus, for Whites, the range of images we have is large and diverse. In contrast, because the only African American men we

ever see are either criminals or sport heroes, it makes sense that the sport
hero becomes the image for the role model.

Yet any set of contradictory images like these is inherently dangerous
for a variety of reasons. First, it leads to the development of dangerous
stereotypes for Whites, who believe that African American men are of
only two types: the good and the bad. Second, this contrast in images
can also serve to limit the development of talent in the African American community because the only options for young men appear to be
"thugs" or athletes. Finally, it sets up an inherent set of mutually exclusive roles: African American men are either bad ("thugs") or they are
good ("athletes"). What happens when some of them are both? It not
only disrupts the social construction, but it also begs us to question the
utility of pigeonholing African American men in this diametrically opposed system.

It is important to note that the issue of whether athletes should be role
models did not start with Charles Barkley. Discussions about role models
date back to the 1940s, with the development of the role model thesis. The
role model thesis originated in several places in the 1940s, but it most directly comes from the doctoral dissertation by Herbert Hyman in the area
of social psychological research at Columbia University. While his dissertation, *The Psychology of Status* (1942), did not cause a stir at the time,
today we know that he put in place our understanding of the reference
group. A reference group is any group to which we compare ourselves. A
reference group can be our classmates or colleagues, but it can also include members of the culture who are so high in profile that we feel like
we know them and thus can compare our lives with theirs.

For our purposes, we will define "role model" as an individual whose
behavior in a particular role provides a pattern or model upon which another bases behavior in performing the same role. Like reference individuals more generally, role models can be a source of norms and values and
serve as standards for comparison.

This definition is ours, but the general tenor of it comes from Columbia University sociologist Harriet Zuckerman (1988). It helps place in
context just what is meant by a term that has caught on and is now a part
of common parlance or the everyday language of the street. A more suc-
cinct definition comes from the world of sport and legendary coach John

Wooden (1997), who put it a bit differently: "A role model is someone that those who love you would want you to be like" (p. 157).

The main problem with applying the role model thesis to athletes is that it is taken at face value. Many young African American males who participate in sports are very much aware of the role model thesis because of the overplay of quotes such as Barkley's on the 24-hour sport and news networks such as ESPN and CNN. When it is applied to sport, it is clear that these young people imitate those athletes that they have come to love in terms of their athletic prowess, including the often brash Barkley.

One unscientific indicator of this imitation is the sporting of player jerseys. If you walk through any mall (suburban or rural), you will see young people, primarily men, of any ethnic group wearing the jerseys and shoes of their favorite players in football, basketball, hockey, and soccer. Many of these young African American males (and now females) see the glory of athletic achievement that comes in the form of money, celebrity, privilege, and media notoriety, but fail to see the need for talent, integrity, hard work, and just plain luck in making it in the world of commercial sport. (For a more in-depth discussion of the issue see Michael Sokolove, 2005. In this major magazine article Sokolove lays out the problems inherent in professional basketball as inner-city players come to the game having learned little of the fundamentals of good, sound basketball. He attributes this to the ESPN "highlight reel" that shows only the most dazzling individual play, and in basketball it is the dunk.)

Perhaps at one time in history, athletes as a class would have been as good a place as any to look for role models. In those days, before 24-hour-a-day television and the need of the media to entertain instead of inform (Herbert, 2005), young people had access to role models in sport as well as politics, science, education, and religion. Today, the news is dominated by crime and entertainment (Glassner, 2000), and thus sports figures are imbued with the qualities of leaders, when in fact there is no correlation between athletic prowess and the kinds of qualities we associate with role models and leaders. For example, at a recent conference on sport sociology, some asked if we should expect Michael Jordan to pick up the mantle of civil rights leadership. Why? Why should Michael Jordan or Bill Cosby or Puff Daddy be encouraged to take up that mantle any more than Martin Luther King or Henry Louis Gates should play basketball or make rap videos? This confusion between high profile and of good character gets blurred in the media. This would not be a problem if people were critical consumers. But it is pretty clear that as a culture, we are not critical. Thus, these images of professional athletes as role models are not only unfair and misplaced but can also have dire consequences. The reality is that when we look at behavior *off* the fields of play, the question arises, would those who love us want us to behave like Mark Chmura, Kirby Puckett, Tonya Harding, Mike Danton, Jennifer Capriati, Kobe Bryant, O. J. Simpson, or Latrell Sprewell? We are confident that the answer to that question is a resounding *no*!

LEADERSHIP, ROLE MODELS, AND ILLICIT BEHAVIOR

The tension noted in this chapter created by the difference in behavior on and off the playing field of individuals who have been elevated to the rank of "role model" is evident outside the institution of sport as well. Many sport sociologists argue that sport is both a reflection of and an influence on the larger society. It is a microcosm of social relations as they play out in other institutions and in the society at large. A brief illustration from outside the world of sport will serve to illustrate this idea.

President Bill Clinton and NBA Star Kobe Bryant

What, might you ask, do Bill Clinton and Kobe Bryant have in common? In terms of our analysis, they have much in common. In 1998, Monica Lewinsky, a 23-year-old intern in the White House, charged that then President Bill Clinton had sex with her in the Oval Office. In the summer of 2003, an 18-year-old woman in Eagle, Colorado, charged that she had been raped by Kobe Bryant. Both men had sex outside their marriages. Both men engaged in carefully scripted and publicly televised "explanations" of what did not happen, although both changed their stories over time. In January 1998 Bill Clinton said, "I did not have sexual relations with that woman—Monica Lewinsky." In the midst of a grand jury hearing, on August 17, 1998, Bill Clinton confessed that he did have sex "with that woman." The nation saw the confession on national TV in September 1998. On July 18, 2003, Kobe Bryant, on national television, holding his wife, Vanessa's, hand, said, "I am innocent of the charges filed today. I did not assault the woman who is accusing me. . . . I made the mistake of adultery." Yet 6 months later, Kobe Bryant was charged with felony sexual assault, and though the criminal case has been dropped, at the time of this writing, Bryant is currently facing a civil suit.

None of us will ever know what transpired between President Bill Clinton and White House intern Monica Lewinsky, or between Kobe Bryant and the young female hotel clerk in Eagle, Colorado. What we do know is that both men had sex outside their marriages. And what we know is that in Clinton's case he had sex with a very young woman whom he "supervised," and in Bryant's case, he had sex with a woman he had known for only 45 minutes. It is difficult to imagine that most Americans would want their children to grow up to behave this way, yet the attention on both men's "off-court" behavior eventually waned, and they both returned to their status as "role models," based largely, we suppose, on their "on-court" successes.

Why compare Bill Clinton and Kobe Bryant? First, the antics engaged in by Bill Clinton are not new, for in fact they are part of the historic fabric of the U.S. presidency. And for the most part, White men of power and privilege, White men who have been designated role models, have been able to ride out these sorts of antics. (John Kennedy, for example, remains one of the most popular U.S. presidents of all time.) The antics of Kobe Bryant, however, are new. For in our not so distant past, a Black man accused of sexually assaulting a White woman would have been lynched, guilty or not. So what has happened? Among other things, through the conduit of sport, some African American men have been elevated to the position of role model, and thus they are immune to or protected from being cast as the usual stereotypes even when they engage in behavior that has such a strong and potent history. We argue here that given the possible roles for African American men—thug versus athlete—Kobe Bryant has always been a role model, and thus he is able to retain the worship of his fans. Think for a moment, for example, about how many young and not so young men you saw wearing Kobe Bryant jerseys while his trial for felony sexual assault was under way!

ENDORSEMENTS AND THE ATHLETE ROLE MODEL

Fueling the role model thesis are money and the power of advertising and the media. And while there is much talk about the explosion of athlete salaries, with many stars in the NFL, NBA, and MLB making in excess of $10 million per year on multiyear contracts, the real money is to be made in endorsements. The role that product endorsements play is important both to the athlete (as this is how he—or rarely she—will make the most money) and to the culture, as the endorsements not only sell products but also promote powerful individual athlete images: the way the athlete is perceived.

Many products these days are being pushed by high-profile athletes: from cookies to cars to underwear to milk to shaving cream and soap to chewing tobacco and of course McDonald's hamburgers. We see Michael Jordan, Serena Williams, Kobe Bryant, Charles Barkley, Tiger Woods, and other easily recognizable high-profile athletes selling these goods. Some of the corporations even "sponsor" athletic events, such as Buick, which sponsors golf tournaments in which their pitchman Tiger Woods plays.

For at least the last 3 decades advertisers have recognized the enormous power high-profile athletes have in the effort to sell countless products. In the 1970s, for example, O. J. Simpson, who was considered one of the best athletes of all time to play the game of football and who had "crossover appeal" (see especially Patterson, 1998), was used in advertising campaigns to sell everything from rental cars to orange juice. More importantly, however, these advertising campaigns sold the image of a "good" African American man, an African American man who was indeed worthy of the title, role model. Recall how many admirers of O. J. lined the highway where he was embroiled in a high-speed police chase holding signs that read, "Go Juice Go!" Though O. J. did suffer a fall from grace, nevertheless his fall was a cushioned one (see especially Johnson & Roediger, 1997). A decade after he was tried for the murder of his ex-wife, and a decade after the world learned he was a batterer, he continues to inspire young running backs. He has even been rewelcomed in the University of Southern California football locker room to give inspirational speeches before home games. Who among us would hope our sons will grow up to be batterers and accused wife-murderers, even if they can also run the football in ways no one has ever seen before? Yet we continue to disconnect O. J.'s on-the-field behavior from his off-the-field antics, just as we did with President Kennedy.

We argue here that in the current state of binary oppositional categorizations of African American men (thug and athlete), even these lines are beginning to blur. For example, more recently, advertisers seem to be less sensitive about negative associations with their spokespeople, at least certain kinds of negative associations. In fact, some "negative" images are actually considered to be "positive" when associated with certain athletes and with the selling of certain products. Perhaps Latrell Sprewell provides the best illustration of this point. Latrell Sprewell has always had a sort of "thug" reputation. Then, in 1997, Sprewell choked coach P. J. Carlisiemo during practice. He was suspended for the rest of the season and fined for the assault. Compared to the "clean-cut" images of his peers, athletes such as Kobe Bryant, one might assume Sprewell would not get many endorsements. Not true! Just a few years after reentering the league, Sprewell, who now plays for the Minnesota Timberwolves, earns $15 million per season and has a new shoe named after him.

Dada Footwear is the Los Angeles–based shoe company that made the flashy metallic shoes Chris Webber wore in the all-star game two years ago. With less than 0.5% in market share, Dada has the shoe that figures to turn some heads on and off the court. They're called the Sprees—named after their endorser. The shoe features a to-scale model of the custom spinning rims on Sprewell's car—with the small wheels appearing on the outside ankle of the shoe.

In contrast, San Antonio Spur Tim Duncan, a repeat league MVP, a consistent member of the NBA All-Star Team, and World Championship ring holder, has almost no advertising endorsements. If athletic prowess sells shoes, then why does a player like Duncan have little to no advertising appeal? We think it is because he is not a thug.

CONCLUSION

When "role models" such as Kobe Bryant and Ruben Patterson can negotiate multiyear, multimillion-dollar contracts while they are on trial for felony sexual assault and other "off-court" antics, something is terribly wrong with our capitalist economy. When Kobe Bryant can have a judge organize the trial schedule around Mr. Bryant's game schedule, something is wrong with our system of justice! Yet, when athletes make more in endorsements than in salary, what good is a suspension or a fine in curtailing these aberrant behaviors? One way to end the disastrous behavior of athletes is to stop promoting them in public spaces. When a true athlete such as Tim Duncan cannot get big-time endorsements because he is not mean enough, that tells us something about what the problem is.

One of the outcomes of being in the spotlight is that people take notice of what you do both on and off the court, fair or unfair. If athletes such as O. J. Simpson, Kobe Bryant, and Jennifer Capriati (who was arrested for drug possession while at the peak of her teenage tennis career) are to be role models or people whom we want those we love to be like, namely our children, then we must no longer turn a blind eye to their behavior off the court. Wilt Chamberlain and Magic Johnson may not have broken any laws by sleeping with literally thousands of women (Wilt claims to have slept with 20,000 women or 1.2 per day), but their casual approach to sexual intimacy, having sex with women they didn't even know, is not the type of behavior most Americans would like to encourage in their young sons and daughters. In fact, based on the outcome of the 2004 presidential election, Americans as a whole seem to be more conservative on sexual issues (abortion and gay marriage) today than a decade ago.

How, then, can we explain our idolizing of men such as Kobe Bryant? As a culture, we have chosen to ignore their off-the-court antics, as if the athlete's entire reputation as a person is based only on the athletic prowess that he displays on the field of play. And this goes all the way back to the beginning of sport, with men such as Babe Ruth and Ty Cobb. Until we, as a culture, hold athletes to the same standard of behavior that we hold each other, until we, as a culture, stop ignoring their off-court antics, we will continue to raise our sons and daughters to be "like Mike." As long as we continue to confuse the qualities it takes to play basketball with the qualities it takes to be a leader, or a role model, then we will continue to ignore the violent behavior of athletes such as Ruben Patterson, and we will continue to dismiss the violence that young athletes participate in, including gang rapes like that in Glenridge, New Jersey. And, as long as we ignore their criminal cases while they are negotiating their contracts and continuing to come into our homes via TV advertising endorsements, we will continue to see the proliferation of violence, sexual assault, drug use, illicit sex (see especially Jeff Benedict's book *Out of Bounds*, which details the sexual assaults, domestic violence, drug use, and illicit sex of NBA players from Wilt Chamberlain to Kobe Bryant), and even homicide (for example, Mike Danton, a professional hockey player, who arranged a "hit" on his lover and is now in prison).

As a society we need to do better, not worse. We should do more, not less.

REFERENCES

Benedict, J. (2004). *Out of bounds: Inside the NBA's culture of rape, violence, and crime.* New York: HarperCollins.

Glassner, B. (2000). *The culture of fear: Why Americans are afraid of the wrong things.* New York: Basic Books.

Herbert, B. (2005). *Promises betrayed: Waking up from the American dream.* New York: Times Books.

Hyman, H. (1942). *The psychology of status.* PhD Dissertation. Columbia University.

Jackson, B. (with Schaap, D.). (1990) *Bo knows Bo.* New York: Doubleday.

Johnson, L., & Roediger, D. (1997). Hertz, don't it?: Becoming colorless and staying Black in the crossover of OJ Simpson. In T. Morrison (Ed.), *Birth of A Nation'hood: Gaze, Script, and Spectacle in the O. J. Simpson Case* (pp. 197–240). New York: Pantheon Books.

Patterson, O. (1998). *Rituals of blood.* Washington, DC: Civitas.

Sokolove, M. (2005, February 13). Beware the dunk. *New York Times Sunday Magazine*, p. 42.

Smith, E. (2003). *The African American student-athlete.* Paper presented at the 27th Annual Porter L. Fortune Symposium, University of Mississippi, Oxford, MI. Sponsored by the Department of History & the Center for the Study of Southern Culture. Symposium Topic: "Race and Sport: The Struggle for Equality On and Off the Field."

Wooden, J. (with Jamison, S.). (1997). *Wooden: A lifetime of observations and reflections on and off the court.* New York: Contemporary Books.

Zuckerman, H. (1988). The role of the role model: The other side of a sociological coinage. In H. J. O'Gorman (Ed.), *Surveying Social Life: Papers in Honor of Herbert H. Hyman* (pp. 119–144). Middletown, CT: Wesleyan University Press.

VI

SPORT AND SCHOOLS

19

The Scholar-Baller Approach: A Cultural Map for Academic Success in America

C. Keith Harrison, Arizona State University; Eddie Comeaux, University of California, Los Angeles; Jean A. Boyd, Arizona State University; Cliff J. Parks Jr., Long Beach Unified School District; and Dave Heikkinen, Eastern Michigan University

Feature films such as *Varsity Blues, Friday Night Lights*, and *Coach Carter* all project the American socialization of student-athletes in high school with aspirations of matriculating to college with the dream of playing professional sport in America. These representations of sport in American society enable educators, youth, teachers, coaches, and fans to examine the values that sport and society teach through athletics and other cultural organizations (Coakley, 2004; Sammons, 1994).

As high school and college athletics become increasingly commercialized with a greater urgency to produce winning seasons, secondary and postsecondary institutions are currently facing the challenge of addressing the increasing lack of academic productivity among some populations. Specifically, the student-athlete culture in higher education possesses some subcultures that underachieve educationally (Bowen & Levin, 2003). This issue, compounded by the recent NCAA Academic Reform Movement (ARM), requires new *cultural* paradigms to be explored that challenge the student-athlete to apply the competitive spirit beyond the game, in the classroom, and in the development of life skills (Brand, 2003). Hence, the purpose of this chapter is to (1) define and explain the implicit and explicit theory and practice of scholar-baller as a unique identity and lifestyle of education, sport, and entertainment; (2) present a collegiate case study of the scholar-baller success at one university; (3) apply to interscholastic sports the scholar-baller ideology;

and (4) contextualize the meaning of emblems and patches in American culture in relation to the scholar-baller patch and the future of this "tipping point" in society.

SCHOLAR-BALLER

C. Keith Harrison, director of the Paul Robeson Research Center for Academic and Athletic Prowess, first introduced the term "scholar-baller" in his continued discussion on Paul Robeson's incredible commitment to education and sport (Harrison, 1995; Harrison, 1996; Harrison, 1997; Harrison as cited in NCAA, 1998; Harrison & Lampman, 2001). While on the surface one could argue that "scholar-baller" is synonymous with student-athlete, we would like to expand upon this notion. We propose to consider "scholar-baller" as an innovative concept for repackaging the current model of intercollegiate athletics, creating an identity and mindset among students in terms of their perceptions about education, sport, and occupational aspirations.

In order to better understand and conceptualize "scholar-baller," we must first examine the term. "Scholar" is a term used to describe an individual who possesses academic prowess or commitment to education. For example, Paul Robeson, a 1919 graduate of Rutgers University, possessed the intellectual capacity and political awareness to earn the status of Phi Beta Kappa scholar, valedictorian of his class, gifted orator, and legendary political icon. Robeson represented a "scholar" on many levels, including his law degree from Columbia University and his numerous speeches and lectures throughout the world.

Moreover, the urban vernacular "baller" is an image that resonates with individuals of all origins and has taken on global meanings. For the purposes of our discussion, we define "baller" as a term that can be used as a noun, adjective, or verb ("ballin'") signifying aspects of achievement or success. For example, an individual who is considered a high achiever in any task or vocation (usually sport and entertainment) could be labeled a "baller." The "baller" label has until recently been excluded from such spaces as academe and other traditional mainstream arenas, and a baller is only one of several identities that develop in urban spaces that deal with cultural stresses such as unemployment, violence, poverty, and hopelessness (Kelley, 1997). To borrow a street term for someone who excels in

entertainment, business, sports, or life in general, being a baller means being successful. In today's world, people, especially young people, view a
baller as someone who has gone to the top, won the biggest prize, and just
simply made it. Ask a room full of football players, "Which one of you is
a baller?" and all the hands in the room reach sky high. It's a concept
young players understand and embrace.

Together, scholar-baller is a concept that promotes the willingness of
students to accept the challenge of harmonizing academics and athletics.
At a pragmatic level, scholar-baller is about cultivating education, sport,
and entertainment consumption into one lifestyle. As utilized by scholars
such as Taylor (1999), this concept suggests that sport and athletic principles (i.e., character, determination, perseverance, and commitment)
should be applied to academics, which would improve the motivation of
student-athletes in the classroom. This motivation for academic excellence is enhanced through popular culture and the lifestyles of today that
shape youth and young adults (music, film, athletics, and the arts). This is
a key aspect of hip-hop culture's influence on Thinkman, who wears a
backwards cap, biceps-hugging T-shirt, and baggy jeans as he puts pen to
paper in a collegiate-style desk chair (see Figure 19.1). The goal of this
representation is to affirm scholastic excellence, not inhibit it.

IMPLICATIONS FOR PRACTICE:
A COLLEGIATE-LEVEL CASE STUDY

The researchers and scholar-baller intervention strategy have set forth to
impact first the mindset of student-athletes, and second, matriculation and
graduation patterns, while addressing the development of the critical life
skills of student-athletes. Pilot implementation of the scholar-baller program began in August 2001 at one major Division I institution with its
football program.

Student-athletes on the football team were first introduced to the concept
of scholar-baller during fall camp, prior to the 2001 season. The team was
asked how many of them considered themselves to be "ballers"; approximately 85 out of 105 raised their hands. When asked how many of them saw
themselves as "scholar-ballers," only several raised their hands. Typically, a
portion of "revenue sport" student-athletes tends to focus narrowly on their

athletic prowess while trivializing their academic and social development experiences in college.

However, with the introduction of the scholar-baller concept, it was immediately evident that this concept resonated with the student-athletes who participated in revenue and major college sports, in this case football. Within the next several days, multiple student-athlete football players approached both the head football coach and the football academic counselor and communicated sincere interest in attaining scholar-baller status and recognition. The football student-athletes at this institution were challenged to employ their competitive spirit in the arenas of academics and social development. A series of strategies were utilized to establish a consistent message that subpar or even average performance in academics was simply unacceptable.

Some of these strategies included

- helping student-athletes examine their social and self-identities to reinforce that they were complete human beings with a multiplicity of abilities beyond athletics
- exposing student athletes to scholar-baller icons (i.e., Paul Robeson, Ralph Bunche, Vince Carter, and others)
- displaying academic goals for the football program in the locker room alongside football goals
- engaging in an academic team competition in which subteams of football student-athletes competed against each other

Additionally, the head football coach and assistant coaches embraced the scholar-baller term and soon incorporated it into some of their pedagogical vernacular, including utilizing the term in memorandums and letters to the team during the off-season, encouraging academic excellence during team meetings, and including it in the player's manual. More importantly, an incentive and disincentive system was established that rewarded the student-athletes for high performance in the classroom. This same system parallels internally what the NCAA academic reform movement is attempting to do externally with its new incentive/disincentive system to increase academic achievement and graduation rates.

A scholar-baller was defined as a person in a given academic year who earned a fall, spring, or cumulative GPA of 3.00 or above. First-year scholar-ballers earned a T-shirt. After completion of the academic team competition during their 2nd year, the top three academic teams earned sweat suits that lauded them as "Scholar-ballers—Competing in the Classroom." Needless to say, this was very well received and reinforced that it really was a benefit to compete and perform well in school. Scholar-ballers were acknowledged by the head football coach at the beginning of each semester, and at the end of the most recent term, the scholar-ballers were rewarded with a steak dinner, hosted by the athletic director. In fall 2004, football student-athletes who achieved scholar-baller status were recognized with the ThinkMan logo jersey patch, the first known time in the history of Division I football that academic prowess had been acknowledged on the jersey.

In the 3 years this program has been implemented, there have been significant increases in team cumulative GPA, fall team GPA, freshman cohort GPA, and retention rates of student-athletes. For example, retention rates skyrocketed to 80% for the three classes that have entered under the coaching staff. The number of football student-athletes earning a GPA of 3.0 rose from figures in the teens in 2000 to 38 in 2004. Another shift occurred with decreases in the number of football student-athletes on probation, which went from 5 after spring semester in 2000 to 8 after spring semester 2001, to 0 in 2004. The number of those disqualified was also 0 in 2004, and the number of student-athletes ineligible to compete due to academics plummeted to only 1 out of 70 recruited student-athletes from 2001 to 2003. Finally, 33 student-athletes earned B or better averages after the 2004 football season and academic semester. Student-athletes in this football program understood from day 1 that they had entered a culture in which it is not okay to do the minimum work required to pass classes and remain eligible. Academic excellence has become the verbal and written goal of most players in the school culture. The following are some quotes and narratives from 2004 scholar-baller participants (N = 28) who were interviewed (open-ended survey question that was transcribed) about becoming the first NCAA Division I school to acknowledge academic success on the front of a football jersey:

> It feels good because of the stereotypes that have been set that f-ball players can't be smart but society always changes. Happy to represent [support the program's image and concept] by wearing the patch.

It feels good to be recognized for something positive. Many people think of football players as dumb jocks so this was a way to prove that they were wrong. It gave me something to push for.

I feel it is a great honor to wear this patch. The patch is not about separating yourself from others, yet its purpose is to glorify those who work hard in all phases of life. This is a motivation for those who do not have one. I think the patch is a great idea and should be continued through the years.

At first I didn't like the idea of the razzing we would get on the field. After the first game I played in, no one said anything. After realizing that we are the only school to do so, I felt proud to have the patch on my jersey. My mom also feels that way, more so because she always preaches school to me.

IMPLICATIONS FOR PRACTICE AT THE HIGH SCHOOL LEVEL

As implied by the scholar-baller, it is assumed that this paradigm will serve as a resource for academic and athletic success for all student-athletes (scholar-ballers) at any educational institution across the nation. Because this model is being used at the intercollegiate level and has been proven to be successful, it can be assumed that it would be effective at the high school level. However, the model would have to be flexible enough to fit the needs of any interscholastic program in which implementation would take place.

There are many things to consider related to the implementation of the scholar-baller program at the high school level, many of which have already been discussed in this chapter. Other aspects to be considered in the implementation process of scholar-baller would include the socioeconomic status, ethnic background, demographic region, and overall morale of the students at the particular high school in which implementation of the scholar-baller would take place.

Implementation Process of the Scholar-Baller at the High School Level

The scholar-baller implementation process and intervention begin with high school coaches, administrators, counselors, and teachers involved in a life skills curriculum designed to challenge student-athletes to create powerful visions for their future. The curriculum covers content standards such as (1) self-identity, (2) the competitive spirit, (3) the scholar-baller paradigm, (4) purpose/vision/mission and goals, (5) decision-making system, (6) living the scholar-baller way. The goal of scholar-baller would be to create an environment on high school campuses that will allow student-athletes as well as other students to view education and athletics as means to success. The scholar-baller will empower student-athletes to be better prepared for the rigors of college and the many challenges that it has to offer; grade point averages will increase, and parents will be empowered to support their children not only athletically but also academically. Finally, the scholar-baller will develop critical life skills and give student-athletes the ability to make positive future decisions relating to career and other aspects of life.

THE SCHOLAR-BALLER PATCH: THE NEW BADGE OF "COOLNESS"

The Motivational Entertainment Educational (MEE) Report (1992) found that urban youth ages 13–18 (N = 387) spent most of their disposable income on clothes, food, music, shoes, and jewelry. This finding has significant implications. One, urban youth set the trends for popular culture, and hip-hop culture is currently one of the most consumed products and commodities in American society (Boyd, 2004; Dyson, 2003). Specifically, marketing, fashion, language, and urban styles in general permeate the most mainstream cultural spaces (Simmons & George, 2002). In addition, athletic identity is a valued status symbol in secondary education. Thus, the desire to be "cool" often involves the attainment of some of the material items found in the MEE Report. Through the previously mentioned cultural facts about urban styles and athletics in secondary education, we hope to see the scholar-baller logo become a "tipping point" and trend (Gladwell, 2000) in American culture. We think this is possible if scholar-baller continues to become aligned, associated with, and embedded in social things youth and young adults value the most.

The essence of the main scholar-baller logos, such as the ThinkMan and ThinkWoman logos, are of a student-athlete sitting at a desk studying—representations that are powerful in their simplicity, with or without additional wording.

These logos, when applied to a piece of apparel, are meant to be a badge of honor that can be proudly worn, a statement of the acceptance of the scholar-baller ideals and the related accomplishments made by each individual. The scholar-baller logos and their related marks and graphics will continue to evolve with recognition, acceptance, specific individual or team needs, and the trends of style.

To date, ThinkMan and ThinkWoman have adorned polo shirts, sweatshirts, sweat suits, shorts, hats, coffee cups, duffel bags, dress shirts, visors, and more. For team uniforms, these logos are placed in a shield of sorts, much like the crests on the shields of battle of honorable warriors in history. The scholar-baller shield, or patch as it is often called, can then be easily worn on any part of a team uniform.

Examples of this already include Arizona State University, which became the first NCAA Division I football team to recognize academic achievement during athletic competition. Hampton University and Morgan State University also "rocked" the patch during the New York Urban League (NYUL) classic, becoming the first of the Historically Black Colleges and Institutions to participate in the scholar-baller patch recognition. Finally, during the 2004 Vitalis Sun Bowl, Arizona State and Purdue University became the first Bowl teams to recognize academic achievements on players' jerseys based on the scholar-baller concept. (Purdue created a minor version of the scholar-baller patch that was significantly smaller and imageless but based on the ideology and foundation of the scholar-baller incentive system.)

The basic colors of scholar-baller are black and white; the patch is nondenominational yet includes all cultures, teams, sexes, and apparel and gear manufacturers. This is the reason members of the scholar-baller executive team wear white logos on black items or black logos on white items; as a team we really are all-inclusive and quite proud of our collective diversity and accomplishments. However, when a scholar-baller individual or team makes a request for an adaptation of the logo to better blend in with team or organization colors, corresponding color schemes are easily developed, with great attention paid to detail. For example, Arizona State University sent an actual home and away football jersey to the scholar-baller executive team so that a well-coordinated color scheme could be developed. This resulted in "home" and "away" patches being prepared. Patches were then produced in an appropriate volume and sent to the team equipment manager to attach to the uniforms, something that equipment managers often do. As other teams and organizations join the scholar-baller program, this process will be repeated over and over.

A scholar-baller patch or shield on a uniform is but one small piece of the possible recognition offerings. Working closely with representatives from Arizona State University's athletic department, and understanding their desires for motivational and recognition items, a set of items was prepared: a backpack with a patch applied in ASU colors, a ThinkMan hat in ASU colors, a T-shirt with the ThinkMan on one side and the team goals on the other, and a pair of Nike basketball/street shorts with Thinkman added on the lower leg. Each scholar-baller on the team received one of these sets in a special ceremony.

Much more is planned for the scholar-baller logo set, including continued evolution of the base logos, creation of complementary logos such as the emerging "It's Cool to be Smart" logo, and development of additional recognition and motivational items. Not only do we want the scholar-baller ideals and related curriculum to be embraced by many, but we also want those who are christened scholar-ballers to be able to proudly express this recognition in a variety of ways.

CONCLUSION AND IMPLICATIONS

For over a century, the academic success of student-athletes has been a complex challenge for American postsecondary education. The disconnect and gap between academics, athletics, and popular culture is poignantly articulated by Coleman (1960) in three powerful narratives. First, speaking of adolescence, Coleman said,

> In effect, then, what our society has done is set apart, in an institution of their own, adolescents for whom home is little more than a dormitory and whose world is made up of activities peculiar to their fellows. They have been given as well many of the instruments which can make them a functioning community: cars, freedom in dating, continual contact with the opposite sex, money, and entertainment, like popular music and movies, designed especially for them. The international spread of "rock-and-roll" and of so-called American patterns of adolescent behavior is a consequence, I would suggest, of these economic challenges which have set adolescents off in a world of their own. (p. 338)

This world of their own often consumes American youth in nearly all cultural forms except the lifelong engagement and acquisition of knowledge—educational development. Student-athletes are even more influenced from elementary to postsecondary education by the bombardment and messages about material gain from the athletic and entertainment identity (Gerdy, 1997). What are the effects of a cultural system that reinforces athleticism and not intellectualism? The second narrative by Coleman is key to understanding this question.

Coleman (1960) continues to frame the incentive and reward system of American education and society by having a vision that "the fundamental change which must occur is to shift the focus: to mold social communities as communities, so that the norms of the communities themselves reinforce educational goals rather than inhibit them, as is at the present case" (p. 338). Presently, the social communities have learned to consume athletics, material objects, and immediate gratification at such an influential rate that education is overlooked and neglected as a viable option for success (Harrison, 2002). In a Coleman culture the movies, music, video games, and athletic contests would complement the pedagogy of schools systems with competency in reading, writing, and arithmetic, commonly known as the 3 Rs. This method could easily enhance educational goals instead of inhibiting them— hence, a method that inspires youth to desire learning and intellectual development throughout their life span. This leads to the third and final narrative.

In the final analysis, Coleman (1960) exposes the bias in American sport and entertainment by indicating the cultural fact that "the outstanding student has little or no way to bring glory to his school" (p. 347) (in comparison to athletics). This is where the scholar-baller paradigm may theoretically and practically influence the culture of American sport by ending the silence around academic success. This is an approach that will, we hope, become the new map for success in America.

REFERENCES

Boyd, T. (2004). *Young, Black, rich and famous*. New York: NYU Press.

Bowen, W., & Levin, S. (2003). *Reclaiming the game: Sports and our educational values*. Princeton, NJ: Princeton University Press.

Brand, M. (2003). *Sustaining the collegiate model of athletics*. Paper presented to the NCAA membership. Retrieved in January 2003 from www2.ncaa.org/releases/MylesBrand/20031210sportsbus.html.

Coakley, J. (2004). *Sport in society*. Denver, CO: McGraw Publishers.

Coleman, J. S. (1960). The adolescent subculture and academic achievement. *American Journal of Sociology, 4*(35), 337–347.

Dyson, M. (2003). *Open mike: Reflections on philosophy, race, sex, culture and religion*. New York: Basic Books.

Gladwell, M. (2000). *The "tipping point": How little things make a big difference*. New York: Back-Bay Books/Little, Brown & Company.

Gerdy, J. (1997). *The new standard*. Phoenix, AZ: Onyx Press.

Harrison, C. K. (1995). *African American male student-athletes*. Paper presented at the North American Society for the Sociology of Sport Annual Meeting, Sacramento, CA.

Harrison, C. K. (1996). *Time capsule: Perceptions of Paul Robeson, Arthur Ashe, and Grant Hill*. Paper presented at North American Society for Sport History, Auburn, AL.

Harrison, C. K. (1997). *Philosophy of African American males in sport: Time for change*. Paper presented at the International Sport Conference, Seoul, Korea.

Harrison, C. K. (2002). Scholar or baller: A visual elicitation and qualitative assessment of the student-athlete mindset. *National Association of Student Affairs Professionals Journal, 8*(1), 66–81.

Harrison, C. K., & Lampman, B., (2001). The image of Paul Robeson: Role model for the student and athlete. *Rethinking History 5*(1), 117–130.

Kelley, R. (1997). *Yo mama's disfunktional: Fighting the cultural wars in urban America*. New York: NYU Press.

Motivational Educational Entertainment Report. (1992). Philadelphia.

NCAA (1998). *Role model for athletes*.

Sammons, J. (1994). Race and sport: A critical historical examination. *Journal of Sport History 21*, 203–298.

Simmons, R., & George, N. (2002). *Life and def.* New York: Three Rivers Press.

Taylor, E. (1999). Bring in da noise: Race, sport and the role of schools. *Educational Leadership, 56*, 75–78.

20

Rethinking the Role of Sports in Our Schools

John R. Gerdy
Ohio University

For close to 100 years, highly competitive, elite athletic programs have been a part of our nation's educational system. It is notable that the United States is the only country in the world in which such programs are sponsored by secondary schools. In Europe, for example, the responsibility for the development of elite athletes and teams is borne by private sports clubs or professional teams. The purpose of this chapter is to explore the following question. In the case of the development and promotion of highly competitive, elite athletics, could it be that the Europeans, rather than we Americans, have it right?

While we tend to think of sports as simply fun and games, the fact is that organized athletics have a tremendous impact on our lives. Their influence ranges from the culture that exists within our educational institutions to the taxes we pay, to our public health, to the lessons we teach our children, to the types and tenor of the communities in which we live. Thus, the way in which our schools handle the cultural subject matter of athletics is an important public policy issue with far-ranging and long-lasting effects.

At issue is not whether athletics are good or bad, but whether the current system is best suited for making the most of athletics' potential to meet our nation's education and public health needs. Undoubtedly, fitness activities should be a part of our nation's educational system. The Greek ideal of a sound mind/sound body is, in fact, sound. And there is definitely a place for elite athletics in our culture. The question is simply whether that place should be in our schools. As an alternative, what would be the educational and societal cost of restructuring our nation's athletic system to mirror those of European countries?

To answer this question requires that we identify the justifications for the incorporation of interscholastic athletics into the fabric of our educational institutions. There are four supposed benefits of this relationship. First, involvement in athletics is educational for, and builds the character of, participants. Life lessons in discipline, sportsmanship, teamwork, communication skills, and sacrifice are being taught on the playing fields and courts by coaches who are educators. Second, athletic programs unify the school and surrounding communities, generating a healthy school and community spirit. Third, school sports provide entertainment. Last, participation in athletics is not only healthy for the athletes, but also serves an important public health function by promoting the value of being fit.

AN HONEST ASSESSMENT

Despite widespread belief that elite athletics have the potential to contribute greatly to the missions of our educational institutions in vibrant and meaningful ways, and by doing so, have a positive impact on our society, it is increasingly apparent that many elite athletics programs fall far short of their potential. The extent to which organized sport subverts our nation's educational interests is enormous. At the grade school and high school levels, it is the passing of athletes who have not mastered the work. The prevailing notion is that it is acceptable if Johnny can't read as long as he can play. Coaches plead the case of a "good kid, whose only chance at a better life is through an athletic scholarship, and he won't be eligible unless he passes this course." (I use a male example here because this problem is more prevalent with males, although with increased participation of females in sport we may begin to see the same thing.) Far too often, the teacher or principal complies, not wanting to be responsible for denying a youngster his "only chance." Unfortunately, everyone knows — classmates, parents, coaches, teachers, and Johnny himself — that Johnny did not deserve to pass. The impact on the academic credibility of the institution is significant. Such acts — and they are far from isolated — serve to cheapen the value and standing of education in our communities.

This academic fraud is perpetuated when our institutions of higher learning spend substantial resources recruiting and later admitting Johnny, despite the fact that he is unqualified to perform college work and unlikely to graduate. Once the "student-athlete" is enrolled, it becomes all too clear that the reason for being at college is to produce on the fields of play. All else—education, social life, and personal development—occupies a distant place on the list of priorities for what in reality is an "athlete-student." All this in the name of "educational opportunity." All at the expense of academic integrity.

H. G. Bissinger, in his 1990 book *Friday Night Lights*, explains how athletics undermine educational priorities at Permian High School in Odessa, Texas. He noted that the cost of boys' medical supplies at Permian was $6,750. The cost for teaching materials for the English department was $5,040, which included supplies, maintenance of the copying machine, and any extra books besides the required texts that a teacher thought might be important for students to read. The cost of game film was $6,400. Meanwhile, the English department had just received its first computer, which was to be used by all 25 teachers. An English teacher with 20 years experience earned a salary of $32,000 as compared to the football coach, who also served as athletic director, earning $48,000 and having the free use of a new Taurus sedan each year. And, during the 1988 season, Permian spent $70,000 for chartered jets for the football team's travel (Bissinger, 1990, pp. 146–147).

Such imbalance prompted one teacher to fume,

"This community doesn't want academic excellence. It wants a gladiatorial spectacle on Friday nights." As she made that comment, a history class meeting a few yards down the hall did not have a teacher. The instructor was an assistant football coach. He was one of the best teachers in the school, dedicated and lively, but because of the pressures of preparing for a crucial game, he did not have time to go to class. That wasn't to say, however, that the class did not receive a lesson. They learned about American history that day by watching *Butch Cassidy and the Sundance Kid*. (Bissinger, pp. 147–148)

And while in this case, the football coach was a good teacher, there are countless examples of teachers being hired, not based upon their ability as teachers, but rather as coaches. This is simply another example of a contributing factor in the evolution of a culture within our schools that demands nothing less than the best on the fields of play at the expense of excellence in the classroom.

Further, a growing body of research casts serious doubt on whether the win-at-all-costs culture that permeates elite athletic programs has a positive impact on the teaching and development of character. According to a 1999–2000 study by the University of Rhode Island's Institute for International Sport, 26% of NCAA Division I basketball players agreed that their teammates would *expect* them to cheat if it meant the difference in winning a game. This example demonstrates that the culture surrounding sports in America has become more about winning and providing entertainment than about education and building character. In today's world of sports, cheating is winked at, a lack of civility toward opponents is considered a positive attribute, violence is glorified, and the promotion of the individual, often at the expense of the group, is tolerated. In sports, there are no rules of civility. There is no trust. There are no standards of acceptable behavior, or if there are, they can easily be bent, broken, or amended if the player is good enough. In the athletic culture, there is no order and but one rule: Win at any cost. The question is whether that cost has become too high.

The claim that athletic programs unify educational institutions can also be disputed. There are just as many students, faculty, parents, and taxpayers who would rather see institutional resources and energy devoted to improving their school's art, music, science, theater, or English departments than to buying new uniforms for the football team. Further, there are risks in relying on athletic teams to unify educational communities. Schools that use athletics to solve the problems of a fragmented community run the risk of making athletics, rather than educational and academic excellence, the primary purpose of the institution. Although a football or basketball team can unite a high school in a way that an English department cannot, the primary purpose of the institution remains, as it always has been, educational. In short, a winning football team does not make a quality educational institution.

Of all the justifications for educational institutions to sponsor athletics, it is the entertainment function that programs are meeting most effectively. This, however, begs the larger question of whether educational institutions should be in the entertainment business, particularly when so many of the values and attitudes of the entertainment culture run counter to those of the educational community.

But it is in the area of public health that the current structure of athletics in our school systems fails most dramatically. For example, the vast majority of health, physical education, and athletic-related extracurricular school spending funds football. It is a sport in which the final high school game is the last time that 99% of the participants ever play the game. Yet football flourishes while high school gym class requirements are reduced or eliminated. The *New York Times* reported in 2000 that in the nation, "only 29 percent of high school students had daily physical education in 1999, down from 42 percent in 1991. Two years ago, Virginia stopped requiring physical education in elementary school. In 1996, Massachusetts did so for high school. By 1999, only 61 percent of Massachusetts high school students had gym class even one time per week, down from 80 percent five years earlier" (Rothstein, 2000, p. A29).

Today, Illinois is the only state that still requires daily physical education classes for students in K through 12. And Colorado, along with South Dakota, does not have any mandate for physical education on any level— elementary, middle school, or high school (Reed, 2004). In short, an official policy of encouraging students to pursue a healthy life through exercise is no longer a priority in our nation's schools. Meanwhile, our nation becomes more obese. The Centers for Disease Control and Prevention report that the number of obese children ages 6 to 11 has increased nearly 300% over the last 25 years. And the numbers are nearly identical for teenagers (Reed, 2004).

The disturbing question is whether the justifications for elite athletics within our national educational system are being met. Again, at issue is not the value of elite athletics in our culture, but whether our educational institutions should be saddled with the responsibility of developing our future college and professional athletes.

RETHINKING OUR EDUCATIONAL MISSION

Given these concerns, we face a nagging truth about athletics in our educational system. What if the traditional justifications for keeping elite athletics as an integral part of our educational system are no longer relevant in a world that is much different from the one that existed when they were incorporated into that system? Or, if the justifications remain relevant, what if our athletic programs are not meeting them? What does this mean for athletics, our nation's educational system, and our society? As elite athletics in America acquire more of the values and practices of the entertainment industry and less of the educational community, we must assess their influence on our educational system. We must also be willing to restructure our educational and societal investment in organized athletics accordingly.

To be specific, as our nation struggles to meet rapidly changing economic, business, educational, intellectual, and social demands, shouldn't we be investing our time and precious educational resources to ensure that our students have the best educational resources, equipment, and instruction? Shouldn't this be our focus, as opposed to a new weight room for elite athletes? The information-based, high-tech, global economy of the future will require all of us to be better educated. As we enter this new age, an age where intellect, education, and the ability to manage and communicate large amounts of highly technical information will power our growth and continued development as a world leader, it is intellectual muscle, not gladiatorial feats, that will be the currency of the future.

In short, the challenges we face in educating our children and maintaining our economic status as a world power are simply too great for our school systems to invest in activities that, however entertaining, have demonstrated a consistent tendency to undermine academic values. It is against this backdrop that we must reconsider whether our tremendous investment in athletics continues to be a sound one.

Thus, we must ask the following questions: Is our obsession with and investment in organized sport endangering the educational and economic health of our society by promoting values and encouraging behaviors within our schools that run counter to sound educational principles? By embracing the values and behaviors of a gladiator class, have we become less able to meet the intellectual challenges of the new millennium? Will a nation full of dumb jocks and passive fans fare well in the fast-paced, information-based global economy of the 21st century?

And perhaps our nation's general health needs are better met through other exercise and athletic programs. The fact is, the health benefits associated with exercise are not exclusive to highly organized, ultracompetitive youth, high school, college, and Olympic sports. Positive health benefits can be derived from involvement in exercise and fitness programs that are less competitive and less expensive, such as intramural sports, wellness programs, or local club teams. To maximize sports' potential to positively influence the health and fitness of our populace, the focus of our investment should be on involving the maximum number of participants rather than spending an increasingly large commitment of time, effort, and emotion on only those athletes who might have the potential to play at the major college or professional level.

What if, for example, rather than spending an increasingly large commitment of time, effort, and emotion on the development of elite athletes and teams, our nation's schools concentrated on conducting programs that emphasized broad-based participation in health and fitness activities that could be practiced for a lifetime? Inasmuch as the health and fitness of our nation's youth is a vital societal issue, the effectiveness with which our school systems are fulfilling this function should be evaluated carefully and critically. To that end, intramural, physical education, and wellness programs should be expanded. The result would be far more students making use of health- and exercise-related resources. Such a change would place our educational system in the position to more effectively serve the broad, long-term health and fitness needs of America.

Given the ever-increasing economic challenges facing our educational systems, educators and school boards will face mounting pressure to justify spending precious resources on extracurricular activities. Specifically, the burden of proof that such activities have a direct, vital, and productive impact on the institution's fundamental educational purposes will increase dramatically. This educational cost-benefit analysis will cut two ways. First, the educational return on dollars invested in the elite athletics for entertainment model versus athletics designed to encourage broad-based participation in physical activities that can be enjoyed for a lifetime must be considered. And, second, funding for athletics versus other extracurricular activities such as the arts and music must be taken into account.

Undoubtedly, cultural and community attitudes against moving interscholastic athletics out of the educational system will be strong. Regardless, it is imperative that we critically assess our nation's educational priorities and outcomes, including elite interscholastic athletics and their tremendous influence on those priorities and outcomes. Ultimately, American education must structure itself according to what will best enable it to meet its responsibility to provide leadership in addressing the many challenges facing our society.

WHAT DO WE LOSE?

So, what would we lose if our schools, and colleges for that matter, relinquished the responsibility for the development of elite athletes and teams? Very little. Contrary to what the avid sports fan might believe, our nation's educational system would not collapse if the responsibility for developing elite athletes and teams were "privatized." While our school systems might be less dynamic and, in some ways, less fun without elite athletics, they would continue to go about the business of educating. In fact, the education of students would likely improve with the elimination of such programs, as the focus on academics would intensify.

Athletes and coaches would continue to have the opportunity to hone their skills, as elite sports activities and training would simply shift to other local sponsoring agencies. As in Europe, local sports organizations would develop and sponsor more comprehensive athletic programs, and professional teams would develop feeder systems and programs, similar to the one that currently exists in baseball.

Further, there is nothing to suggest that athletic programs must be a part of an educational institution for a young person participating in that program to learn the lessons being taught by coaches in discipline, sportsmanship, teamwork, and sacrifice. The potential to utilize athletics as a tool to build character and teach those lessons will remain, regardless of the team's sponsoring agency.

Finally, after an initial outcry from those who do not fully appreciate the fundamental purpose and responsibility of our nation's schools, fans would come to identify with the team of their choice, despite the fact that it might be sponsored by the local car dealership rather than the high school. And it is likely that supporters of the institution would display their school spirit by supporting other activities such as music or theater groups.

The positive benefits for the institution as well as for our society would be enormous. Our educational system would be rid of a highly visible and expensive source of hypocrisy and scandal. As a result, the credibility of, and public trust in, our educational system would increase dramatically, as such change would signify that our schools and communities have strong educational values and priorities. Such a shift would better enable our schools to fulfill their mission, which to this day remains education, without the distractions and drain on resources that go along with sponsoring elite athletics.

The fact is, our educational institutions will teach far more, far more clearly, and to far more people, about the importance of education by relinquishing the responsibility of developing a small number of elite athletes. The mixed messages sent and the educational compromises made, all for the athletic development of a small fraction of our student population, have increasingly undermined educational values and our long-term civic priorities, cultural welfare, and public health.

MEETING OUR LEADERSHIP RESPONSIBILITIES

There is no American institution better suited than our school system through which to promote public health through participation in exercise. Thus, we must ask whether our nation's health interests are being met by the current emphasis, in terms of time, effort, emotion, and money that is being spent on entertainment-based, elite interscholastic athletics, as opposed to physical education, intramural athletics, and wellness programs. Expanding exercise and fitness programs that have as their primary focus broad-based participation would result in far more students being able to avail themselves of health- and exercise-related resources. With such a change in our athletic and health and physical education priorities, our educational systems would be better positioned to begin the process of serving the broad, long-term health and fitness needs of our nation.

Our societal investment in organized, elite sport is enormous. That investment has been justified largely by the health, educational, and socialization benefits both to the participants and to the larger society. But in the face of Nike commercialism, NCAA Final Four hype, ESPN highlights, and daily reports of athletes' scraps with the law, it is increasingly difficult to see any connection between athletics and such "higher purposes." Sport in America has become more about money, winning, and ego than about education, sportsmanship, and ethics; more about commercialism, sneaker deals, and trash talking than about personal development and educational opportunity; and more about being a passive spectator than an active participant.

In the final analysis, society looks to our educational institutions to provide leadership on a broad array of issues, including the proper role of athletics in our culture. That being the case, it is time to consider seriously whether our current system of elite athletics, sponsored mainly through our educational system, continues to be in our best interests. A move toward the European model of elite athletics would send a very clear and important message to our sports-crazed populace that as much as we love highly competitive, elite sports, we must love and value the education, health, and fitness of our children more.

REFERENCES

Bissinger, H. G. (1990). *Friday night lights: A town, a team, and a dream*. New York: Addison Wesley.

Institute for International Sport. (1999–2000). *Men's college basketball sportsmanship research*. Kingston, RI: Author.

Reed, K. (2004, February 1). Back talk: Elitism in youth sports leads yields physical fatness. *New York Times*, Sports section, p. 1.

Rothstein, R. (2000, November 29). Do new standards in the three R's crowd out P.E.? *New York Times*, p. A29.

21

The Meaning of Success in Academics and Athletics

Rob Renes
Muskegon High School

Before a person can accurately label an endeavor a success, one must be able to define success. Although I have come across many definitions of the word, I am consistently disappointed with either the vagueness or the narrow scope that most definitions imply. While most of us have a personal belief about what constitutes success, I believe that it's difficult to pin down a consistent and accurate definition of something that is so important to so many in our society. With these discrepancies in mind, I believe it is difficult to qualify a student-athlete's collegiate experience as successful or unsuccessful. Few would argue that a football player who receives consistent all-American status experiences success, but how many believe, as I do, that a struggling third-string player may be just as successful? For this reason, I believe that success can be considered only a relative term.

A LESSON LEARNED

Like many young people, I grew up dreaming of a day when I could represent my favorite college team on the field of competition. Through hard work and perseverance and with a tremendous amount of support, I was determined to become a student-athlete at the collegiate level. When I finally received a full scholarship, I began looking to the future, where I assumed I could finally attain a true sense of being successful. Naively, I discredited my prior accomplishments, both in the classroom and on the field, as mere prerequisites to success. In addition, I had mistakenly come to believe that accomplishment led not only to success, but also to happiness. Therefore, I had begun to equate attainment of success with my own personal happiness. I believe it was this immature association that led to unnecessary stress and discontent.

During the first 2 years of my college experience, I endured a tremendous amount of pressure. There was the normal level of anxiety associated with being a freshman student-athlete at a Division I institution, but in addition, there was an enormous amount of self-imposed stress, which was the result of my inability to disassociate accomplishment from success and happiness.

During my first semester of college, I was very unhappy. Most, including my family and friends, attributed this to being homesick. While being homesick certainly played a role in my angst, I now understand that my sense of anguish had a great deal to do with my self-evaluation of personal accomplishment. I had a difficult time accepting the fact that two things I had always held as strengths, academics and athletics, were now areas in which I needed a great deal of improvement. I began to give in to self-doubt and contemplated whether or not I had made a mistake. At that point, more than at any other point in my life, I began to view all my prior accomplishments, especially the scholarship, as undeserved. I wondered how I ever could have thought that I deserved to be there, or whether or not I would ever enjoy a sense of being happy.

Despite my growing belief that I was failure, I held tight to the understanding that my being in college was a tremendous opportunity. After many hours of counsel from my parents and friends, I was determined to approach the remainder of my stay in school as if I were working to earn it, every day. I surrounded myself, as I had in high school, with people who I felt wanted the same things out of life that I did. I sought out academic support and I committed myself to the football program, while heeding nearly every piece of advice I could garner from veteran players and coaches alike.

The changing of my approach to school and sport served me well. During my second semester, I started to come into my own. I began doing better in school, and I was working my way up the depth chart. Unfortunately, despite my change in attitude, neither my opinion of what success was nor my understanding of the origins of happiness changed. As time passed and opportunities were taken, I accomplished a great deal. By my 3rd year, I was a starter; I was on the dean's list; and I believed that I was finally becoming successful. With this belief in hand, a sense of happiness began to grow in me. I had finally achieved what I had set out for. All the sacrifices I had made were seemingly worthwhile, and I believed I could accomplish anything I put my mind to.

My last 2 years of school continued to be enjoyable. I went on to become team captain, I earned both academic and football all-American status, and I graduated from a world-renowned university. And if that wasn't enough to qualify as a dream realized, just before graduation, I was drafted into the NFL. I left college on an extremely high note. I left college feeling that I had gained success.

Early in my rookie season in the NFL, I sustained a career-ending injury. With more time on my hands than I could ever recall having, I began a long period of introspection. As time passed, without the reward of either football or school, my sense of being a successful person began to fade, and so, too, did my sense of happiness. It wasn't until I finally put football behind me and took a position as a teacher and coach that I finally began to put things into perspective again. It was through working with others, while teaching and coaching, that I believe I came to realize that I had always viewed success in a distorted manner.

I had always looked at success as something to be achieved as an end result. I believed that people could be successful only if they accomplished what it was they had set out to do. While I had long believed this in terms of my own life, I had a great deal of trouble applying it to my students and players. I believed that most, if not all, of the kids I worked with were successful even if they didn't reach their goals. It was this inconsistency in my attribution of success that prompted me to reevaluate my view of what it means to be successful.

I am now very comfortable with, and confident in, viewing success as something experienced through defying attrition. Therefore, those who are successful are not only those who win the game or have a grade point average of 4.0, but also those who, despite the result or outcome, embody perseverance and determination. We all, at one time or another, experience failure. This in and of itself doesn't signify a lack of success, but an unwillingness to forge ahead does. Those who consistently pull themselves up after they fall personify success.

I consider my current understanding of the concept of success to be one of the most empowering aspects of my life. Looking at success from this perspective allows me to better appreciate every aspect of my life, including my past. I work very hard to instill this in the young people with whom I work. I firmly believe that with this outlook one can better focus on the tasks at hand, rather than the impending outcome, therefore ensuring success.

Conclusion: Sport, Society, and Social Justice

Brian Lampman
Saline Middle School

THE JOURNEY

Noted sports attorney Leigh Steinberg spoke on the campus of the University of Michigan the fall of my freshman year in college; I was enthralled with his presentation. The dream quickly crystallized for me: I would become a sports attorney. Like Steinberg at the University of California, Los Angeles, I would have a client base that would grow at another of the beacons for academics and athletics: the University of Michigan. One courier job at a local law firm, one circuit court internship, and one nasty divorce by my parents changed everything for me. I felt disillusioned about my decision to enter the legal profession; I knew I could not have the impact I wanted to achieve. Although my legal dreams were deferred, I was fortunate to discover a new passion: a passion for teaching. The decision to teach became an easy one; why I had turned my back on it for so long, I have never quite understood. Although the chain of events leading to this decision was painful, I would not have changed them for the world. I gained vision. I gained perspective. I gained a passion for working with young adults. I would also, unknowingly, find a way to fuse my passion for sport, social justice, and educating young adults.

Upon entrance into the University of Michigan School of Education, all candidates were encouraged to have as much interaction with children as possible. Therefore, when the girls' freshman soccer coaching position opened at the high school where I was student teaching, I jumped at the opportunity. I had participated in a number of different sports in high school and even briefly flirted with Division I athletics as a walk-on member of the University of Michigan track and cross-country teams, but soccer had been my lifelong passion. Little did I know that coaching would consume me and 12 years later still be such a precious part of my life. Little did I know that I would be granted the academic freedom by my school district to create and teach a sports sociology class for secondary education students. This conclusion reflects on my experience as a middle school educator who also coaches high school athletes to engage in a critical assessment of our sporting culture, and ultimately, to develop a broader understanding of our society and the role sport can play for positive social transformation.

OUR SPORTING CULTURE

When our country was devastated by the tragedy of September 11, the New York Yankees' postseason run into the baseball playoffs helped ease our country's wounds, particularly those of shell-shocked New Yorkers. As we struggled with the pain inflicted by that fateful day, stories emerged. Stories of joy that sport brought to the families of the loved ones who perished that day. Stories of the hope that a baseball team playing in the shadow of the smoldering twin towers could bring a temporary diversion to a city grasping for answers—sport as promise for a better day.

When a war-torn Iraq struggled with a new identity after the ouster of the brutal Hussein regime, the country looked for a way to uplift its spirits. The success of the Iraqi National Soccer Team in the 2004 Summer Olympics did not restore electricity or sanitation services or bring clean drinking water to remote villages. But the team's success did serve as a point of pride for Iraqis during the Olympic Games in Greece. A sense of unity enveloped a country thirsty for an affirmation of its future on the world stage—sport as hope.

When Lance Armstrong pulled away from the competition in the French Alps in last year's Tour de France and pedaled gracefully down the Champs Elysées, he earned his record seventh straight Tour victory. But his crowning achievement meant so much more to the thousands of cancer victims, survivors, and families mourning the loss of loved ones. Arm-

strong's victory resonated with these families, the victory over insur-
mountable obstacles. His victory served notice that anything is possible.
His charity bracelets have raised millions and added another layer of re-
silience for those stricken with cancer—sport as cure for the soul.

And when Muhammad Ali lit the torch at the 1996 Summer Olympics
in Atlanta in front of 3 billion people worldwide, he saw his life turn full
circle and considered it one of his most memorable moments. In his career, Ali endured knockout blows from gifted opponents, racism and discrimination, and a government that stripped him of his title after his re-
fusal to be inducted into the army and fight in Vietnam. He took a stand
and he paid dearly for his position. He was jeered, but as he lit the torch,
he was cheered—and even drove many to tears of joy—sport as a catalyst
for social transformation.

Whether we recognize it or not, sport plays a critical role in our lives.
One could certainly make a case for sport being one of the most powerful
social forces in our country. From the millions we spend on sports equipment, to the millions who watch the spectacle known as the Super Bowl
each year, sport is an incredibly influential force. Just as Olympians captured the attention of ancient Greeks, our modern-day athletes participate
in sport—and we are mesmerized with every slam dunk, home run, and
touchdown. Sport can sometimes serve as a unifying force for communities and at other times as a divisive wedge. We have a unique relationship
with the institution of sport that has such an immense presence in our culture. Boys and girls emulate their heroes and with every cut, fake, and ges-
ticulation, dream of being like "Mike" or "Mia." We live in a sporting culture and often place our athletes on a pedestal whether we should or not,
whether they want to be there or not. We take their athletic accomplishments as proof of their inherent potential as role models. Young adults emulate their stars on dusty dirt fields and cracked asphalt courts across the
country.

As an educator, I am also acutely aware that our culture touts the importance of education yet often lionizes the accomplishments of its athletes. Students are fed a steady stream of media images that sensational-
ize athletics. Unfortunately, as educators, we cannot say the same
messages about academics are always presented. In fact, there are even
times that schools, communities, and our government may serve to perpetuate an overemphasis on athletics. When is the last time you heard of

a pep rally for the honor roll students? Is it not far more common to enter a community filled with welcome signs boasting of sport titles rather than academic achievements? Do referendums for high-tech stadium projects routinely pass with little opposition, while school millage proposals leave supporters anxiously holding their collective breath? It would be unheard of for the military to hold a fund-raiser for basic supplies, yet schools must consistently resort to such tactics. As is customary for the opening pitch of baseball's World Series, have you ever heard of a president throwing out a stack of pencils at the steps of the schoolhouse doors on the opening day of school? Many have forgotten that South Dakota Senator Tom Daschle's office received an envelope containing anthrax in January of 2004, but no one has forgotten the Super Bowl halftime show the same month, when Janet Jackson's infamous "wardrobe malfunction" occurred.

Sport is an unequivocal social force in our country. We must be willing to recognize its behemoth presence in our culture. As an educator and a coach, I want to know how we can harness this force as a teaching tool to create positive change. Is there a way to use sport as a mechanism for better understanding and appreciating the diverse world in which we live? Can we flip the script? Can we change the game? And if we could, would we? And if we would, how would we?

EXPLORING SPORT AND SOCIETY

I have always considered it an educational travesty in our country that most students have little or no exposure to a class in sociology until they attend college. I wonder how we expect students to develop empathy toward others and a desire to work for social justice when they are not afforded opportunities to grow in their appreciation for social awareness and compassion. I feel fortunate to have the academic freedom in my classroom to use sport as a teaching tool. Integrating sports sociology (using sport as a vehicle to teach about race, gender, social class, and our nation's history) into a classroom engages the student in creative, relevant, and stimulating curriculum. Our country's fascination with athletes, the media's saturation on the airwaves with the accomplishments of athletes, and record numbers of students who participate formally (as participants) or informally (as fans) in sporting activities make sport a valuable and viable teaching tool.

As a secondary educator who has taught a sports sociology course for 6 years, I have a unique lens through which to view the union of sport and our society and reap numerous benefits from its use as a learning instrument. I am able to glean valuable information from my students and stimulate meaningful discussion through a critical assessment of our sporting culture. For instance, students can be hesitant to discuss their true feelings about racial hiring practices in the United States. A conversation on this topic last year was jumpstarted in my class using Tyrone Willingham's abrupt dismissal at the University of Notre Dame. Students were intrigued to learn that Willingham was only one of five Black Division I head college football coaches in 117 institutions at the time—an even more alarming figure when it is noted that approximately 51% of the scholarship athletes are Black! (Black College Association, 2005). As of fall 2005, the number has dwindled to three: Karl Dorell at the University of California, Los Angeles; Tyrone Willingham, now at the University of Washington; and Sylvester Croom at Mississippi State.

My students are also invested in the discussion of the use of American Indian mascots in many high schools, collegiate, and professional teams. They recognize the contradiction when a sacred American Indian headdress is acceptable for a mascot to flaunt, while a Catholic Rosary would cause a firestorm of controversy. They understand the dominant cultural ideology that constructs and frames representations of non-Whites, and the inherent problems associated with challenging these representations. These discussions can be invaluable avenues for exploring race in our country, well beyond what any textbook could offer.

My students know that women have faced many challenges on the road to gender equality. Our Title IX discussion generates probing dialogue and questions involving inequities for women in sport and in the workforce. We question historical representations of what it means to "play like a girl" and speculate what the future may hold for strong, able-bodied female athletes.

My students may consider a current discussion on same-sex marriage to be an unwelcome venture into the politically and socially charged subject of homosexuality. When these same students are given a cartoon of a male figure skater and female hockey player, they are quick to note the challenges to gender constructions that are represented. They are very honest and open when stating that the word "fag" is a very common put-down in our middle school. This discussion helps them to understand the importance of more inclusive school environments, school environments where students recognize the positive change among their peers they have the power to effect. Sports sociology can be a mechanism for engaging students in these difficult conversations and can push them to think critically about the world and their proactive role in it.

We must equip students with the tools to navigate difficult issues such as race, gender, social class, and sexuality. Sport can be the bridge to stimulate that dialogue and facilitate students' understanding, acceptance, and vigilance, as well as their commitment to work for change. If we choose to ignore these issues, we are doing our students a disservice—one for which society will pay the price in the long run. As teachers, coaches, parents, and community members, we must intervene and question the negative messages many students are consistently bombarded with by the media and pop culture to facilitate positive change in sports and in society.

MAINTAINING PERSPECTIVE

I still think about "the letter" from time to time. It was 2 months after coaching the fall season that it arrived, surreptitiously dropped in my school mailbox. Parent complaints certainly come with the territory when coaching; however, I was unprepared for the venom in this letter. It read,

> Six months after the fact, I am still in shock that my son was cut from the team. He was probably the most valuable player on his previous (youth) team. How does he go from M.V.P to being cut? I would say it was from your ignorance and the biased opinion of your advisors and the lackadaisical attitude of your punk evaluators. . . . If my son were just an o.k. player, I could understand him not making the team. But that wasn't the case—you and your gang of [expletive] just totally screwed him.

While only an excerpt from the seven-page, handwritten letter, this passage serves to characterize this parent's displeasure with my coaching decisions. When I first received it, I was shocked. Over time my shock has turned to sadness—sadness that I did not have the impact I wanted to have with this young man and his family. As a coach, I recognize how vested a parent can be in a child's success on the playing field. Knowing this, at times, can prove to be as useful a skill to a coach as knowledge of the game. As coaches, educators, and parents, we certainly experience times when the connection with a student, player, or child does not develop in the way we would ideally hope. Coaching kids can sometimes be as challenging as teaching, if not more so. I have often found that a student who underachieves in my class, and receives a poor grade, can frustrate a parent. The same child who does not receive the playing time parents feel he or she deserves may infuriate them.

Parents often become so consumed with their children's participation that they lose perspective. The stakes appear to be so much higher; the investment for families seems to take on an uncharted new level of importance. The disappointment and dejection of not making the team and fulfilling the role as the "star" are magnified by every snap of the ball, swing of the racket, or swish of the net. Major newspapers routinely splash sensational headlines across their pages about the high school football player who, unhappy with his minutes on the field, takes the coach to court. The grounds for the lawsuit: potential loss of scholarship dollars as a collegiate athlete. We hear about the peewee soccer coach attacking a referee over a call, and subsequently, insurance carriers offering special "at-risk" insurance coverage for referees. Current NCAA statistics illustrate the staggering odds (roughly 1 out of every 600,000 players) of a high school basketball player turning into the next Cleveland Cavaliers basketball star LeBron James; however, many parents drive their sons and daughters as if this will happen with full certainty in their child's life (National Collegiate Athletic Association, 2005). Sport, as we know it, appears to have spiraled out of control in front of our very eyes. Or has it?

I like to reference the letter as an example of love, not hate. Instead of seeing it as an example of the evils of sport and the by-product of an athletic environment gone terribly wrong, I choose to look at it from a different perspective. This is a perspective that I have acquired from a lifetime of participation in sport, a perspective that perhaps one acquires when one becomes a parent for the first time, as I recently did. I believe the parent who wrote this letter deeply loves his child; he sees the hurt in his child's eyes, and instinctively he goes after the one who caused that pain—me. While I fault this parent for the delivery, I value his passion for his child's happiness. While this interaction was certainly difficult (and is one that I will never forget and would love not to repeat), it was far from the norm. I have coached almost 500 young athletes including Special Olympians, elementary children, middle schoolers, and high schoolers; this is the only letter of this kind that I have ever received. Sport has its dark clouds, but it also has its shining moments. Our society loves to talk about the dark clouds, and we often overlook our shining moments. As a coach, I have had a positive impact on hundreds of lives. As a coach, these positive relationships, not one letter, will be my mark.

COACHING AND TEACHING AGAINST THE GRAIN

In part I coach and teach because I want to work for positive change. I recognize the many problems still associated with sports in this country, but I want athletes to take an active role in changing the negative practices that are still too prevalent in schools and sports in this country. That is why I actively coach and teach against gendered, racist, and homophobic practices, which are all too common in high school sports. I try to ensure that my athletes understand the discriminatory nature of gendered language and its consequences not only for young women, but also for young men. I want athletes to understand why hazing activities are not motivational ploys, nor true bonding experiences. I want them to understand that an athlete's excellence must extend far beyond the playing field into the classroom. I want them to see themselves as role models in the community and active participants in social change. I want them to debunk the image of athletes on pedestals and instead ensure that all students are treated respectfully and with the value they deserve. To accomplish these goals, I ask that my athletes read books that explore the problems and possibilities that sport has to offer. They read books such as *Season of Life* by Jeffrey Marx, which deals with images of false masculinity, and *The Big Picture* by Ben Carson, which examines race, compassion, and empathy. We volunteer in the community, hoping to make a difference in the lives of others. I also work hard to ensure that my athletes respect others both on and off the playing field. It is not acceptable for them to adopt a Lombardian win-at-all-costs mentality, and I hope they learn lessons about what it really means to be a successful athlete through these activities. The goal here is to create a ripple that will have lasting effects, not only during their tenure as athletes in the school district, but also beyond, as they live their lives and influence others.

I am also very proud of efforts to use sport as a teaching tool through the creation of a lecture series for my school district this calendar year. The Saline Sports in Society Lecture Series uses sport as a means to teach about race, gender, social class, and the history of our nation. Prior to the publication of this book, two speakers have addressed the community of Saline. Our first speaker, Dr. Richard Lapchick, CEO of the National Consortium of Academics and Sport, is an internationally known human rights activist and expert in issues of race and sport. He challenged students, parents, faculty members, and community leaders in attendance to reflect on ways they can work for social justice in their communities. Lapchick himself was a victim of a hate crime and spoke passionately about the need for tolerance and acceptance of all races. One of the country's leading antisexist male activists, Jackson Katz, followed Lapchick two months later. Katz energetically delivered his message about gender violence prevention education programs and discussed strategies to navigate the treacherous images of masculinity and femininity in our country, images many youths are conditioned to embrace as the socially accepted representation of a man or a woman.

Our next three speakers will all bring a wealth of expertise in the realm of sport and society. Dr. Donna Lopiano, executive director of the Women's Sports Foundation and a decorated athlete herself, will discuss the historical barriers that many women have faced. She will address the state of Title IX in our country and what she believes will be the greatest challenges to women's participation in the future. Former NBA player Bob Bigelow, author of *Just Let the Kids Play*, will then bring his unique experience concerning youth participation in sport. He teaches strategies for putting the "fun" back in youth sports and meaningful perspective for adults who help coach. Olympic gold medalist in soccer and World Cup champion Julie Foudy will be our final lecture series speaker. Foudy will bring her important message concerning the importance of hard work and goal setting, coupled with the inspirational story of her own success as an Olympian. The lecture series is an extension of my conviction about the value and power of sport as a vehicle for positive social change.

FINAL REFLECTIONS

As one might have anticipated by now, I believe in the power of sport. I believe in the beauty of a collection of individuals striving toward a common goal. I hold the conviction that sport is a tremendous arena for personal growth. Yet for all the reasons that sport has been so valued in our country—fun, building character, teaching teamwork, learning to embrace euphoric highs and disappointing lows, and developing leadership qualities—it often falls short of these goals. I am convinced that our society does not have to accept this; parents, teachers, and coaches are in a position to make a significant, positive impact. We cannot expect our athletes to learn the positive values of sport without a supportive environment and collective encouragement by peers, coaches, and parents. Whether fair or not, athletes must accept their tremendous influence on the youth of our country. Our news media must stop glorifying sport violence and highlighting the transgressions of our athletes. Parents must recognize that sport best serves as an outlet for fun, exercise, and healthy competition. Coaches must recognize the tremendous influence they have on their athletes, an influence that extends far beyond the confines of the playing field. Sport will always be imperfect because it is a reflection of our society, but we must expect, in fact demand, more. Sport can be a powerful learning tool and a mechanism for change, but we must support and educate athletes, parents, coaches, and teachers about how to change the game. When we strive to make these changes, sport will truly live up to its potential for positive social transformation.

REFERENCES

Black Coaches Association. (2005). Division I coaching statistics. Retrieved from www.bcasports.org/micontent.aspx?pn=FAQs&#stats.

National Collegiate Athletic Association. (2005). Odds of competing in collegiate and professional sports. Retrieved from www.ncaa.org/research/prob_of _competing/.

About the Editors and Contributors

Natalie G. Adams is an associate professor in the Department of Leadership, Policy, and Technology Studies at the University of Alabama. Her major fields of interest are adolescent girls, the construction of a gendered identity, and young women and sports. She is coauthor of *Cheerleader! An American Icon* (2003) and coeditor of *Geographies of Girlhood: Identities In-Between* (2005), both with Pamela J. Bettis.

Doug Abrams is a professor of juvenile and family law at the University of Missouri and has coached youth ice hockey at all age levels since 1968. Doug has written four books, including *Children and the Law*, and currently publishes his free, online e-newsletter, *Today's Articles*. Hundreds receive Doug's compendium of newspaper and magazine stories from around the country about issues in youth sports.

Quaylan Allen is a doctoral student in the Division of Educational Leadership and Policy Studies at Arizona State University and a former student-athlete and graduate of California State University, Sacramento. Allen is currently examining the academic success patterns of African American males in football and basketball.

Eric Anderson is a lecturer in the Department of Education at the University of Bath. He uses qualitative methods to investigate the construction of masculinity and sexuality in feminized and masculinized terrains.

His most recent book, *In the Game: Gay Athletes and the Cult of Masculinity* (2005), examines the construction of masculinity in the sport setting and how openly gay male athletes navigate and challenge this institution.

Pamela J. Bettis is an assistant professor in the Cultural Studies and Social Thought in Education program at Washington State University. Her current research focus is an exploration of the meaning of nice for girls and women. She is coauthor of *Cheerleader! An American Icon* and coeditor of *Geographies of Girlhood: Identities In-Between*, both with Natalie G. Adams.

Bob Bigelow is a former collegiate and NBA player who has conducted thousands of clinics over 20-plus years, served for over 10 years on youth boards, and conducted extensive research into youth sports. Bob is a longstanding advocate for change, delivering over 600 community talks in the past 10 years, and coauthored the book *Just Let the Kids Play*.

Jean A. Boyd has a master's degree from Arizona State and is a former Sun Devil football player. He is in his 3rd year as assistant athletics director for Student-Athlete Development. Boyd works closely with the football program, helping student-athletes develop critical academic and life skills, in addition to overseeing the academic and life skill development of all student-athletes. Boyd is cofounder of Scholar Baller.

Jay Coakley is a professor of sociology at the University of Colorado, Colorado Springs. He earned a PhD at the University of Notre Dame and has studied the social aspects of sport since 1970. He has written many books and more than 130 papers and chapters primarily on sport, society, and culture.

Eddie Comeaux recently completed his PhD at the University of California, Los Angeles. Dr. Comeaux's dissertation findings, *Unveiling Stereotypes of Nontraditional Student Groups on College Campuses: An Organizational and Critical Race Theory Analysis of Faculty Attitudes toward Male and Female Student-Athletes*, was recently cited in the *Indianapolis Star*.

Bill Curry graduated from Georgia Tech in 1964 and played 10 years in the NFL, mostly with the Green Bay Packers and Baltimore Colts. He then coached for 22 years, at Green Bay as an assistant, then at Georgia Tech, Alabama, and Kentucky as head coach. He has been a football analyst at ESPN for the past 8 years.

Margaret Duncan is an associate professor at the University of Wisconsin, Milwaukee, in the Department of Human Movement Sciences. The focus of her research is representations of girls and women in sport media, sport spectatorship, and an interpretive analysis of play and sport texts. She is currently working on a project about the significance of physical activity and sport in the lives of girls for the University of Minnesota's Tucker Center for Research on Girls and Women in Sport.

Fred Engh is the founder and president of the National Alliance for Youth Sports (www.nays.org), a nonprofit organization that works to provide safe and fun sports for children around the world. He is also the author of the book *Why Johnny Hates Sports*.

Martha Ewing is a professor in the Department of Kinesiology at Michigan State University. She is also a faculty member of the Institute for the Study of Youth Sports and current president of the Association for the Advancement of Applied Sport and Exercise Psychology. She also serves as a sport psychology consultant on the MSU Sports Medicine team. Previously, Martha was a collegiate coach.

Steve Fisher has many years of experience in variety of positions in the American Youth Soccer Organization and youth soccer. Steve has an extensive background in organizational development and has assisted the Partnership for Youth Development through Sports in creating new youth sports play models that reduce adult incentives for overinvolvement.

John R. Gerdy is a former all-American (Davidson College) and professional basketball player, NCAA legislative assistant, and associate commissioner of the Southeastern Conference. He is currently a visiting professor in sports administration at Ohio University, Athens, and has authored several books, most recently *Sports: The All-American Addiction*.

Joe Gervais is coordinator of Student-Athlete Services at the University of Vermont. Prior to this appointment he was an assistant coach of men's ice hockey for 8 years. He received his MEd from the University of Vermont in 2000 and is currently working toward his doctoral degree there in educational leadership and policy studies.

C. Keith Harrison conducts research and teaches at Arizona State University in the Division of Educational Leadership and Policy Studies. Dr. Harrison first established the Paul Robeson Research Center for Academic and Athletic Prowess at the University of Michigan, and his scholarship is well published and frequently quoted by mass media. Harrison is cofounder of the nonprofit Scholar Baller.

Angela Hattery holds the Zachary Smith Reynolds Associate Professorship in Sociology at Wake Forest University, where she teaches the following courses: Social Stratification and Social Inequality; Gender, Power, and Violence; Contemporary Families; Sociology of Gender; and Research Methods. She is currently working on a book with Earl Smith, *African American Families: Health, Wealth, and Violence*, which examines the outcomes of many systems of oppression on African American families.

Dave Heikkinen is a motivational wear expert and former student-athlete at the University of Michigan, where he earned a BA. Dave is currently a graduate student at Eastern Michigan University and owns the company Heikk's Embroidery.

Richard Irving is the founder of Character Through Sports and director of the Laconia (New Hampshire) Area Youth Basketball League (LAYBL). Rich has extensive high school and collegiate play experience and has developed successful approaches for community change that help transform youth sports to an educational/mentorship model.

Kyle W. Kusz is an assistant professor in kinesiology at the University of Rhode Island whose work examines the racial and gender politics of sport, film, and media culture in the United States, and he is still trying to figure out the appeal of *Viva la Bam*.

Brian Lampman is a middle school history teacher in Saline, Michigan, where he also coaches high school boys' soccer. In addition to teaching history, Brian also teaches sports sociology and challenges students to think critically about issues of race, gender, sexuality, and social class as they relate to the history of our country.

Richard Lapchick is the DeVoss Eminent Scholar Chair and director of the Business Sports Management graduate program in the College of Business Administration at the University of Central Florida. He founded both the Northeastern University's Center for the Study of Sport in Society and the National Consortium for Academics and Sport and is now director emeritus of the Center and the director of the Consortium.

Peggy McCann is a doctoral candidate at Michigan State University. Prior to her graduate work she was an administrator and youth sport coach. She has been involved with the Institute for the Study of Youth Sports, including developing coaching education materials and instructing coaching education workshops. She is currently studying how having a parent as coach impacts the relationship between that parent and child.

Stephen D. Mosher is professor and coordinator of the Sport Studies program at Ithaca College, where he teaches a variety of courses in sport and popular culture. He is engaged in studying sport from a dramaturgical perspective and has won several awards for his cultural poetic videos, including *Bread and Circuses in America* (1993).

Cliff J. Parks Jr. is a counselor and special projects coordinator at Long Beach Unified School District, where he is an expert on increasing the retention rate of urban males of color in K–12 public institutions. Parks earned a BS in psychology from Louisiana Tech while playing football, and an MS, PPS from LaVerne University in California. Parks is cofounder of Scholar Baller.

Sandra Spickard Prettyman is an assistant professor at the University of Akron, where she teaches courses in multicultural education, sociology of education, and qualitative research methods. She is also a mother of three whose experiences prompted her interest in and passion for how sports and athletics are currently experienced and understood by young people.

Rob Renes is a former academic and football all-American (University of Michigan) and professional football player. He currently enjoys his role as a teacher and coach in Muskegon, Michigan. In addition to working in the field of education, he has begun work toward a master's degree in counseling.

Earl Smith holds the Rubin Distinguished Professorship in American Ethnic Studies and is professor and chairman in the Department of Sociology at Wake Forest University, where he teaches the following courses: Ethnicity and Immigration; Social Stratification; Gender, Power, and Violence; and Sociology of Sport. His forthcoming book, *Race, Sport and the American Dream*, addresses the ways that sport is intertwined with race in American society.

Maureen Smith attended Ithaca College as an undergraduate, where she also received a master's degree in physical education. She earned a master's degree in Black studies and a PhD in cultural studies of sport, both at Ohio State University, and is currently an associate professor at California State University, Sacramento, in the Department of Kinesiology and Health Science.

Ellen J. Staurowsky received her undergraduate degree in health and physical education from Ursinsus College, a master's degree in sport psychology from Ithaca College, and a doctorate in sport management from Temple University. Since 1992 she has worked at Ithaca College. Her research interests focus on gender equity, Title IX, the exploitation of athletes, the representation of women in sport media, and the misappropriation of American Indian imagery in sport.

Bruce Svare is professor of psychology and neuroscience at the State University of New York, Albany, and founder of the National Institute for Sports Reform (NISR). Bruce has over 20 years of experience as a coach and administrator in youth and amateur sports and recently published his book *Reforming Sports Before the Clock Runs Out*.